Free Will and Consciousness

Free Will and Consciousness

How Might They Work?

Edited by
Roy F. Baumeister
Alfred R. Mele
Kathleen D. Vohs

2010

OXFORD
UNIVERSITY PRESS

Oxford University Press, Inc., publishes works that further
Oxford University's objective of excellence
in research, scholarship, and education.

Oxford New York
Auckland Cape Town Dar es Salaam Hong Kong Karachi
Kuala Lumpur Madrid Melbourne Mexico City Nairobi
New Delhi Shanghai Taipei Toronto

With offices in
Argentina Austria Brazil Chile Czech Republic France Greece
Guatemala Hungary Italy Japan Poland Portugal Singapore
South Korea Switzerland Thailand Turkey Ukraine Vietnam

Published by Oxford University Press, Inc.
198 Madison Avenue, New York, New York 10016

www.oup.com

Library of Congress Cataloging-in-Publication Data
Free will and consciousness : how might they work? / edited by Roy F. Baumeister,
Alfred R. Mele, Kathleen D. Vohs.
p. cm.
Includes bibliographical references.
ISBN-13: 978-0-19-538976-0 (acid-free paper)
ISBN-10: 0-19-538976-X (acid-free paper)
1. Free will and determinism. 2. Consciousness. I. Baumeister, Roy F.
II. Mele, Alfred R., 1951– III. Vohs, Kathleen D.
BF621.C75 2010
123'.5—dc22

2009039649

9 8 7 6 5 4 3 2 1

Printed in the United States of America
on acid-free paper

We dedicate this book to the three As: Alex, Angela, and Athena.

ACKNOWLEDGMENTS

The preparation of this book was greatly facilitated by financial support from the John Templeton Foundation. It began with conference sponsored by that Foundation under the Humble Approach Initiative, held at Amelia Island in April 2008. Additional support by the foundation contributed to the writing and editing of this book. The authors and editors are highly grateful to the foundation, both for the financial support and for its encouragement of open-minded inquiry into topics of profound interdisciplinary interest.

We also wish to thank Mary Ann Meyers of the Templeton Foundation for her guidance and hard work to facilitate the conference and the book. We thank Tyler F. Stillman, Ph.D., for his diligent and scrupulous efforts to summarize the transcripts of discussions. We thank Lori Handelman of Oxford University Press for her help in making this book a reality.

TABLE OF CONTENTS

CONTRIBUTORS

Roy F. Baumeister
Florida State University

Jim Blascovich
University of California
Santa Barbara

Stephanie M. Carlson
University of Minnesota

Merlin Donald
Queens University

Erik Helzer
Cornell University

Richard Holton
Massachusetts Institute of Technology

Alfred R. Mele
Florida State University

David A. Pizarro
Cornell University

Adina L. Roskies
Dartmouth College

Jonathan W. Schooler
University of California
Santa Barbara

John R. Searle
University of California
Berkeley

Kathleen D. Vohs
University of Minnesota

Free Will and Consciousness

1 Free Will and Consciousness: An Introduction and Overview of Perspectives

Alfred R. Mele
Kathleen D. Vohs
Roy F. Baumeister

Free will and consciousness may seem so familiar to you as to need no introduction. Even so, it has been argued that free will is an illusion and that consciousness does little work. One of us (Alfred Mele) began a recent book defending the thesis that scientific arguments for the nonexistence of free will are unpersuasive and that conscious intentions and decisions do make a difference, by quoting the following e-mail message; it fortuitously arrived out of the blue while he was writing the book:

> Dear Dr. Mele,
> I recently purchased a DVD by Dr. Stephen Wolinsky.... He explains from the point of neuroscience that there is no such thing as free will, as we can only perceive an action after it has already occurred. Can you please help me with this? I can understand that I don't know what thought will occur next. But that that has already happened is beyond comprehension. Thank you as I am in a lot of despair. (Mele, 2009a, p. vii)

This is not an isolated incident. The belief that scientists have shown that there is no such thing as free will is disturbing, and two of us (Roy Baumeister and Kathleen Vohs) have produced evidence that lowering people's subjective probability that they have free will increases misbehavior—for example, lying, cheating, stealing, and socially aggressive conduct (Baumeister, Masicampo, & DeWall, 2009; Vohs & Schooler, 2008).

One thing we worry about is that most people who read in newspapers or hear on DVDs that scientists have shown that free will is a myth might understand the expression "free will" very differently than those scientists do. Consider the following from neuroscientist P. Read Montague:

> Free will is the idea that we make choices and have thoughts independent of anything remotely resembling a physical process. Free will is the close cousin to the idea of the soul—the concept that 'you', your thoughts and feelings, derive from an entity that is separate and distinct from the physical mechanisms that make up your body. From this prospective, your choices are not caused by physical events, but instead emerge wholly formed from somewhere indescribable and outside the purview of physical descriptions. This implies that free will cannot have evolved by natural selection, as that would place it directly in a stream of causally connected events. (2008, p. 584)

If, instead of reading that scientists have demonstrated that there is no "free will," people were to read that there is scientific proof that we have no magical, nonphysical, nonevolved powers, would they respond with despair? We doubt it, and there is evidence that most people do not understand free will in the way Read Montague does. Rather, the layperson's belief in free will is closer to the legal concepts, namely that the person could do something different from what he or she eventually does and is mentally competent to know the difference between right and wrong (e.g., Baumeister, 2008; Nahmias, Morris, Nadelhoffer, & Turner, 2006; Nahmias, in press; Paulhus & Margesson, 1994).

All three of us have taken positions elsewhere on how the expression "free will" should be understood and on the bearing of consciousness on free will (Baumeister, 2005, 2008; Baumeister, Sparks, Stillman, & Vohs, 2008; Mele, 2006, 2009a, 2009b). But, of course, generating a consensus on how to define "free will" or "consciousness"—much less a consensus on how the apparent phenomena are related—is no mean feat. We invite readers to approach the following chapters with an open mind on these issues. Our plan for this volume sidesteps definitional struggles to some extent.

We asked our contributors to refrain from arguing about whether free will exists and whether consciousness has any effects, to assume a positive answer to these questions, and to tackle questions about how free will and consciousness might work. (Predictably, none of the contributors endeavored to explain how magical, nonphysical, nonevolved powers might work, so P. Read Montague and his fellow travelers will be disappointed!) This volume draws from philosophy and psychology, arguably the two fields that have grappled most fundamentally with these questions. Most though not all of the chapters are based on the talks at an exciting small conference held on Amelia Island in April 2008. The conference was deliberately organized for people who had made positive and diverse contributions to the questions of how free will and consciousness might function. The critics and skeptics were known to the participants, and their objections were respected, but the goal was to promote forward movement by gathering together a group of relatively like-minded thinkers who could therefore focus on "how" questions rather than "whether" questions. This book is intended for readers who wish to move beyond debates about the existence of free will and the efficacy of consciousness and who wish to move closer to appreciating how free will and consciousness might operate.

The conference was funded by a small grant from the Templeton Foundation. Although we think the ideas should speak for themselves, some recent public remarks in various contexts have questioned the motives of that foundation and of people who take its money. For example, one of us (Baumeister) debated the question of free will with John Bargh of Yale University at a major scientific conference in February 2009, and Bargh thought it fitting to insinuate that the research Baumeister might be doing must have a hidden agenda of a possibly religious or right-wing nature. Bargh drove this point home by livening up his critique of Baumeister's work with a picture of Karl Rove, President Bush's erstwhile chief of staff (later indicted) and someone who was suspected of conspiring to advance ideological goals even at the expense of science. Possibly this was nothing more than a dirty debating trick, but perhaps some hearers may have thought that there was some hidden agenda.

In our experience, the Templeton Foundation seeks only to promote the best possible scientific research on profound questions of the human condition. Baumeister (who, incidentally, is a tentative atheist and also so apolitical that he has not voted for over a decade) received a grant from them to conduct experiments on free will—but only after the foundation insisted on his assurance that he would follow the data wherever they led and would be quite happy to publish any findings that came out against free will. The various editors of this book may disagree with individual members of the foundation (and probably with each other) over matters of personal faith and political values, but they enthusiastically share the desire to find out whatever science can tell us about deep, fascinating questions.

This book is thus one product of the effort to pursue ideas without knowing where the data and analyses will lead. The idea of leaping past the questions of whether free will exists and whether consciousness has any effects was not based on an assumption that those questions have been definitively answered, nor on the assumption that such debates are not worth pursuing. Rather, we simply assume that those questions are already being debated in abundance elsewhere (see, for example, *Does Consciousness Cause Behavior?* [Pocket, Banks, & Gallagher, 2006], and *Are We Free?* [Baer, Kaufmann, & Baumeister, 2008])—and that they are not the only questions worth discussing.

Indeed, it is our hope that this book will be of interest to readers across the full range of views and opinions. For those who already believe that free will is a reality, this book is intended to put flesh on the bones and show how it might operate. For those who are already certain that free will is an illusion, then this book can contribute to showing what are the real psychological phenomena and processes that produce the experiences and actions that are often mistaken to be the products of free will. As for consciousness, the usefulness of this book to all sides is a bit less obvious than it is for free will because readers who are convinced that consciousness is a useless, feckless epiphenomenon may not think there is any value in trying to understand how it operates. But we think that in the long run, science and philosophy will probably decide that consciousness is good for something, and so it is worth beginning to ask, now, what that might be. Moreover, the chapters that focus on consciousness here typically seek to incorporate the evidence from the critics and skeptics in order to fashion a new, improved understanding of what consciousness is good for.

Each chapter presents the authors' perspective on the free will process. Some also take the opportunity to offer thoughts on the free will–consciousness interplay. Each chapter is followed by a summary of highlights from the discussion that followed the author's presentation at the Amelia Island conference. It is our hope that these summaries will enable readers to appreciate the chapter more fully and to taste a bit of the excitement of the lively exchanges that went on at the conference.

Next we provide a brief overview of each chapter to help guide readers toward those chapters that they may find most intriguing or challenging.

Donald starts the book by emphasizing the centrality of culture in building consciousness and free will. Working from the notion that conscious integration of social events is fundamental to complex learning, and that language is a prime example of this process, he departs from mainstream neuroscientific theories in proposing that the symbolic process is imposed by culture, which increased the brain's ability to plan behavior, control attention, and maintain longer-term control over cognition itself.

Baumeister's chapter dovetails with Donald's in discussing free will and consciousness as products of evolutionary processes that enabled humans to create and sustain their new kind of social life, including culture. Culture, in this view, is the main biological strategy that the human species has developed to deal with the basic biological problems of survival and reproduction. Free will is an advanced form of agency that is suited to culture, including its increased demands for self-regulation and rational choice. Indirect control of action and processing information already in the mind (thus not incoming and separate from the here and now) may be the crucial functions of consciousness and therefore may constitute key features of free will.

Mele's chapter addresses two primary aims. The first is to develop an experimentally useful conception of conscious deciding. The second is to challenge a certain source of skepticism about free will: the belief that conscious decisions and intentions are never involved in producing corresponding overt actions. The challenge Mele develops has a positive dimension that accords with the aims of this volume: It sheds light on a way in which some conscious decisions and intentions do seem to be efficacious.

Vohs focuses her chapter on operationalizing free will as executive functioning. In this model, free will is for goal-directed, future-oriented behaviors, including rational choice, planning, intelligent thought, and self-control. She links the notion of free will to a limited stock of energy that appears to guide executive functioning processes. Overall, then, she claims that the system that allows people to perform behaviors and responses aimed at the decision making and future orientation—those that are relatively free—appear to operate via use of scarce psychological resources.

Holton's argument is that it is unwise and just plain false to think that free will can mean the (a) capacity experienced by agents when they act freely, (b) property possessed by agents when they are morally responsible, and (c) an agent's ability to behave otherwise. His paper focuses on the first two aspects. He comments that if freedom is something that is experienced, then one should ask what it is an experience of. Regarding morality, he comes to the conclusion that moral agency cannot be derived from the factors that give rise to the experience of freedom.

Pizarro and Helzer wrestle with the psychological relationship between freedom and moral responsibility. They contend that in moral judgments, people assign responsibility first, then adjust judgments of freedom to accord with their judgments of responsibility. Ultimately, judgments of freedom matter most because they allow people to justify judgments of responsibility and blame that they have already made and not, as it is often argued, to determine whom to hold responsible.

Searle offers definitions of both consciousness and free will. He begins by suggesting that free will is a mystery: Free actions are caused; and how can that be, given that they are not deterministically caused? He ends by observing that the hypothesis he develops in his chapter is a system whereby the mystery of free will is explained by the mystery of consciousness, which is in turn explained by the mystery of quantum mechanics. This is heady stuff indeed.

Coming from developmental psychology, Carlson's chapter uses consciousness and a domain-specific approach to study free will. She discusses the paradox that less consciousness can index more advanced forms of thought. Her core claim is that development in the case of consciousness is not only an upward-bound process in achieving an objective sense of self (i.e., the more choice and control, the better), but rather can be characterized as a balance between objectivity and personal, tacit knowledge.

Roskies is a philosopher-cum-neuroscientist whose unique stance offers combinations of these two core disciplines. Her chapter brings together free action ideas from the philosophy side and mechanistic routes from the neuroscience side. Both angles, she claims, can be understood in terms of a view of freedom that is independent of the question of determinism. Moreover, she brings in consciousness of reasons during deliberation as essential for decisions that are made freely and for which people can be held responsible.

Virtual worlds are the centerpiece of Blascovich's piece, as he has devoted over 10 years to building and exploring the ramifications of them for understanding human behavior. He notes that humans have long consciously and unconsciously transported themselves psychologically to "worlds" other than the grounded conventional realities in which they are physically situated. Moreover, this psychological movement is typically functional or adaptive. It helps people time travel in the sense of revisiting the past and planning for the future. In short, virtual reality is an important, yet underused, technique for understanding free will and consciousness.

Schooler's chapter rounds out the book by asking questions about what science can and should say about free will. The first section considers research examining the impact of telling people that science has ruled out the existence of free will. The second section reviews evidence for the three major perspectives on free will: hard determinism (determinism is true and free will is an illusion), compatibilism (free will and determinism are not mutually exclusive), and libertarianism (free will and determinism are mutually exclusive and free will exists). Compelling arguments for all three views are presented, indicating that it is premature for scientists to claim that science has definitively ruled in favor of one.

We hope that you will read on. Our preference is that you read consciously and freely. Unconscious reading is likely to be less rewarding. Also, we do regard this volume as compelling, but not in a way that would render your reading it unfree.

REFERENCES

Baer, J., Kaufmann, J., & Baumeister, R. F. (Eds.) (2008). *Are we free? Psychology and free will.* New York: Oxford University Press.

Baumeister, R. F. (2005). *The cultural animal: Human nature, meaning, and social life.* New York: Oxford University Press.

Baumeister, R. F. (2008). Free will in scientific psychology. *Perspectives on Psychological Science, 3*, 14–19.

Baumeister, R. F., Masicampo, E. J., & DeWall, C. N. (2009). Prosocial benefits of feeling free: Disbelief in free will increases aggression and reduces helpfulness. *Personality and Social Psychology Bulletin, 35*, 260–268.

Baumeister, R. F., Sparks, E. A., Stillman, T. F., & Vohs, K. D. (2008). Free will in consumer behavior: Self-control, ego depletion, and choice. *Journal of Consumer Psychology, 18*, 4–13.

Mele, A. R. (2006). *Free will and luck.* New York: Oxford University Press.

Mele, A. R. (2009a). *Effective intentions: The power of conscious will.* New York: Oxford University Press.

Mele, A. R. (2009b). *Free will.* In W. Banks (Ed.), *Encyclopedia of consciousness* (Vol. 1, pp. 265–277). Oxford, UK: Elsevier.

Montague, P. R. (2008). Free will. *Current Biology, 18*, R584–R585.

Nahmias, E. (in press) Why "willusionism" leads to "bad results": Comments on Baumeister, Crescioni, and Alquist. *Neuroethics.*

Nahmias, E., Morris, S., Nadelhoffer, T., & Turner, J. (2006). Is incompatibilism intuitive? *Philosophy and Phenomenological Research*, 73, 28–53.

Paulhus, D. L., & Margesson, A. (1994). Free will and determinism (FAD) scale. Unpublished manuscript, University of British Columbia, Vancouver, BC, Canada.

Pocket, S., Banks, W. P., & Gallagher, S. (2006.) *Does consciousness cause behavior?* Cambridge, MA: MIT Press.

Vohs, K. D., & Schooler, J. W. (2008). The value of believing in free will: Encouraging a belief in determinism increases cheating. *Psychological Science, 19*, 49–54.

2 Consciousness and the Freedom to Act

Merlin Donald

"The only states of consciousness that we naturally deal with are found in personal consciousnesses, minds, selves, concrete particular I's and you's. Each of these minds keeps its own thought to itself. There is no giving or bartering between them. No thought ever comes into direct *sight* of a thought in another personal consciousness than its own. Absolute insulation, irreducible pluralism, is the law. It seems as if the elementary psychic fact were not *thought* or *this thought* or *that thought,* but *my thought,* every thought being *owned.*"

—William James, *Principles.*

The denial of personal efficacy is an old theme in Western civilization. Quite apart from the concept of fate, which dominated the ancient world, much post-Enlightenment thought has viewed scientific determinism as axiomatic. La Mettrie wrote *L'Homme Machine* almost three centuries ago. Skinner wrote *Beyond Freedom and Dignity* almost 40 years ago. Recently the attack on the concept of free will has resumed, and while earlier claims were argued mostly from questionable a priori principles, the new ones are supposedly supported by empirical research.

A number of modern cognitive scientists have argued that consciousness is merely a comforting illusion. Recently, volition and voluntary movement have been relegated to the same status (Wegner, 2002). The claim is that, although we may have the illusion of being free and fully aware when we make a decision to act in a certain way, this is contradicted by empirical evidence. Even so small a matter as a decision to move a finger is said to be outside our conscious control, determined by unconscious brain processes. The illusion of having "caused" the action is useful for us as a somatic marker in memory, and may indeed be comforting, but it is, after all, an illusion.

This idea has a precedent in the behavioristic movement that dominated the first half of the twentieth century. This crude application of deterministic principles claims to avoid dualism. The central argument is that we are unconscious automatons, and worse, deluded automatons. Brain activity, inaccessible to conscious awareness, always precedes action of any kind, including voluntary action. Even a decision to act must be preceded by an inaccessible brain signal, and therefore we are not truly free. Our awareness of such a decision comes too late to influence the choice we make; the brain has already initiated the action, and consciousness is only informed of this event after the fact. Moreover, our thoughts and behavior are constantly being shaped by unconscious factors. Unseen influences permeate the background of behavior and determine many of the choices we make. There is nothing new in this idea. Perhaps it just reflects a periodic shift in the *Zeitgeist* back to a new variant of positivism. Behavior is shaped unconsciously, and the unconscious is, by definition, not free.

The empirical evidence cited to defend this idea comes mainly from two findings: the timing of brain signals, relative to action, and strong evidence of unconscious influences on cognition. Recordings of brain electrical activity are often cited as conclusive negative evidence against the efficacy of consciousness in action. This is the heart of the timing argument. The claim is that consciousness always lags behind action and therefore cannot play a causal role in guiding it. The next section will concern this evidence, and its interpretation.

The other argument, that there are many powerful unconscious influences on awareness, is not fatal for free choice in its own right because it is an inductive argument. There are many instances of unconscious influence. The most convincing and elegant are found in the recent literature on priming, where countless experiments show subtle changes in perception and behavior induced by exposure to prior stimuli that are outside the subject's awareness at the time (Bargh & Ferguson, 2000). Social psychology courses are now full of such demonstrations. The problem is that they only show the ubiquity and importance of unconscious influence; they do not, and cannot in themselves, disprove the possibility of freedom of choice, or free will.

Another well-known experimental demonstration of unconscious influence concerns the automatization of performance. It is well established that highly skilled tasks are best performed when overpracticed, or automatized. If a subject directs second-by-second attention to skilled performance, the result can be disastrous. A pianist or gymnast who becomes self-conscious during a performance is less likely to do well. It is better to let the unconscious do the work. Similarly, creative thoughts often come in an unplanned, apparently unguided (therefore unconscious) free-associative manner. And so on. Priming effects and free-associative effects outside of awareness have been standard fare in psychology for a half a century or more—but there is a current thrust to overgeneralize such unconscious influences, so that they become the explanation for every aspect of thought and behavior, and no role is left for consciousness.

This type of demonstration is still inductive: it leaves the door open to some efficacious role for awareness. In order to rule out free will altogether, there must be convincing negative evidence that can be generalized, so that every kind of behavior and cognition has been accounted for, and consciousness has been left with no apparent function, and no empirical foundation. For some, that evidence has come from the timing argument.

THE TIMING ARGUMENT

The apparent freedom entailed in voluntary action has been questioned on the basis that there is an inherent temporal distance between awareness and the brain processes that create it. In other words, awareness comes after the fact, and too late to influence choice. The most popular example used to support this idea consists of well-known experiments on finger movement carried out by Libet (1985, 1993). These experiments claim to show that brain activity "decides" to initiate a movement before the observer even becomes aware of having made a decision to move. If this were the case, it would constitute a possible death knell for the notion of conscious efficacy. Therefore it is important to examine these studies carefully.

The evidence for this claim is that a build-up of electrical activation in the premotor cortex occurs several seconds before the observer decides to initiate a movement. The technical name for the electrical wave that Libet recorded was variously labeled the "readiness potential" or "*Berietschaftspotential*" (BP) by its discoverers (Kornhuber & Deecke, 1965); another version of this was also known as the "expectancy wave" (Walter, Cooper, Aldridge, McCallum, & Winter, 1964). The activation takes the form of a surface-negative wave that peaks just before the action is performed and discharges just as the act is initiated. This effect has been replicated many times, in many laboratories, with various kinds of movements and electrical recordings. In my own laboratory, for instance, we studied this effect in the context of foot, hand, and mouth movement (Brooker & Donald, 1980; Donald, Inglis, Sproule, Young, & Monga, 1980). The results are similar in all three modalities of action. In a self-paced movement paradigm, when the subject freely decides to move, a surface-negative activation wave often begins well over a second before muscle contraction is initiated. It is true that it takes some time, in this case much less than 100 milliseconds, to send a motor command from the cortex to the hand muscles. It is the additional residual delay, between the onset of a BP and the movement, that must be explained.

Libet's special contribution to this paradigm was to add a subjective judgment to the self-paced movement task. The actors performing the movement were required to report the precise time when they decided to initiate the action, by reading the position of a moving second hand on a clock face. This subjective report was compared to the timing of muscle contraction, and the actual physical movement of the hand, as well as BP onset. Invariably, the subjects reported their decision to move long *after* the preparatory electrical activity had already begun. The delay between brain activity and awareness was consistently measured as three-quarters of a second or more. In parallel experiments on perception, Libet reported a time lag of approximately one-third of a second between electrocortical response to a cutaneous stimulus, and the time of subjective awareness of that stimulus. In both cases, conscious experience lagged behind brain activation.

Thus, it seems that consciousness only "catches up" with an action or a stimulus after it has already been processed thoroughly by the brain. Many theorists have used this result to infer that unconscious brain processes had already made the decision and started the movement, before subjects experienced the illusion that they had consciously decided to move. The implication here is that, in both sensation and action, awareness has no say in what happens. Awareness seemed to follow a physical brain event and always trailed behind the action. A more general proposition often follows: consciousness is inherently too late, after the fact, and powerless to influence behavior. Since there is no freedom without a conscious decision, there is no such thing as true freedom of choice.

These experiments have been criticized many times, and some of my own objections to this interpretation of Libet's work have appeared in print elsewhere (Donald, 2001). I have suggested that Libet's paradigm overemphasizes the sensorimotor interface and ignores the slower time range within which human conscious awareness matters most, within which executive and supervisory operations such as planning, metacognitive oversight, and social communication take place. I have also suggested that we do not yet know enough about the slower-acting brain mechanisms that mediate such operations (Donald, 2008) to make pronouncements about the neural basis of consciousness. I will not repeat these points at length here.

However, there is another, more fundamental criticism of Libet's movement paradigm. In it, subjects are sitting in a room with their hands on a platform, and the only thing they have to do is move a finger, without moving anything else (not easy). For subjects trapped in such a situation, this decision to move becomes the sole focus of attention. It is an excruciatingly boring task, and it is not easy to sustain interest in it; as a result, there is much subjective anticipation of each decision to move.

The key fact here is that this kind of anticipation is very general. It is not really specific to the hand movement. The BP that it generates is not actually a motor command signal. Rather, it is a generalized preparatory wave that precedes any major self-initiated cognitive event. Libet's studies showed only that *the making of such a decision* was anticipated by the observer's brain long before the decision was made. This is hardly surprising, given the nature of the task, and the properties of the BP. It is also completely irrelevant to the question of conscious efficacy or free choice in moving the finger. While it is true that a BP appears several seconds before the action, the conclusion drawn in most studies of this effect prior to Libet's unusual claim, and by most investigators afterward, was that the BP was generated in anticipation of making a decision to move, rather than of moving per se.

In the commentaries on his 1985 BBS article, Libet had already been criticized for mistakenly judging that his subjects actually initiated a movement when the BP started to develop. They had not. Libet apparently confused the slow-moving BP with a later, last-minute spike known as the "command potential," which precedes a specific voluntary hand movement by approximately 100 ms and has both a different wave shape and a different cortical origin (Kornhuber & Deecke, 1965). The BP has been shown to be a sign of a very general state of anticipation. The fact that this mistake is still in circulation provides us with a very good example of how a misinterpretation of scientific evidence can be perpetuated and duplicated widely if the error matches the current expectations of scientists. The truth is, the timing argument fails on all counts.

MONISM, DUALISM, AND PSYCHOPHYSICAL SIMULTANEITY

But the conceptual problem goes deeper. However we may regard the meaning or validity of Libet's work, there is a more important challenge that haunts this field of research: the simple fact that brain activity is inaccessible to awareness. The implications of this fact have not been fully accepted or digested by many investigators.

Conscious observers can never be directly aware of the brain activity on which their awareness depends. One reason for this lies in simple anatomy. We are only able to sense things for which we have sensory receptors, and there are no specialized receptors to detect and record brain activity. Thus, there are no neural projection systems that could possibly inform some receptive region of the brain about its own electrical or chemical activity. Even if there were such receptors, their inputs would return home where they started, in another flurry of cortical activity, in an endless (and pointless) loop.

Surely this is a clear principle on which most scientists and philosophical schools of thought can agree: Brain activity as such cannot be directly experienced by the owner of that brain. While conscious experience has access to the *cognitive contents* of certain classes of brain activity, it cannot access the electrochemical activity itself. The subject experiences only the phenomenal outcome of the brain's activity. The brain's actions themselves—the firing of neurons, multidimensional changes in synaptic activity, exchanges of transmitter substances, changes in local current flow, and so on—are permanently out of bounds.

Brain activity can never be the direct object of conscious experience. This principle is basic, and not on the table. It is equally obvious, especially when examining electrical activity during epileptic seizures and observing the close temporal correlation between experience and behavior, that conscious experience is very much contingent on brain activity, and closely tethered to it in real time (because of this, cortical electrical activity was once the primary neurological criterion of brain death).

Thus, brain activity, while not consciously accessible, is essential for any kind of mental activity. A subset of that activity, as yet not properly identified, is dedicated to conscious mental activity. Consciousness thus seems to be produced by something that it cannot observe. Does this negate freedom of choice, reducing it to the status of an illusion? Does the mere fact that brain activity goes on outside of our awareness mean that we are automatons that live with the pleasant delusion that we are free?

These questions lead us back to a discussion of two old philosophical workhorses: monism and dualism. Monism is the position that most scientists claim to support in principle. It asserts the unity of science and denies dualism, which holds that body and mind are separate ontological domains. A monist stance on consciousness must therefore assert that brain activation and experience reflect a single underlying reality. Every experience must therefore have a corresponding brain state. No neuroscientist will question this.

If a given brain state and its corresponding experience are aspects of one and the same event, viewed from different vantage points, *there can be no direction of causality involved.* Neither aspect could precede the other in the causal chain leading to awareness—they are one and the same link in that chain. Nor could there be a temporal lag between brain and phenomenal experience. A specific brain state could not "precede," "lag," "trigger," or "lead toward" its corresponding subjective aspect. This has consequences for experimental design. An experience does not, could not, and should not be expected to follow or precede its corresponding brain aspect, as if it were crossing some mysterious ethereal divide. The two aspects, physical and phenomenological, must be simultaneous and identical.

Any other position amounts to dualism. This exposes the dualism in Libet's interpretation of his timing experiments. In a monist world, if an experimenter does not find simultaneity of brain activity and experience, he is looking in the wrong place!

There are many theories of consciousness compatible with a strict monist view. These include the "global workspace" hypothesis of Baars (1988) and Newman & Baars (1993), the "dynamic core" hypothesis of Edelman & Tononi (2000), and several theories of binding, which, while preliminary, provide hints of a possible physical correlate of consciousness. They also include some wider theories, such as my own (Donald, 2001), which try to unite the neural and cultural sources of awareness into a single theoretical framework.

This returns the discussion to the significance of studies like Libet's. Why would it matter that an expectancy wave was generated long before a decision? In a monist framework, such a finding could only imply that the real neural event corresponding to the experience of making a decision had not been found in that particular experiment, and that the experimenters should continue their search for the neural events related to the phenomenon under investigation. Any alternative conclusion would be dualistic.

As we move forward in building a neurocognitive theory of conscious choice, these issues will continue to come to the fore. Dualism should always be taken off the table in advance. Adherence to a monist approach to consciousness at our current stage of knowledge demands optimism and persistence. At present, we have not yet made enough progress even to know what the important neural variables are. But there is no reason to reject the possibility of developing a successful theory.

CULTURE AND FREEDOM OF CHOICE

There is no evidence that would enable us to dismiss the possibility of free will and conscious choice. However, this fact does not result in an explanatory theory of any kind, nor does it resolve the issue, in the sense of "proving" that choices are truly free. It merely leaves the question open. Awareness, when viewed in terms of its physical or phenomenal aspect, must meet certain criteria before it can be called free. It is far from clear how a nervous system; that is, a physical system subject to the laws of physics and chemistry, can act in a manner that we would call free. It is equally uncertain how to apply a reasonable criterion of "freedomness" to a subjective experience.

But there are strong reasons to adhere to an evolutionary approach to consciousness. Consciousness exists in some form in many animals, and the expansion of the powers of conscious processing in evolution is mostly about improving the capacity for learning, especially the capacity to integrate complex new material that must be assimilated by the brain. The ultimate product of wider conscious integration (this principle applies to many species) is an expanded "world model" by which an organism can guide action, including its own future cognitive activity (thought is always potentially manifest in action). By implication, freedom of choice is linked to the breadth of an organism's worldview. The reach of consciousness, and freedom, is graded and flexible.

An evolutionary approach inevitably results in a graded theory of choice. As the individual mind's model of the world expands to include more and more possibilities and variables, so does freedom of choice. The window of awareness is narrow in simple organisms, and so choice is very restricted, perhaps limited to such things as control over emotion, or inhibition of response. This situation becomes wider and deeper with the emergence of more complex nervous systems, which must be equipped to deal with many more options and variables in determining any course of action.

The assessment of the width of awareness in animals is based on several variables, including sensitivity, curiosity, and the duration of working memory. The latter variable draws on Hebb's (1963) notion that what we experience as awareness is really the memory of immediate past experience, and depends on short-term memory. As the temporal integration of events in the world becomes more advanced, encompassing larger events, especially social events such as changing alliances, or shifts in the dominance hierarchy, awareness is confronted with many more possibilities. Choice must cut through this incredible complexity and resolve an adaptive pattern of action, and it must do this quickly and efficaciously.

Culture complicates this picture, especially in the case of humans. Humanity's uniqueness lies in our collective cognitive systems, that is, in our cultures. We have mind-sharing cultures, in which alliances of trust can be based on such cognitive things as a shared belief in the same ideas.

A simpler way to put this is that, as the hominid brain widened the range of experiences it could integrate in a single act of synthesis, it eventually reached a point where the collective interaction of such brains triggered a cultural chemistry that fed back onto the individual mind and brain. Cognitive-cultural interactions amplified the powers of individuals, who in turn amplified the collective powers of society, and so on, in what cyberneticists might have called a positive evolutionary feedback loop.

This feedback process stepped through a series of cognitive-cultural stages (cf. Donald, 1991), building more and more abstract networks of cognitive activity distributed across many brains, and eventually, across a hybrid system that included artificial memory technologies, and external symbolic devices, such as the cinema, that have effectively re-engineered experience itself.

The key adaptation enabling the emergence of human mind-sharing cultures, and eventually language itself, was an evolutionary expansion of the range of primate working memory. This expansion involved a qualitatively new neural "slow process" that was unique to social mammals and became very highly evolved in human beings. This process is constantly running in the background of awareness, while traditional mechanisms of attention, perception, and short-term memory run in the foreground. It is the ultimate governor of human mental activity.

The neural mediator of this slow process is still unknown, but such a process is a theoretical requirement to explain the cognitive properties of human culture (Donald, 2008). It operates in the very long time range of minutes and hours, and none of the known active electrochemical processes that have been related to cognition can operate in that time zone. Among the known properties of neurons, there are many possible candidates for such a process, but much work remains to be done in this area before it will be understood.

Apes share a similar cerebral architecture with humans but cannot master more than a fraction of human culture. This could be because their slow process is less fully evolved. There are very large differences between humans and apes in the complexity and temporal extent of the kinds of social events they can understand, and this is a crucial variable in determining the degree to which culture can be penetrated. Moreover, humans are much more accomplished learners, and much of that increased learning capacity depends upon slower-acting executive brain processes identified with conscious cognitive control.

In the case of humans, the claim of free will is based on special evidence and usually conveys the human subject's personal power to reflect upon, and choose, the direction of action, especially in the long term. We might agree that human beings do not normally wage war or build skyscrapers unconsciously! We plan, execute, and design such major adventures in groups, and do so very deliberately. There is no question that we also have the option to veto many choices that have already been made. While there are many, including myself, who defend the existence of some free will in animals, these claims are typically much less confident than in the human case and are usually expressed in terms of approximating, in varying degrees, human freedom of choice.

It is useful to treat the human case as special because it is the template, the standard to which others species are held. What is it that makes the human mind unique, and human choice uniquely free? The answer is that human uniqueness is founded in *the depth of our enculturation*. Culture has set the brain free in various ways, and allowed it to redeploy its resources. One major role for culture is found in language. Languages are inventions of the group; that is, they emerge from distributed cognitive networks. There are no documented cases in which isolated human individuals have invented languages or symbols in any form. Individuals have an innate potential for language, but it cannot be realized except in an interactive group. Therefore, inasmuch as language makes us more capable of free choice, this freedom must be attributed in part to collective cognitive processes, that is, culture, including its major cognitive offshoot, language.

Does language acquisition affect awareness? This is one question that can be answered affirmatively, and definitively, on the basis of empirical evidence. This effect can be seen most clearly in deaf people who acquired sign language as adults. Once they have language, they experience reality very differently and have great difficulty remembering anything of their previous lives. Helen Keller referred to her prelanguage self as "Phantom," and her experience has been corroborated in several other late language learners studied by Schaller (1991). It is possible that, to some degree, these subjects were capable of free choice before they had language, but there is no question that their experience of feeling free after learning language was directly related to their sense of empowerment over consciousness itself, especially over the power to consciously recall events and other items from memory. This power is affected by having language.

Moreover, autobiographical memory depends upon language, or more precisely, on the highest language capacity, the ability to construct a personal narrative. Neither narrative ability nor autobiographical memory can develop without early immersion in human culture (Nelson, 1993, 1996). Our sense of having freedom of choice, while not inconceivable outside the wide temporal framework of autobiographical memory, is apparently greatly constrained without it.

Another enormous source of cultural influence is found in the effect of symbolic memory technologies, including such things as writing and mathematical notations, on conscious awareness. Written displays reorganize working memory in the reader, who becomes plugged into a temporary distributed system. This distributed system reallocates the cognitive load imposed by various tasks, amplifying the parameters of working memory, and the powers of choice we experience. This is a direct function of having representations in artificial memory media (Donald, 2001). External displays leave the observer freer to reflect on representations in a way that is not available to natural, or biological, working memory. This is achieved by reorganizing the task, and offloading some operations to external media. The acquisition of literacy skills imposes a novel functional architecture on the brain. It actually reorganizes the way neural tissue is deployed in cognitive tasks (Donald, in press). In a variety of ways, symbol-using cultures liberate the brain, creating options that extend freedom of choice. Daniel Dennett (2003) has reached a somewhat similar conclusion about the importance of culture in evolving freedom of choice.

On the representational level, human awareness seems to be unique because of the effects of symbolization on the stream of consciousness. How could a capacity for symbolically mediated awareness have evolved in a brain that remains nonsymbolic in its internal workings? I proposed long ago that the symbolic process is imposed by culture, and that it evolved from the "outside in," consistent with a Vygotskian approach to language phylogenesis, as well as ontogenesis. In essence, the developing human brain is programmed by cultural immersion, in a process that has evolved through several successive stages. As this process widened the reach of awareness, it also increased the brain's ability to plan behavior, control attention, and maintain longer-term control over cognition itself.

IMPLICATIONS FOR HUMAN FREEDOM OF CHOICE

The act of making a decision might be taken as the one major paradigm in which we might be able to examine a wide range of brain–culture interactions. Decisions are the final resolution events of a variety of cognitive scenarios that can engage, in theory, the entire voluntary action repertoire of human beings. Essentially, decisions occur at choice points in a cognitive sequence. Thus, one could, in theory, "decide" which memory to retrieve, which stimulus to attend to, whether to inhibit an impulse, which perceptual set to activate, which emotional attitude to assume toward a social scenario, and which pattern of action to pursue in a variety of contexts. Choice occurs everywhere in the higher cognitive system.

Choice engages most subroutines and subsidiary systems concerned with memory, symbolic representation, and thought. Thus, it constitutes an abstract category that cuts across all of cognition. Decisions are sometimes imposed from above on innate emotional brain systems—for instance, whether to release a smile in a particular social context—and are sometimes embedded in algorithms and mental habits with purely cultural origins—for instance, decisions involving numbers or other symbolic systems, or those that must obey complex symbol-based rules, such as buying stocks, filling out crossword puzzles, or choosing materials for a tool. Human choice is most commonly a culturally determined process in which many basic cognitive operations play a part, and the mechanisms of such decisions must be regarded as hybrid systems in which both brain and culture play a role. When the individual "makes" a choice, that choice has usually been made within a wider framework of distributed cognition, and, in many instances, it is fair to ask whether the decision was really made by the distributed cognitive cultural system itself, with the individual reduced to a subsidiary role.

This is not a simple issue to resolve. The individual brain and mind contain within them a great deal of history and structure that can be brought to bear on how decisions are made in specific cases. The differentiation of brain regions engaged in a specific kind of decision may be determined as much by this history as by innate brain growth patterns, both because of the epigenetic impact of culture on cognitive architecture, and because the actual task imposed on the brain by a given decision can be changed by redistributive effects that occur within the networks of culture.

In this way, distributed systems are able to change where in the system each component that influences a certain decision is located. This applies to such things as the locus of memory storage for a specific item, the locus of a specialized cognitive operation, and the locus of the choice mechanism itself. When all these components are located in a particular individual brain, decision making is one thing; when they are distributed across the brains of various people and information media, it is quite another, even if the final "decision" is made by one person. For this reason, and because decision making is so wide in its application, we should not predict the existence of a specialized brain region or subsystem that is devoted to resolving decisions in any general sense of the term. Rather, decisions can be made in a variety of ways that involve different anatomical subsystems of the brain.

Choice may be made automatically, without conscious engagement, in highly overpracticed routine situations. But, even in such situations, when necessary, an actor can intervene consciously at any level in the cognitive hierarchy of control. Thus, a pianist might play a well-rehearsed piece automatically but might also choose to consciously modify his playing online at the level of finger position, heaviness of touch, phrasing, formal interpretation, or emotion, depending on the feedback he gets from listening to his own performance. The important conclusion is that the possibility of conscious intervention in every choice remains viable, even after the automatization of a particular skill.

Certain kinds of choices must be made consciously—especially those involving novelty or learning. But, for the larger distributed systems of culture to operate smoothly, the rule seems to be: the less conscious engagement, the better. Conscious intervention is needed for acquisition and feedback control, but most individual cognitive operations should be made as automatic as possible in such systems. This constitutes a kind of industrialized cultural-cognitive network coordination, with concomitant efficiencies and increased collective power.

The superior powers of spontaneous intuition are often cited in studies of decision making (cf. Engel & Singer, 2008). Such intuitions are sometimes considered unconscious. But this is a rigged argument. In most examples, these cases of superior intuitions are clearly the outputs of deeply enculturated routines that have been learned by means of extensive and repetitive conscious rehearsal and refinement. This applies in principle to examples such as face recognition (an acquired, highly culture-specific skill), chess playing, various kinds of social judgment, business decisions, the composition of poetry, and so on. In each case, the task hierarchy is typically acquired in the context of a distributed cognitive-cultural system, with extensive pedagogy and training, and highly conscious, or deliberate, practice and rehearsal (sometimes in the form of imaginative play), to the point of automatizing the response, which affords the temporary release of conscious monitoring. In short, one of the main objectives of human conscious supervision is to make itself less important in future performances of the same activity.

However, as in all things, there is an associated caveat: While there are obvious advantages to abandoning personal conscious control in overlearned performances, under some circumstances (especially in novel situations), there are equally obvious dangers. The conscious individual is still the ultimate arbiter of choice, and the systems that remember networks of cultural practice and transmit their functions to new generations cannot be constructed without a great deal of conscious deliberation. This is where freedom gains an especially meaningful degree of traction. The advantages of a loss of conscious control in many short-term actions should not overshadow the oversight role of consciousness in creating and maintaining the elaborate cognitive apparatus of culture, keeping it on course, and preventing it from becoming unstable. Call it distributed metacognition. Whatever the label, it is at the very heart of human freedom to choose.

DISCUSSION WITH MERLIN DONALD

Might there be a way to aid children in learning how best to navigate the possibility space of modern conscious experience?
The main feature of modern conscious life that stands out from the past is the invasion of the highly engineered products of the electronic world into personal experience. One possible way to help children deal with this is to expose them early to this environment in a benign and protected manner. Interactive computer games and even use of the Internet can train up attention and memory management skills that are very important in this society. In addition, this kind of experience develops metacognitive skills that will be helpful in dealing with the rapid turnover of information so characteristic of this age.

There are probably trade-offs in placing emphasis on this type of experience at such a young age, but it does seem to cultivate the kind of mental skills that help meet the challenges presented by the "engineered" experiences afforded by the new electronic environment. So long as this does not interfere with their social development, it might be seen as constructive.

Would a robot that demonstrated sensitivity, curiosity, and autonomy be a candidate for consciousness?
Yes. In principle, it is possible that a robot might meet these criteria. However, the criteria for consciousness referred to in this paper, (sensitivity, curiosity, and autonomy) were developed mainly from an evolutionary perspective. Other species, and not robots, were the context for developing them.

Rather than contemplating imaginary robots, it might be more useful to consider the kinds of robots that currently exist. These do not come anywhere close to meeting these criteria. Some existing robots are capable of extraordinary sensory and perceptual sensitivity, but none are curious or autonomous, and none has the sensitivity to nuances of meaning found in human beings.

How are humans different from other species?
In many ways, which I have discussed at length in my two books. One important difference that is often overlooked is the high speed of automatized attentional management that human beings are capable of sustaining. The neural basis for this capacity probably has some connection with the selective evolution of the frontal-cerebellar tract in humans, which is around 10 times larger in us than in chimpanzees.

Humans and other species are qualitatively different in their surface cognitive capabilities, such as language and other skills. But, more fundamentally, humans are fantastically fast and nimble at automatized attentional management of all kinds. It is the capacity for this kind of attention that stands out as a cognitive precondition for the complex behaviors that define us. Piecing together a conversation, or playing a game of baseball or soccer, is a feat that requires a unique high-speed, multchannel, automatized attentional system. This is why even chimpanzees cannot match the skills of children at such things.

Are attention and consciousness the same thing?

No. Complex cognitive actions involve an attentional hierarchy. Some of the attentional acts in the hierarchy are conscious, and some are not. One example that illustrates the difference between consciousness and attention is reading. When children learn to read, much of their early training is concerned with where to look, and what to notice on the page. This requires conscious control of visual attention. However, once children have learned to read, their eye movements no longer need to be consciously controlled, at least under normal circumstances. The focus is on meaning.

Nevertheless, even in skilled readers, visual attention remains essential to the act of reading. There is a complex and specific sequence of eye movements that enable the brain to integrate what otherwise would be confusing images into a meaningful text. The point is that in a literate person those eye movements become part of an automatized attentional hierarchy that controls the act of reading. The hierarchy of attention is thus not entirely "in" consciousness. The eye movements still constitute an attentional act, and yet they are no longer in the focus of awareness (of course, if necessary, they can return there). The subject is normally "aware" only of the top end of the hierarchy of attention. Attentional acts at lower levels in the reading hierarchy are not fully conscious, but nevertheless operate effectively at some less conscious level of the mind.

REFERENCES

Baars, B. J. (1988). *A cognitive theory of consciousness*. New York: Guilford Press.

Bargh, J., & Ferguson, M. J. (2000). Beyond behaviorism: On the automaticity of higher mental processes. *Psychological Bulletin, 126*, 925–945.

Brooker, B. H., & Donald, M. (1980). The search for scalp-recordable speech potentials. In H. Kornhuber and L. Deecke (Eds.), *Progress in brain research, Vol. 54, Motivation, motor and sensory processes of the brain: Electrical potentials, behaviour and clinical use* (pp. 782–789). Amsterdam, The Netherlands: Elsevier, North Holland.

Dennett, D. (2003). *Freedom evolves*. New York: Viking.

Donald, M., Inglis, J., Sproule, M., Young, M., & Monga, T. (1980). The averaged movement potential in stroke hemiplegia: Comparison of intact and pathological hemispheres. In H. Kornhuber and L. Deecke (Eds.), *Progress in brain research, Vol. 54, Motivation, motor and sensory processes of the brain: Electrical potentials, behaviour and clinical use* (pp. 487–490). Amsterdam, The Netherlands: Elsevier, North Holland.

Donald, M. (1991). *Origins of the modern mind: Three stages in the evolution of culture and cognition*. Cambridge, MA: Harvard University Press.

Donald, M. (2001). *A mind so rare: The evolution of human consciousness*. New York: W. W. Norton.

Donald, M. (2008). The slow process: A hypothetical cognitive adaptation for distributed cognitive networks. *Journal of Physiology (Paris), 101*, 214–222.

Donald, M. (in press). The exographic revolution. In C. Renfrew and L. Malafouris (Eds.), *Becoming human - Innovation in material and spiritual cultures*. Cambridge, UK: McDonald Institute, University of Cambridge.

Edelman, G., & Tononi, G. (2000). *A Universe of Consciousness: How matter becomes imagination*. New York: Basic Books.

Engel, C., and Singer, W. (2008). *Better than conscious? Implications for performance and institutional analysis*. Cambridge, MA: The MIT Press.

Hebb, D. O. (1963). The semi-autonomous process; its nature and nurture. *American Psychologist, 18*, 16–27.

Kornhuber, H., & Deecke, L. (1965). Hirnpotentialandeerungen bei Wilkurbewegungen und passiv Bewegungen des Menschen. Beritschaftspotential und reafferente Potentiale. *Pflügers Archiv, 284*, 1–17.

Libet, B. (1985). Unconscious cerebral initiative and the role of conscious will in voluntary action. *Behavioral and Brain Sciences, 8*, 529–566.

Libet, B. (1993). *Neurophysiology of consciousness*. Boston: Birkhauser.

Nelson, K. (1993). Psychological and social origins of autobiographical memory. *Psychological Science*, 4, 7–14.

Nelson, K. (1996). *Language in cognitive development: The emergence of the mediated mind*. New York: Cambridge University Press.

Newman, J., & Baars, B. J. (1993). A neural attentional model for access to consciousness. *Concepts in Neuroscience, 4*, 255–290.

Schaller, S. (1991). *A man without words*. New York: Summit Books.

Walter, W. G., Cooper, R., Aldridge, V. J., McCallum, W. C., & Winter, A. L. (1964). Contingent negative variation: An electric sign of sensorimotor association and expectancy in the human brain. *Nature, 203*, 380–384.

Wegner, D. (2002) *The illusion of conscious will*. Cambridge, MA: MIT Press.

3 Understanding Free Will and Consciousness on the Basis of Current Research Findings in Psychology

Roy F. Baumeister

Free will and consciousness are two perennial and challenging problems that have attracted attention from many great thinkers. Often, people have debated whether and in what sense free will and consciousness can be regarded as realities. In this chapter, however, I shall sidestep those questions. I shall merely assume that there are some genuinely real and effective phenomena that are commonly associated with free will and consciousness. Instead of debating the ultimate reality of free will or possible utility of consciousness, I shall draw on empirical findings in psychology in the attempt to understand how they function.

In a nutshell, free will is a particular form of action control that encompasses self-regulation, rational choice, planned behavior, and initiative. Evolution found a way for humans to use the body's basic energy supplies to fuel complex brain processes that override simple impulses and alter the stream of behavior based on meaningful contemplation of distal outcomes, abstract rules, and enlightened self-interest. (I am not taking sides as to whether this fully deserves the label "free will" in the most sophisticated sense.) Consciousness, meanwhile, is the brain making input for itself, which is neither for the direct perception of the environment nor for the direct control of action. Rather, consciousness is an internal mental process that facilitates cross-communication across different segments of brain and mind. It enables sequential thought. Its most far reaching function involves creating simulations that are useful for upstream input into the control of actions and for helping the individual operate in the complex social and cultural worlds that humans create.

FREE WILL

In practical terms, free will is the assumption that more than one course of action is possible for a given person in a given situation. Hence, the person really makes a choice, in the sense that some act is possible and then ceases to be possible. Free will is the capacity to choose between different possible acts.

Understood in that way, belief in free will is woven into the fabric of human social life. People believe that they and others make choices. Some determinists may contend that that common belief is mistaken, that the multiplicity of options is illusory, and that causal processes are in motion that ensure that only one outcome is truly possible. And there is abundant evidence that sometimes people are swayed by causes of which they are not aware (e.g., Freud, 1933/1964), so that their sense of freedom to choose is exaggerated. In contrast, others believe that people actually do make choices, that multiple outcomes are possible, and that the future is not set in stone but rather depends on what choices people make.

Evolution of Freedom

I start with the assumption that human psychological capabilities and tendencies were shaped by natural selection. This view is widely held among scientists today. Building on this, I believe that the major force guiding the evolution of the human psyche consisted of the demands for the specifically human forms of social life, including culture (see Baumeister, 2005). Therefore, the traits that are distinctively human are largely adaptations to enable the human animal to create and sustain culture and to survive and reproduce effectively in a cultural environment. In short, nature made us for culture. Free will (and consciousness; see below) are both best understood in this light.

What is culture? There are many definitions. In general, however, culture is understood as an information-based system that enables people to live together in organized fashion and to satisfy their basic needs, ultimately including survival and reproduction.

Culture is, in an important sense, humankind's biological strategy. It is how our species solves the universal problems of survival and reproduction. Even today, if new problems of survival and reproduction arise, people typically turn to the culture for solutions: They go to hospitals and clinics, they vote for money for research on problems, they institute tax breaks for families with small children, and so forth.

Culture is not unique to humans. De Waal (2001) noted that cultural behavior has been observed in several dozen species of animals, if one adopts a very loose definition of culture. However, culture is usually a minor and optional aspect of life for most of these animals, whereas in humans alone it is a pervasive, defining aspect of social life. Only humans have made culture into a central biological strategy. This pattern fits the evolutionary argument quite well: The beginnings of culture emerged in other species, presumably before the first humans appeared. Culture was therefore part of the selection environment in which humans evolved.

Culture has served humankind extremely well. In scarcely 200,000 years, the human population has ballooned from one woman to nearly 8 billion. Life expectancy has perhaps tripled. Thus, measured by the biological yardsticks of survival and reproduction, it has been a very effective strategy.

In order for culture to work, however, people must be able to free themselves from natural impulses and other prepotent response patterns. No other species has been able to utilize culture as effectively as humans, despite the obvious benefits. The most likely reason for their failure is that they lack the psychological capabilities to overcome the natural response patterns so as to behave culturally. This is roughly analogous to the inability of older computers to access the Internet.

The ability to overcome natural response patterns in order to behave culturally is an important meaning of freedom. In my view, this ability represents the pragmatic problem associated with free will. Free will, in a psychologically useful and adaptive sense, is therefore an advanced form of action control that can incorporate cultural prescriptions and execute them behaviorally. It enables the human animal to pursue its enlightened self-interest amid a cultural environment characterized by rules and other abstract, socially meaningful considerations.

Belief in Free Will

Two empirical facts have recently emerged that are quite relevant, regardless of one's metaphysical beliefs about free will versus determinism. First, most people believe in free will. Second, that belief has behavioral consequences.

A seminal investigation by Vohs and Schooler (2008) manipulated students' belief in free will. Some were encouraged or persuaded to shift toward greater belief in free will, while others were persuaded to believe in determinism and reject free will. Subsequently, the latter (i.e., induced determinists) were relatively more likely to lie, cheat, and steal.

Subsequent work using similar procedures has found that (manipulated) disbelief in free will leads to increased aggression and to decreased willingness to help someone in need (Baumeister, Masicampo, & DeWall, 2009). Likewise, participants induced to disbelieve in free will were subsequently more likely than others (including induced libertarians) to conform mindlessly to what others have said, rather than thinking for themselves (Alquist & Baumeister, 2008). Disbelieving in free will makes people anticipate that they would not feel as guilty over possible misdeeds, as compared to when believing in free will (Stillman & Baumeister, 2008). It makes people less likely to learn lessons (colloquially called "morals") from their misdeeds (Stillman & Baumeister, 2008). It reduces their tendency to engage in counterfactual thinking (Alquist, Daly, Stillman, & Baumeister, 2009).

Thus, alterations in belief in free will seem to have behavioral consequences. The general thrust of findings is that determinists behave in relatively antisocial ways: cheating, stealing, aggression, not helping, and so forth. Conversely, then, belief in free will supports prosocial behavior, of the sort that is most advantageous for culture. This is consistent with the view that the purpose of free will is to facilitate culture, though of course it is hardly proof of that.

In these studies that manipulate belief in free will, the neutral control condition generally yields the same behavioral results as the pro–free will condition. The implication is that belief in free will is the norm (so promoting that belief does not really change anything). Disbelief departs from the norm and produces the change in behavior—and, mostly, a change for the worse. It is not an accident that people ordinarily believe in free will, because that belief is useful for society. It makes people behave better and treat each other better. It helps them follow the rules by which society survives and culture becomes possible.

Further evidence that most people believe in free will comes from simple questionnaire data. Measures of chronic belief in free will and determinism (see Paulhus & Margessen, 1994) generally reveal that respondents score on average significantly above the scale midpoint, indicating belief in free will.

Free Acts Differ from Other Acts

A next empirical fact is that free actions differ from non-free ones. Hence, it is meaningful to speak of freedom of action. We have conducted studies to show that people can reliably distinguish free from non-free actions.

Opponents of the idea of free will like to focus on the causal issue and say that a truly free act would have to be (and be proven to be) independent of all external influences and all prior events. In essence, this would be just a random action. Our work on how people rate actions has confirmed that participants do rate an act as highly free if it is presented in this way, as random and thus independent of all influences (e.g., Stillman, Sparks, & Baumeister, 2008). But this is not the only definition.

More broadly, we find that people associate free will with several important patterns First, actions that show the person resisting temptation (and thus exercising self-control) draw high ratings on freedom. Acts that resist external pressures likewise are characterized as free. Acts that involve pursuit of long-term gain and self-interest, rather than short-term impulse, are seen as free. Also, acts that indicate conscious reflection and thought are regarded as free.

To be sure, the results across many studies and scenarios are not entirely consistent. There seems to be some variation based on how questions are phrased and other seemingly minor matters. Still, the mere fact that some significant differences are obtained indicates that people can reliably distinguish certain actions from others along the dimension of how free they seem. Moreover, and perhaps more important, these broadly show certain distinctive patterns: internal agency, self-control, and rational, conscious choice.

The concept of freedom of action thus has social meaning. Even a dogmatic determinist must recognize that people have a belief in something they call free will and that they can reliably distinguish some free actions from others. Put another way, there are genuine, legitimate phenomena associated with the idea of free will, and the determinist merely objects that they do not properly deserve to be called free will.

One other implication is relevant. The fact that people differentiate actions along a continuum of freedom means that not all actions are equally free. The view that all human action is inherently, inevitably a result of free will (e.g., that humans are "condemned to freedom," in Sartre's famous phrase) does not mesh well with the view that people rate some actions as free and others as not free.

Variation in freedom of action is centrally important to my understanding. Humans may be cultural animals, but they are nonetheless animals, and as such they come equipped by nature with instincts, animal learning patterns, and the like. Free will may enable people to act culturally rather than naturally to some degree and on some occasions. But freedom will be partial at best. Partial freedom, fortunately, is sufficient to enable the cultural system to work.

Different Processes: Self-Control and Rational Choice

Thus far I have argued that people believe in something they call free will, that that belief has behavioral consequences, and moreover, that actions can be reliably differentiated as relatively more or less free. A fourth empirical fact is that the inner, psychological processes that produce the actions regarded as free differ from those that produce the relatively unfree actions.

Here let me return briefly to the conception of free will as random action, that is, something the person does that is unrelated to any prior cause or external influence. As already noted, our scenario studies show that students will rate an action high on freedom if it is presented as just such a completely random action.

My view is that this is an unhelpful conception of free will and one that probably should be discarded. The uncaused random action is one theory that is unlikely to correspond to any reality. Let us assume that evolution shaped the human psyche, and that, indeed, the distinctively human traits (of which free will would presumably be one) were developed to adapt to the distinctively human forms of social life (see Baumeister, 2005). Imagine for a moment that it were possible for a genetic mutation to create the capacity for purely random action. Would a baby born with the capacity for random action survive and reproduce better than its peers, especially in the social and cultural environments that humans create and live in? It is hard to see why it would. Culture as practiced by most human groups does not favor random action. Thus, even if biology could produce random action, there is serious doubt as to whether natural selection would favor that capability, and hence it is unlikely that humans would have it.

Instead, I suggest that the most useful forms of free will would include self-control and rational choice (see Searle, 2001). These undoubtedly pay off in human social life—indeed, intelligence and self-control predict success in life across many spheres. These two are also operative definitions of free will held by the general public, in the sense that laboratory participants give high ratings for freedom to acts that reflect self-control and rational choice (Stillman et al., 2008).

Our research has established a powerful link between self-control and rational choice—in their underlying processes. We first discovered that self-control consumed a limited energy resource, which is presumably behind the folk concept of willpower. When people perform a task that requires self-control, they perform relatively poorly if they have recently exerted self-control in any other sphere, even one completely irrelevant (e.g., Baumeister, Bratslavsky, Muraven, & Tice, 1998). Thus, the first task depletes energy, so there is less remaining for the second task. Subsequent work has indicated that this willpower resource involves glucose in the bloodstream, which is the basic fuel for brain processes (in the sense that neurotransmitters are made from it). Acts of self-control depend on and consume blood glucose, leaving the body's fuel temporarily depleted (Gailliot et al., 2007).

The connection to rational choice has emerged more recently. We found, first, that intelligent thought depends partly on the same resource: After exerting self-control, people perform worse on tests of logical reasoning (Schmeichel, Vohs, & Baumeister, 2003). And, crucially, making choices depletes the same resource. After making decisions, people are relatively poor at self-control (Vohs et al., 2008).

We coined the term *ego depletion* to refer to the state of reduced resources that results from exerting self-control or making decisions. Possibly other activities by the self draw the same resource and produce ego depletion also. Likely candidates would include making ad hoc plans and responding actively instead of passively. These would also be adaptive and plausible forms of free will.

Viewed in that way, how did free will evolve? I would speculate along the following lines. The capacity to inhibit an impulse and its incipient response was probably needed fairly early in evolution, so that an animal could benefit from learning that something was dangerous. Social uses for inhibition likewise probably arose before humans evolved. For example, when a hungry animal sees good food, the natural response would be to eat it, but in a social group, the animal may have to wait until the alpha male has eaten. (Otherwise it risks a beating!) Self-control may have evolved in order to enable just such adjustments to social life.

Self-control allows the creature to alter its behavior to conform to the rules of the social group. In a sense, rational choice allows a person to think up his or her own rules and then follow them. Hence, rational choice likely used the same mechanism that had been developed for self-control, only with the aid of the more advanced cognitive capacity to formulate rules for oneself.

It may sound paradoxical to suggest that free will is for following rules. But I think that is an accurate and useful way to understand it. Human social life in the form of culture is saturated with rules, and the ability to function in culture depends on the ability to conform one's behavior to rules.

CONSCIOUSNESS

The sense that one's conscious self is in direct control of all one's actions is a familiar and comforting feeling, but it is almost certainly mistaken.

Viewed up close, and in terms of direct execution, behavior occurs when muscles move bones, as directed by neuronal activation. Consciousness is nowhere to be seen in those processes. You may decide consciously to walk somewhere, but you do not consciously direct each muscle movement, and you certainly do not consciously specify which neurons should fire into which synapses. If consciousness has any input into behavior, it is at the macro level and far in advance of these actual processes of muscular execution (Donald, 2002).

How does behavior actually occur? Typically, external circumstances activate some response inside the person, most likely involving cognitions and motivations that are associated with possible acts. In a sense, the person interprets the situation and then consults his or her programming to know how to respond. Automatic, nonconscious processes may be largely sufficient to explain these responses.

If consciousness plays a role, it is possibly not in the middle of that response sequence, and it is certainly not as the origin or source of impulses to act, where Libet's (1985) procedures sought it (Mele, in press). It could, however, be useful for revising that bank of programs. It could be useful for learning systems of rules or for planning the action long before it was executed. It can also be useful for resolving conflicts, such as if the person has several separate automatic responses that prescribe different responses to the same stimulus.

Many researchers have concluded from Libet's (e.g., 1985) research that consciousness cannot have any direct impact on behavior. Libet asked his participants to decide when to move their wrist or finger and to make a mental note of exactly when they made this decision (by observing a specially designed clock that was highly sensitive to small time intervals). Brain activity showed an uptick prior to the point at which people claimed to have made the conscious decision. The simple explanation, popular with skeptics of consciousness, is that the brain was already initiating the response before the conscious mind got around to it. Consciousness, in that understanding, may register what the brain has done but does not have any causal role to play.

Libet specifically instructed participants not to plan ahead when to initiate their response, however. This may have seemed reasonable to the investigators. However, my view is that conscious processes are far more useful for planning than for direct initiation of responses. Hence the instructions for that study introduced a serious bias against the possibility of showing what consciousness can do. Libet's study was a bit like asking someone to demonstrate his new piano without making any sound.

Most theories about the functional value of consciousness have sought that value either in the direct control of action or in obtaining sensory information from the physical environment. Our theory

(Baumeister & Masicampo, 2009) looks elsewhere. In the following pages, I present a brief summary of our emerging understanding. In a nutshell, consciousness is a matter of internal information processing, thus several steps removed from both sensory input and behavioral output. Consciousness is for facilitating cross-communication among different parts or regions in brain and mind, so that all the relevant information and processes distributed across it can be integrated. Consciousness is essentially a capacity for constructing sequential thought. Its most important uses are for simulating events away from the here and now. These are done to facilitate dealing with the human social environment, including culture.

Connecting Input to Output

Behavior has long been conceptualized as response to stimulus. The brain makes the essential connection between the incoming stimulus (the input) and the behavioral response (the output). The design of the brain has to enable the input to find the relevant information stores to initiate the output. As long as things are as simple as fight or flight, the design issues seem straightforward. However, if stimuli have multiple layers of possible meaning, and behavioral outputs are subject to multiple constraints and contingencies, then the design problems multiply: How can one get the incoming stimulus properly interpreted and linked to all the relevant stores of information so that the proper output can be produced?

Consciousness is crucial for enabling the different parts of brain and mind to share the information they have. The notion of consciousness as a global theatre or workspace has been articulated by many theorists, notably Baars (1997, 2002). Information is dispersed throughout brain and mind, and so one central signal is prepared and put up on stage (so to speak) where all the different centers of information can take note and produce their relevant contributions.

The transition from a relatively simple set of interpretations and responses to a highly complex one was possibly gradual, produced as the brain developed more and more ways of thinking about the environment. Why would this have happened? After all, the physical environment did not change much across evolutionary history, at least until very recently. For this reason, I assume the extra size of the human brain was not, primarily, for dealing with the physical environment.

The social environment was the driving force between advances in brain size and complexity. Dunbar's (1995, 1998) research tested multiple theories about why natural selection would have increased brain size. After all, brains are highly expensive organs in terms of caloric consumption, and larger brains could cause their owners to starve unless the brains ultimately paid off in terms of increasing the caloric intake. That, incidentally, is why squirrels and rats and bugs and other creatures did not continue to evolve toward ever-greater intelligence: Increases in brain size were metabolically costly and failed to pay for themselves.

Dunbar tested multiple theories about how a bigger brain might pay for itself in terms of bringing in more calories. These included a shift toward more complicated food sources (e.g., fruit, which ripens and rots quickly; the "fruit-seeking brain hypothesis") and expanded territories for roaming. None of these panned out. Instead, he found that the main correlate of brain size was social network size (and complexity). Brains are thus not for understanding predators, prey, or other aspects of the physical environment, but rather for understanding the social environment.

Thus, whereas a squirrel needs only to classify another creature as a dangerous threat (so need to run) or possibly as an opportunity for mating, a human who sees another human has much to consider: not only that person's relationship to the self but also to others (as in alliances and factions), plus possible role complementarities (trading partner, boss, friend, ad hoc partner), perhaps grudges or gratitudes or other dispositions based on prior interactions (again with self or others), and so forth.

Making the Inner Movie

Thus, consciousness is not so much a direct aggregate of incoming sensory information as a moving picture the brain constructs for itself, so that its widely dispersed centers for processing all manner of information can be accessed and can provide useful help. Crucially, these can provide the most help as a function of how much information is contained in the signal they receive. Hence, it pays to construct the conscious image with as much preliminary interpretation as possible.

Light waves strike the retina. One could simply beam this jumble of signals out to the different parts of the brain, but a haphazard set of colors could hardly be expected to activate the brain center that remembers that Sally is holding a grudge against you because of something that happened last week. To activate that information, it is necessary for the signal to be sent out to be identified, already, as Sally. Hence, the brain works up the light waves into an image, identifies it as Sally, and puts that up on the stage or film screen of consciousness. (Baars, 1997, used a stage metaphor, but for reasons that will soon become clear, we prefer a film metaphor.)

The process of making sense of incoming information before it is broadcast across the brain can be called preinterpretation. (In the above example, it includes identifying the image as Sally.) The more extensive preinterpretation is, the more useful the signal will be in terms of activating associations to relevant stores of information dispersed throughout the brain and mind. From a design standpoint, its main drawback is that it is costly in terms of the amount of work it requires.

The cost is greatly reduced, however, if results can be preserved. That is, instead of repeatedly identifying the image as Sally with each new light wave striking the retina, it would be more efficient to identify it once as Sally and then preserve that identification as long as Sally is present.

The difference corresponds roughly to the two ways of making a movie. A conventional movie makes each frame of the film out of the information coming in from the camera each moment. In contrast, animation makes each frame in the movie from the preceding one: The animator copies the previous frame and then makes changes as needed. Our theory is that consciousness resembles animation more than camera filmmaking. The reason is the same: The preinterpretive work that went into making one frame is thus preserved in the next.

The mental apparatus that creates consciousness is therefore largely designed to construct sequences of thought, by which one moment's content is produced out of the previous moment's. When this is a matter of keeping it the same, as in having Sally continue to be Sally, this is simple. However, there is change as well as continuity. The inner filmmaking apparatus is thus designed to model change. One source of change is new information coming in from the external world, such as when Sally sits down.

The apparatus apparently is designed to learn what sorts of change are common and plausible. Sally might sit down or put on a hat, but she will not transform into an alligator. Hence, the mind has to be good at preserving knowledge of who she is while altering her position in space, but it does not need to be able to accommodate her transforming into a member of another species. Learning what follows from what is an important part of learning to have conscious thought and experience.

Once the inner apparatus is capable of constructing sequences of conscious content that include stability and change, the opportunity to break free from the here and now increases. All one needs is a starting point, and the mind can construct sequences of thought even without further input. Moreover, if the starting point can be obtained elsewhere than from direct sensory input, then an entire sequence can be experienced without any dependence on the immediate environment.

It is generally believed, for example, that many animals are not fully conscious in the human sense but do experience dreams. In our view, dreams are an important transitional stage on the road to consciousness. It is no accident that dreams occur during sleep, so that the simple brain does not have to keep track of current sensory input and distinguish it from the mental content. Also, during sleep the animal's actual body itself is not behaving, and so the fact that it is experiencing something away from the here and now will not pose practical problems. (For example, if the animal dreamt of running through a field while it was actually running through a forest, it would crash into the trees, but having such a dream while sleeping, and hence while immobile, poses no such ambulatory dangers.)

Permit me to reiterate that consciousness is removed from both input and output. By this analysis, the content of consciousness is information that the brain already has; consciousness simply puts it into this inner film to make it accessible to many brain areas. Furthermore, the result of consciousness is merely transmission of information to these other parts of the brain and mind, thus not yet behavioral output. Consciousness is thus entirely for inner processing of information. Input and output processes are separate.

Constructed Sequential Thought

The thrust thus far is that consciousness is where the automatic, unconscious mind constructs meaningful sequences of thought. It has learned (though innate preparedness may help) what sequences are plausible, and so it knows what rules to follow in moving from one thought to the next one. As many theorists have noted, whereas the automatic and unconscious mind can do many things in parallel, the conscious mind operates serially and does one thing at a time (e.g., Lieberman, Gaunt, Gilbert, & Trope, 2002).

Several categories of sequential thought appear, in fact, to depend on consciousness and would indeed facilitate human social life. Evidence for these is reviewed by Baumeister and Masicampo (2009) and other sources.

First, multiword speech appears to require conscious processing. The unconscious can understand and respond to single words, but not more. Single words can be processed subliminally, but efforts to slip even two-word phrases into the unconscious have not been successful (see Baars, 2002; also Deutsch, Gawronsky, & Strack, 2006). The difference in power and capability is enormous, indeed infinite: Vastly more information can be represented in sentences than in single words. Thus, consciousness and sequential thought greatly increase the mind's power to process information.

Second, logical reasoning appears to require conscious intervention, as argued by Lieberman et al. (2002). Experimental studies by DeWall, Baumeister, and Masicampo (2009) showed that answers to logical reasoning multiple-choice problems were no better than chance if consciousness were impaired, whereas unconscious load manipulations did not interfere at all. Conversely, conscious motivations improved performance on logic problems, whereas activating unconscious motivations to be logical failed to improve actual performance, even though there was an increase in efforts to seem logical.

Third, counting and quantification appear to require consciousness. Here the evidence can seem misleading, insofar as the unconscious "knows" that 5 times 6 equals 30. But as Winkielman and Schooler (2008) and others have pointed out, nobody believes that the unconscious mind actually performs the computation. Rather, the unconscious simply learns by rote memorization that 5 times 6 equals 30. Studies with the CRT (Frederick, 2005) show that, again, the unconscious may seek to estimate answers to quantitative problems but cannot really solve them, and only conscious rule-based thinking permits correct answers. For example: A bat and ball were purchased for $1.10, and the bat cost a dollar more than the ball, so how much did the ball cost? Although people can get the correct answer of 5 cents, most usually have the automatic thought of "10 cents" and must construct the computation consciously in order to override that and get the right answer. Moreover, when people are distracted or under some condition that pre-empts conscious processing and increases reliance on automatic processes, the wrong answer of 10 cents becomes more common.

Fourth, some forms of causal explanation appear to depend on conscious thought. The issue here is also complicated insofar as certain forms of causal association can be mimicked automatically. Still, full-blown conscious understanding appears to require conscious analysis (e.g., Winkielman & Schooler, 2008).

Two additional forms of thought build on these. First, narrative thought depends on them. A good story is thus logical and causal, and obviously it is almost always made from sentences. If numbers are involved, they also should be consistent with the rules of arithmetic and quantification. To illustrate, we noted earlier that dreams may be an intermediate step toward conscious thought. Dreams have been well recognized to be often deficient in one or more of these respects, such as being irrational or causally implausible.

Second, and last, simulations of events away from the here and now also use these forms of sequential thought. Simulations are often narratives in their own right, and they too are mainly useful if they satisfy the requirements of causality and logic, as well as language and quantification (the latter only if relevant).

The main thrust of the review by Baumeister and Masicampo (2009) is that the capacity for simulating events and processes away from the here and now is the crucial function of consciousness. It is primarily useful for operating in a complex social environment, even a cultural one.

Benefits of Simulations

The benefits of being able to simulate events are extensive, especially for a human being seeking to live in a civilized, cultural society. The argument is that simulations are needed mainly for the sake of adaptation to just such a social environment. I list here several of the main social uses of conscious simulation.

First, when complex decisions are encountered, the mind can simulate each course of action along with its likely consequences and outcomes. Decision making is thus greatly facilitated by conscious thought. Without simulation, it is impossible to anticipate the results of an action, and so the decision about how to act can only be made on the basis of the direct appeal of the action itself (which may include associations based on the reinforcement history for such actions—which may or may not be relevant to the present circumstances). A mental simulation can enable the person to choose the action that promises the best long-term consequences.

Second, by replaying past events, one can learn better from them, so a single experience can constitute many trials of learning. Skinnerian learning occurs when the behavior and its reward (or punishment) occur—or not at all. Moreover, the reward or punishment typically must occur almost immediately after the action, if there is to be any learning (see Roberts, 2002). In contrast, people can replay episodes over and over, in some cases for years, in order to search for lessons and evaluate multiple possible implications.

A (third) related capability is the ability to replay events counterfactually. Replaying a significant event exactly as it occurs may be helpful for learning, to stamp in the lesson, but replaying it counterfactually allows a much greater range of learning. One can think, "If only I had said or done X, the entire episode might have turned out differently," and can imagine how events would have flowed in that case. With such replays, a single event can be the equivalent of many learning trials with different behaviors and outcomes. Hence, the person can learn a great deal from a single event.

Fourth, the conscious human can simulate other people's mental states, experiences, and concerns. Empathy contributes mightily to prosocial behavior. Shared understandings are essential to economic transactions, without which culture would be severely crippled. Human social life and culture depend heavily on shared assumptions, and indeed most conversation assumes that the other person understands what one says the same way one understands it oneself. Simulating the other's perspective and reactions greatly facilitates social interaction.

Fifth, self-control can be bolstered: When the mind is pulled by strong temptations in the here and now, it can simulate future outcomes that can provide an alternative motivational pull. Thus, the ability to forego immediate pleasures for the sake of long-term benefits is fostered.

Sixth, simulating plans or acts can provide guidance for the automatic system, which may execute such plans later or may automatize actions into skills. It seems likely that people generally simulate most specific actions before doing them, and moreover, this is typically adaptive: It is better to think before acting. Mental rehearsal facilitates physical performance and is often a vital step in learning (as noted above, with the example of learning the multiplication tables).

BACK TO FREE WILL AND ACTION CONTROL

Viewed in this way, conscious thought is produced by nonconscious and automatic processes, but it can play a decisive role in deciding what actions are performed. Simulating an action before (or without) doing it can help the person decide whether to go through with the actual performance. Simulating prior events can help extract lessons from them and help foresee how future events might turn out. Simulating the perspectives and mental states of others can help coordinate action and support the sorts of shared understandings on which culture rests.

The "freedom" of free will is linked to consciousness because only with conscious thought can you conceptualize multiple alternatives. Freedom depends on the possibility of doing something else. A basic purpose of consciousness is to enable the person to think of such alternatives (again, in multiple contexts: alternative options in present decision; counterfactual replays; possible future outcomes; alternative perspectives than one's own). The capacity to run conscious simulations frees the person from the tyranny of what one sees and one has actually experienced.

DISCUSSION WITH ROY BAUMEISTER

Can complex problems be solved without conscious reasoning?
Even relatively simple problems, such going to the airport and catching a flight, would be difficult to solve without using conscious thought. To arrive at the airport on time, one has to consider traffic patterns, whether

the destination is continental or international, how busy the airport will be, and so forth. Deciding when to leave requires conscious reasoning, if one wants to arrive at the airport on time. More specifically, a mental simulation in which one walks through all of the necessary steps may be the most common way people solve this kind of problem.

Skeptics may point out that it could be possible for a person to be hypnotized into going to the airport at an appropriate time (so as not to miss his or her flight), which seemingly would suggest that conscious reasoning played no part in getting to the airport on time. Yet the person doing the hypnotism had to do the kind of reasoning necessary so that the person being hypnotized would not arrive at the airport at 4:00 for a 1:15 departure. It may be pointed out that in the hypnotism example, the hypnotized person did not personally reason about when to go to the airport. John Bargh's program of research has found other cases in which it is possible to bypass conscious reasoning and get some behavioral effect. This is like reaching under the hood of a car and getting it to react, bypassing the driver. However, the fact that one can get the car to react without someone in the driver's seat does not constitute evidence that cars do not need drivers.

Does consciousness give humans distinctly different motivations than nonhuman animals?

A lot of nonhuman animals want to get nourishment and eat things that taste good, just as humans do. However, humans desire a conscious experience of eating good food and drinking fine wine, whereas nonhuman animals show no similar inclination. A person in a coma would need to have food and in some way may even get pleasure out of it. Yet conscious humans want more than simply to get food into the body; humans want to have the conscious experience, for example, of a particular wine with a particular food. It seems unlikely that the human desire for gastronomical experiences is only a reflection of a refined palate because it seems unlikely that people would be just as happy with eating a gourmet meal when unconscious as they would be when conscious.

Skiing is another example. Many animals move, and some may get enjoyment out of it. Yet humans seek to entertain themselves by skiing. That is, they want to experience skiing as a conscious experience. If a person went skiing when she was hypnotized, having no conscious experience of it, would that be just as good as skiing consciously? Probably not. Likewise, if a person had sex during sleep and had no recollection of it, that would be a shame. Humans seek conscious experiences in a way that nonhuman animals do not, and there is a loss if desired events are not experienced consciously.

How is consciousness different from experiencing incoming sensory information?

There was a big argument in the history of psychology between the Gestalt school and the introspectionists. Introspectionists trained people to record all of the sensations that they experienced, for example, while looking across the field. They recorded a great number of individual sensations. The big objection from the Gestalt school was, "I don't see 93 sensations. I see a tree." That has continued to astound people. The eye receives sensations in the form of light striking the retina. In other words, the tree as a whole representation is not beamed into consciousness; the individual bits of sensory information are assembled in the constructing/simulating process and are experienced in consciousness as a tree. Consciousness is the picture the brain constructs for itself from a (nearly) impossible number of individual pieces of sensory information.

Is consciousness the exclusive providence of mature human beings, or are nonhuman animals conscious?

Consciousness is most likely not on a continuum. Rather, the best way to think of it is probably as a *step function*. In terms of the evolution of mental capacities, there most likely were discreet steps up. Other species may experience consciousness in some form, but that would be several steps below that of human consciousness.

REFERENCES

Alquist, J., & Baumeister, R. F. (2008). Induced disbelief in free will leads to heightened conformity to others' judgments. Unpublished findings, Florida State University, Tallahassee, FL.

Alquist, J. L., Daly, M., Stillman, T., & Baumeister, R. F. (2009). [Belief in determinism decreases counterfactual thinking]. Unpublished raw data.

Baars, B. J. (1997). *In the theater of consciousness: The workspace of the mind.* New York: Oxford University Press.

Baars, B. J. (2002). The conscious access hypothesis: Origins and recent evidence. *Trends in Cognitive Sciences, 6,* 47–52.

Baumeister, R. F. (2005). *The cultural animal: Human nature, meaning, and social life.* New York: Oxford University Press.

Baumeister, R. F., Bratslavsky, E., Muraven, M., & Tice, D. M. (1998). Ego depletion: Is the active self a limited resource? *Journal of Personality and Social Psychology, 74,* 1252–1265.

Baumeister, R. F., & Masicampo, E. J. (2009). *Conscious thought is for facilitating social and cultural interactions by simulating nonpresent realities.* Manuscript submitted for publication.

Baumeister, R. F., Masicampo, E. J., & DeWall, C. N. (2009). Prosocial benefits of feeling free: Disbelief in free will increases aggression and reduces helpfulness. *Personality and Social Psychology Bulletin, 35*, 260–268.

Deutsch, R., Gawronski, B., & Strack, F. (2006). At the boundaries of automaticity: Negation as a reflective operation. *Journal of Personality and Social Psychology, 91*, 385–405.

De Waal, F. B. M. (2001). *The ape and the sushi master.* New York: Basic Books.

DeWall, C. N., Baumeister, R. F., & Masicampo, E. J. (in press). Evidence that logical reasoning depends on conscious processing. *Consciousness and Cognition.*

Donald, M. (2002). *A mind so rare: The evolution of human consciousness.* New York: Norton.

Dunbar, R. I. M. (1995). Neocortex size and group size in primates: A test of the hypothesis. *Journal of Human Evolution, 28*, 287–296.

Dunbar, R. I. M. (1998). The social brain hypothesis. *Evolutionary Anthropology, 6*, 178–190.

Frederick, S. (2005). Cognitive reflection and decision making. *Journal of Economics Perspectives, 19*, 25–42.

Freud, S. (1964). *New introductory lectures on psycho-analysis.* J. Strachey (Trans). New York: Norton. (Original work published 1933)

Gailliot, M. T., Baumeister, R. F., DeWall, C. N., Maner, J. K., Plant, E. A., Tice, D. M., Brewer, L. E., & Schmeichel, B. J. (2007). Self-control relies on glucose as a limited energy source: Willpower is more than a metaphor. *Journal of Personality and Social Psychology, 92*, 325–336.

Libet, B. (1985). Unconscious cerebral initiative and the role of conscious will in voluntary action. *Behavior and Brain Sciences, 8*, 529–566.

Lieberman, M. D., Gaunt, R., Gilbert, D. T., & Trope, Y. (2002). Reflexion and reflection: A social cognitive neuroscience approach to attributional inference. In M. P. Zanna (Ed.), *Advances in experimental social psychology* (pp. 199–249). San Diego, CA: Academic Press.

Mele, A. R. (2009). *Effective intentions.* New York: Oxford University Press.

Paulhus, D. L., & Margesson, A. (1994). Free Will and Determinism (FAD) scale. Unpublished manuscript, University of British Columbia, Vancouver, British Columbia, Canada.

Roberts, W. A. (2002). Are animals stuck in time? *Psychological Bulletin, 128*, 473–489.

Schmeichel, B. J., Vohs, K. D., & Baumeister, R. F. (2003). Intellectual performance and ego depletion: Role of the self in logical reasoning and other information processing. *Journal of Personality and Social Psychology, 85*, 33–46.

Searle, J. R. (2001). *Rationality in action.* Cambridge, MA: MIT Press.

Stillman. T. F., & Baumeister, R. F. (2008) Induced disbelief in free will reduces anticipation of guilt over possible transgression. Unpublished findings, Florida State University, Tallahassee, FL.

Stillman, T. F., Sparks, E., & Baumeister, R. F. (2008). What makes action free? Determinants of perceived freedom of action. Manuscript in preparation, Florida State University.

Vohs, K. D., Baumeister, R. F., Schmeichel, B. J., Twenge, J. M., Nelson, N. M., & Tice, D. M. (2008). Making choices impairs subsequent self-control: A limited-resource account of decision making, self-regulation, and active initiative. *Journal of Personality and Social Psychology, 94*, 883–898.

Vohs, K. D., & Schooler, J. (2008). The value of believing in free will: Encouraging a belief in determinism increases cheating. *Psychological Science, 19*, 49–54.

Winkielman, P., & Schooler, J. (2008). Unconscious, conscious, and metaconscious in social cognition. In F. Strack & J. Foerster (Eds.), *Social cognition: The basis of human interaction* (pp. 49–69). Philadelphia: Psychology Press.

4 Conscious Deciding and the Science of Free Will

Alfred R. Mele

One source of skepticism about free will is the belief—defended by Daniel Wegner (2002, 2008) and Benjamin Libet (1985, 2004) among others—that conscious decisions (or choices) and intentions never play a role in producing corresponding overt actions.[1] Roy Baumeister writes: "if there are any genuine phenomena associated with the concept of free will, they most likely involve conscious choice. Such a view has to contend with the now widespread belief that consciousness is a useless, feckless epiphenomenon, and that all behavior is guided by nonconscious processes" (2008, p. 76). If all behavior were produced *only* by nonconscious processes, and if conscious decisions (or choices) and intentions (along with their physical correlates) were to play no role at all in producing any corresponding actions, free will would be in dire straits.[2]

Work reporting the pertinent scientific findings tends to show little evidence of careful attention to such conceptual questions as what decisions (or choices) and intentions might be. A clear, precise conception of conscious practical deciding might prove useful both in interpreting data and in designing fruitful experiments. (*Practical* deciding is deciding *what to do*. It differs from deciding that something is the case—for example, that an acquaintance is probably lying about his exploits.) Henceforth, I typically write simply in terms of deciding and count on the reader to remember that practical deciding is the topic.)

Some of the decisions we make are about what to do *right then*. For example, subjects in a Libet-style experiment (Libet, 2004) might decide to flex a wrist at once. These are *proximal* decisions. Other decisions are about what to do later. I might, for example, decide today to see a certain movie tomorrow night. This is a *distal* decision. Distal decisions and intentions have received relatively little attention in the literature on the science of free will.

This chapter has two main aims. The first is to develop a clear, attractive, experimentally useful conception of conscious deciding. The second is to challenge the source of skepticism about free will identified in my opening sentence. The contributors to this volume have agreed to assume that free will is possible and that consciousness is not an epiphenomenon, and to explore ways in which free will or consciousness might operate. Despite the negative ring of my second aim, I do not renege on this agreement in pursuing it. The challenge I develop sheds light on a way in which some conscious decisions and intentions do seem to be efficacious. In Section 1, I provide some conceptual background. Section 2 develops a conception of conscious deciding. In Section 3, focusing on *proximal* deciding, I describe one important way in which that conception may prove to be experimentally useful. Section 4 takes up some conceptual issues surrounding a causal question about conscious proximal decisions. In Section 5, I turn to *distal* decisions and intentions. I make a case there—grounded in empirical work on "implementation intentions" (reviews include Gollwitzer, 1999, and Gollwitzer & Sheeran, 2006)—for the thesis that some conscious decisions and intentions play a role in producing corresponding overt actions. Section 6 wraps things up.

SOME CONCEPTUAL BACKGROUND

What is it to decide to do something? Here is a proposal that I have defended elsewhere: To decide to *A* is to perform a momentary action of forming an intention to *A* (Mele, 2003, Ch. 9). In my view, intentions are executive attitudes toward plans; plans—which range from simple representations of prospective "basic" actions to complex strategies for achieving remote goals—constitute the representational content of intentions (Mele, 1992).[3] The momentary action of intention formation in which deciding to *A* consists is, more fully, an action of executive assent to a pertinent first-person plan of action (Mele, 2003, Ch. 9). I discuss executive assent shortly.

Deciding to *A* is not to be confused with any process that issues in deciding to *A*, including, for example, deliberation about what to do, in the case of deliberation-based deciding. And deciding to *A*, as I conceive of it, does not precede the onset of the intention to *A* formed in the act of deciding. Instead, what it is to decide to *A* is to form—actively—an intention to *A*. The intention arises *in* that momentary intention-forming action, not after it.

Are all intentions formed in acts of deciding? Consider the following: "When I intentionally unlocked my office door this morning, I intended to unlock it. But since I am in the habit of unlocking my door in the morning and conditions ... were normal, nothing called for a *decision* to unlock it" (Mele, 1992, p. 231). If I had heard a fight in my office, I might have paused to consider whether to unlock the door or walk away, and I might have decided to unlock it. But given the routine nature of my conduct, there is no need to posit an action of intention formation in this case. My intention to unlock the door may have been acquired without having been actively formed. In short, it might have been *nonactionally acquired*. If, as I believe, all decisions about what to do are prompted partly by uncertainty about what to do (Mele, 2003, Ch. 9), then when there is no such uncertainty, no decisions will be made. This is not to say that, in such situations, no intentions will be acquired.

I mentioned that, in my view, deciding to do something is an action of executive assent to a first-person plan of action. My notion of executive assent is straightforward.[4] If you tell me that Henrik is an excellent hockey player and I express complete agreement, I thereby assent to your claim. This is overt *cognitive* assent. If you propose that we watch Henrik play tonight at the arena and I express complete acceptance of your proposal, I thereby assent to your proposal. This is overt *executive* assent: I have agreed to join you in executing your proposal for joint action. Possibly, my overt act of assenting to your proposal was a matter of my giving voice to a nonactionally acquired intention to join you in watching Henrik play. For example, upon hearing your proposal, I might not have been at all uncertain about what to do; straightaway, I nonactionally acquired an intention to join you, and I voiced that intention in an overt act of assent. Or I might have weighed the pros and cons, judged that it would be best to join you, and, on the basis of that judgment, nonactionally acquired an intention to join you. However, there is also a distinctly different possibility. Perhaps, because I already had plans and because your offer was attractive, I was uncertain about what to do. Perhaps, upon reflection, I judged that I could revise my plans without much inconvenience but was still uncertain about what to do because my prior plans were attractive as well. And perhaps I performed a mental action of assenting to your proposal and then expressed that inner assent to you. In performing that mental action, if that is what happened, I *decided* to join you: My mentally assenting to your proposal was an act of intention formation, an act of settling on joining you to watch Henrik play tonight.

Readers will have noticed that I have used "decisions [to *A*]" as a synonym for "decidings [to *A*]." That is one use of the term. "Decision" may also be used to refer to the intention formed in an act of deciding and to *what* someone decides, as in "His decision was to go to the arena." I make these points to forestall confusion. In what follows, the context should enable readers to see which sense of "decision" is at work both in passages that I quote and in my own prose.

CONSCIOUS PROXIMAL DECIDING

In the preceding section, I sketched an account of practical deciding. Although some readers may believe that such deciding is always consciously done, that they are right about this cannot simply be assumed in the present context. Libet claims that subjects in a well-known experiment of his become conscious of their proximal decisions over a third of a second after they make them (1985). I have argued elsewhere that this claim is unwarranted (Mele, 2006, Ch. 2; 2009, Chs. 3 and 4). It is not my purpose here to challenge it again. Instead, I intend to develop a conception of *conscious* deciding. If unconscious deciding is possible, the sketch of deciding offered in the preceding section is compatible with it.

What is a good model for a person's becoming conscious of a decision of his? Is the best model becoming conscious of an event in the external world? Consider the Frolich effect: "a slit of light moving at a constant speed from the left edge (say) into a window on a screen is first seen at some distance from the left edge, never at the left edge" (van de Grind, 2002, p. 252). Why? Because, as Wim van de Grind puts it, it takes time for the visual system to determine "a position signal for a moving target and the calculation involves averaging a range of previous positions, so that it never gives you the starting position" (2002, p. 252). Processing input from the external world takes time; so vision lags behind the occurrence of events or event segments that one sees. (In the case of the moving slit of light, it is not as though one does not see the slit move until it has completed its movement into the window, that is, until that event is over; however, one does not begin to see the slit at all until it has already moved some distance, and one's vision of it lags behind its progress across the screen.)

Does it always happen that we become conscious of a decision only after we make it? Is what happens in this sphere just a wholly internal analogue of what happens in the sphere of conscious perception of external events? The following bit of background helps set the stage for an answer. I was once a subject in a Libet-style experiment. My task was to watch a rapidly revolving spot on a Libet clock, to flex my right wrist whenever I felt like it (many times over the course of the experiment), and to report, after each flex, where the spot was on the clock when I first became conscious of a proximal intention to flex. For a time, I waited for intentions to flex to pop up in me, but I found that that was not happening. So I hit on the strategy of silently saying "now!" to myself and then flexing straightaway in response to that silent, conscious speech act. The "now!" gave me a conscious event to report after the flex.

Any occurrence of my silently saying "now!" is undoubtedly the result of a causal process. That process—like any process—takes time. But what that process might issue in is my *consciously performing* the speech act at issue in a sense of "consciously perform" that requires my being conscious of performing the action the whole (very brief) time I am performing it. I know of no sound conceptual argument for the assertion that I become conscious of my silent speech act only after the action itself—*as opposed to a process that issues in it*—is underway. And I know of no sound empirical argument for this. Consciousness of the speech act might not lag behind (segments of) the act in the way that vision of external events lags behind (segments of) the events seen.

Am I a substance dualist (a Cartesian)?[5] Absolutely not. A proper causal, physical account of the production of my conscious silent speech act can diverge from a proper causal, physical account of the onset of consciousness of external events. In the latter case, the external events are among the causes of consciousness of them, and we become conscious of events that have already begun or, in some cases, have already happened. But my consciously saying "now!" to myself might not be a matter of my becoming conscious of a "now!"-saying that has already begun. Again, the causal process at work may instead issue in a speech act that is a conscious action right from its onset. (The onset of an action should not be confused with anything that precedes the action, including any causes of the action. Being conscious of an action right from its onset does not entail being conscious of its causes.)

The view of conscious, silent "now!"-saying that I have sketched provides a model for understanding consciously proximally deciding to *A*. I have suggested that I can consciously perform a silent "now!"-saying action in a sense of "consciously perform" that requires my being conscious of performing the action the whole (very brief) time I am performing it. I now suggest that I can consciously make a proximal decision to *A*—that is, consciously perform the momentary action of forming a proximal intention to *A*—in the same sense of "consciously perform." (Just as my suggestion about conscious "now!"-saying is utterly compatible with a nondualistic, non-Cartesian view of action production, so is this suggestion about conscious deciding.) If the latter suggestion is correct, the time of the onset of a proximal intention to *A* can—at least sometimes—be identical with the time of the onset of the agent's consciousness of that intention. These times are identical whenever an agent consciously proximally decides to *A* in the sense of "consciously decide" just sketched—a sense requiring that the agent be conscious of the deciding-to-*A* action the whole (very brief) time he is performing it.

Incidentally, there is a way of bringing my consciously saying "now!" as a subject in a Libet-style experiment and my consciously proximally deciding to flex even closer together. Perhaps I thought of the "now!" as being in the imperative mood and as short for the self-command "flex now!" Instances of such commanding would seem to be instances of deciding to flex now.

What about conscious *distal* deciding? Because distal decisions are about what to do *later*, consciously saying "now!" silently is not an apt model for them. Consciously saying "Do this!" silently is a better model. If we can consciously perform silent "now!"-saying actions in the sense of "consciously perform" that I have highlighted, we can do the same with silent "Do this!"-saying actions. The corresponding suggestion about distal decisions is that we can consciously make a distal decision to *A*—that is, consciously perform the momentary action of forming a distal intention to *A*—in the same sense of "consciously perform." Again, deciding to *A* is to be distinguished from any processes that issue in deciding to *A* (including deliberation). And, obviously, "Do this!" is not short for "Do this now!" The "this" refers to one of the options for future action that one was entertaining—for example, reading John's chapter tomorrow morning.

EXPERIMENTAL UTILITY

Might the proposed conception of conscious *proximal* deciding be experimentally useful? Some background on Libet-style experiments helps set the stage for an answer. Libet argues that although free will does not initiate actions, it may be involved in "vetoing" conscious intentions or urges to act (1985, 1999, 2004, pp. 137–149). In this connection, he attempts to generate evidence about when his subjects become conscious of pertinent intentions or urges. In some of Libet's studies, subjects are instructed to flex their right wrists whenever they wish. In subjects who are regularly reminded to aim for spontaneity and who report no "preplanning," electrical readings from the scalp (EEGs)—averaged over at least 40 flexings for each subject—show a shift in "readiness potentials" (RPs) beginning at about 550 milliseconds (ms) before the time at which an electromyogram shows relevant muscular motion to begin (1985, pp. 529–530). (These RPs are called "type II RPs" [p. 531].) Subjects are also instructed to "recall ... the spatial clock position of a revolving spot at the time of [their] initial awareness" (p. 529) of something, *x*, that Libet variously describes as a "decision," "intention," "urge," "wanting," "will," or "wish" to move.[6] On average, "RP onset" preceded what the subjects reported to be the time of their initial awareness of *x* (time W) by 350 ms. Reported time W, then, preceded the onset of muscle motion by about 200 ms.

Libet's Results for Type II RPs

−550 ms	−200 ms	0 ms
RP onset	reported time W	muscle begins to move

The following labels facilitate discussion:

E-time: The time at which a proximal decision is made or a proximal intention, urge, etc., is acquired.
C-time: The time of the onset of the subject's consciousness of an item of the kind just specified.
B-time: The time the subject believes to be C-time when responding to the experimenter's question about C-time.

Libet contends that average *E*-time is −550 ms for subjects who are regularly encouraged to flex spontaneously and report no "preplanning." And he arrives at an average C-time of −150 ms by adding 50 ms to his average *B*-time (−200 ms) in an attempt to correct for what he believes to be a 50 ms bias in subjects' reports. (For alleged evidence of the existence of the bias, see Libet 1985, pp. 534–535, and 2004, p. 128.)

There is a lively literature on how accurate *B*-times are likely to be—that is, on how likely it is that they closely approximate C-times (for a review, see van de Grind, 2002). This is not surprising. Reading the position of a rapidly revolving dot at a given time is no mean feat, as Wim van de Grind observes (2002, p. 251). The same is true of relating the position of the dot to such an event as the onset of one's consciousness of a proximal intention to press a button. Patrick Haggard notes that "the large number of biases inherent in cross-modal synchronization tasks means that the perceived time of a stimulus may differ dramatically from its actual onset time. There is every reason to believe that purely internal events, such as conscious intentions, are at least as subject to this bias as perceptions of external events" (2006, p. 82).

One fact that has not received sufficient attention in the literature on accuracy is that individuals display great variability of *B*-times across trials. Patrick Haggard and Martin Eimer (1999) provide some relevant data. For each of their eight subjects, they locate the median *B*-time and then calculate the mean of the premedian (i.e., "early") *B*-times and the mean of the postmedian (i.e., "late") *B*-times. At the low end of variability by this measure, one subject had mean early and late *B*-times of −231 ms and −80 ms and another had means of −542 ms and −351 ms (p. 132). At the high end, one subject's figures were −940 ms and −4 ms and another's were −984 ms and −253 ms. Bear in mind that these figures are for means, not extremes. These results do not inspire confidence that *B*-time closely approximates C-time. If there were good reason to believe that C-times vary enormously across trials for the same subject, we might not find enormous variability in a subject's *B*-times worrisome in this connection. But there is good reason to believe this only if there is good reason to believe that *B*-times closely approximate C-times, and given the points made about cross-modal synchronization tasks in general and the cross-modal task of subjects in Libet-style experiments, there is not.

Another factor that may make it difficult for subjects to provide *B*-times that closely approximate C-times is their uncertainty about exactly what they are experiencing. As Haggard observes, subjects' reports about their intentions "are easily mediated by cognitive strategies, by the subjects' understanding of the experimental situation, and by their folk psychological beliefs about intentions" (2006, p. 81). He also remarks that "the conscious experience of intending is quite thin and evasive" (2005, p. 291). Even if the latter claim is an overstatement and some conscious experiences of intending are robust, the claim may be true of many of the experiences at issue in Libet-style studies. One can well imagine subjects wondering occasionally whether, for example, what they are experiencing is an intention (or urge) to act or merely a thought about when to act or an anticipation of acting soon. Hakwan Lau and coauthors say that they require their subjects to move a cursor to where they believed the dot on a Libet clock was "when they first felt their *intention* to press the button" (Lau, Rogers, & Passingham, 2007, p. 82; emphasis mine). One should not be surprised if some subjects given such an instruction were occasionally to wonder whether they were experiencing an intention to press or just an *urge* to press, for example. (Presumably, at least some layfolk treat intentions and urges as conceptually distinct, as dictionaries do.) Subjects may also wonder occasionally whether they are actually *feeling* an intention to press or are mistakenly thinking that they feel such an intention.

There is much less room for confusion and doubt about whether one is consciously saying "now!" to oneself. This observation, in light of the background just offered, generates both a prediction and a partial test of the utility of the conception of conscious proximal deciding developed in the preceding section. The prediction is that subjects asked to report on when they silently said "now!" to themselves will—individually—exhibit significantly less variability in their reports (relative to time 0) than subjects asked to report on onsets of consciousness of such things as intentions and urges. If the prediction were confirmed, we would have some reason to believe that their reports about when they consciously said "now!" involve *less guesswork* (and, accordingly, additional grounds for skepticism about the reliability of *B*-times in typical studies).

How does this bear on the issue of utility? Elsewhere, I have suggested giving subjects in a Libet-style experiment the following instructions:

> One way to think of deciding to press the button now is as consciously saying "now!" to yourself silently in order to command yourself to press the button at once. Consciously say "now!" silently to yourself whenever you feel like it and then immediately press the button. Look at the clock and try to determine as closely as possible where the dot is when you say "now!" . . . You'll report that location to us after you press the button. (See Mele, 2008, p. 10)

Subjects can also be regularly reminded to make their decisions "spontaneously"—that is, to avoid thinking about when to press. If, as predicted, subjects given these instructions individually show much less variability in *B*-times than subjects given typical Libet-style instructions, the proposed conception of conscious proximal deciding will have proved useful in designing an experiment that provides less questionable evidence about C-times than typical experiments do.

I defined C-time partly in terms of *E*-time, the time at which a proximal decision is made or a proximal intention, urge, and so forth, is acquired. C-time is the time of the onset of the subject's consciousness of an item of the kind just specified. What I now dub C*-time is the time of the onset of the subject's consciousness of a *proximal decision* in particular. Would the proposed experiment give us information specifically about C*-time? I take up this question toward the end of Section 4.

A CAUSAL QUESTION

I opened this chapter with the observation that one source of skepticism about free will is the belief that conscious decisions and intentions never play a role in producing corresponding overt actions. In Section 5, I discuss evidence that some conscious *distal* decisions and intentions are causally potent. The present section's topic is a collection of conceptual issues that surround a causal question about conscious *proximal* decisions.

Saying that my conscious decision caused x leaves open what work, if any, is done by its being a *conscious* decision in causing x. Might the fact that an agent *consciously* makes a proximal decision to press a button in a Libet-style experiment ever have a place in a causal explanation of a button press?

Imagine a study in which subjects are explicitly instructed to make conscious decisions to press and then to press straightaway in response to those decisions. It is made very clear to them that they are not to press unless they first consciously make a proximal decision to press. (They may be given the "now!" instructions about proximal deciding suggested above.) Suppose that Sam, a subject in this hypothetical experiment, succeeds in following the instructions—*literally* interpreted—on a particular occasion. At time t, he makes a conscious proximal decision to press the button and he proceeds to execute that decision.

Consider the following two claims:

Claim 1. If, at t, Sam had not consciously made a proximal decision to press, he would have pressed at the same time anyway, owing, perhaps, to an unconscious proximal decision or intention to press.

Claim 2. If, at t, Sam had not consciously made a proximal decision to press, he would not have pressed the button when he did; instead, he would have consciously made a decision of this kind a bit later and he would have executed that decision.

If we assume that Sam is good at following his instructions, we should view Claim 2 as much more plausible than Claim 1. And Claim 2 supports the following claim:

Claim 3. The fact that, at t, Sam *consciously* made a proximal decision to press the button helps to account for the fact that he pressed the button at $t + n$.

A critic may make the following claim about the proximal decision that Sam made at t: Even if that decision had not been a conscious decision, it would have done the work that proximal decisions do and, accordingly, it would have issued in Sam's pressing the button at $t + n$. Someone who makes this claim may infer that, even if Sam is good at following his instructions, Claim 3 is false.

The inference is misguided. Even if an unconscious proximal decision to press would have been just as effective as a conscious one, it is very likely that if Sam had not *consciously* proximally decided at t to press the button, he would not have proximally decided at t to press the button and would not have pressed it at $t + n$. (Again, given that he is good at following his instructions, it is likely that Sam would instead have consciously decided a bit later to press the button and would have pressed it later than $t + n$.) And this supports Claim 3.

Consider an analogy. Max struck a log with his red ax, thereby causing the log to split. If his ax had been green, it would have split wood just as well. But Max was under strict instructions to split wood only with red axes, and he was committed to following his instructions. If his ax had been green, he would not have used it, and, in fact, he would have looked for a red ax and split the log later, after he found one. In this scenario, the fact that Max's ax is red is causally relevant to his splitting the log *when* he does and therefore to his actual log splitting action, an action that has a specific location in time. Similarly, in the imagined experiment, the fact that, at *t*, Sam made a *conscious* proximal decision to press seems to be causally relevant to his pressing when he does and therefore to the actual pressing action he performs. I should add that although we do know that, other things being equal, red and green axes split wood equally well, we do not know how effective unconscious decisions are. Nor do we know whether unconscious deciding—as distinct from unconscious nonactional intention acquisition—is something that actually happens.[7] Also, for all we know, if there are instances of unconscious deciding, they are far too rare for there to be more than a glimmer of a chance that if Sam had not made a conscious proximal decision to press at *t*, he would have made an unconscious one.

The instructions in the imaginary experiment that I have been discussing are no more peculiar than the instructions in Libet's main study. But they are different. The imaginary instructions encourage subjects to be active in a specific way that Libet's instructions do not. They encourage subjects specifically to make proximal *decisions* to press—that is, actively to form proximal intentions to press.

Despite this feature of the imaginary instructions, it would be difficult to be certain that subjects actually are making such decisions. To see why, consider another imaginary experiment in which subjects are instructed to count—consciously and silently—from 1 to 5 and to press just after they consciously say "5" to themselves. Presumably, these instructions would be no less effective at eliciting pressings than the "conscious decision" instructions. In this experiment, the subjects are treating a conscious event—the conscious "5"-saying—as a "go" signal. (When they say "5," they are not at all uncertain about what to do, and they make no *decision* then to press.) Possibly, in a study in which subjects are given the "conscious decision" instructions, they would not actually make proximal decisions to press but would instead consciously simulate deciding and use the conscious simulation event as a "go" signal.

Ascertaining whether the fact that an agent consciously makes a proximal decision to *A* ever has a place in a causal explanation of his *A*-ing is a difficult task. Among other things, to be confident that data about the output end of things (for example, about the onset of muscle activity) are relevant, we would need to be confident that the agents are actually deciding to *A*, as opposed, for example, to using some other kind of conscious event as a "go" signal. Is this a problem only for those who would like to believe in the efficacy of conscious proximal decisions? Definitely not. It is also a problem for those who claim to have shown with Libet-style studies that the fact that an agent consciously makes a proximal decision to perform an overt action never has a place in a causal explanation of such an action.

CONSCIOUS DISTAL DECISIONS AND CAUSAL POWER

I turn to conscious *distal* decisions. Do any controlled studies yield evidence that the fact that an agent consciously made a distal decision to *A* sometimes has a place in a causal explanation of a corresponding overt intentional action? Peter Gollwitzer's work on distal "implementation intentions" merits special attention in the present connection (Gollwitzer, 1993, 1996, 1999; Gollwitzer and Sheeran, 2006). Implementation intentions, as Gollwitzer conceives of them, "are subordinate to goal intentions and specify the when, where, and how of responses leading to goal attainment" (1999, p. 494). They "serve the purpose of promoting the attainment of the goal specified in the goal intention." In forming an implementation intention, "the person commits himself or herself to respond to a certain situation in a certain manner."[8]

In one study of subjects "who had reported strong goal intentions to perform a BSE [breast self-examination] during the next month, 100% did so if they had been induced to form additional implementation intentions" (Gollwitzer 1999, p. 496; see Orbell, Hodgkins, & Sheeran, 1997). In a control group of people who also reported strong goal intentions to do this but were not induced to form implementation intentions, only 53% performed a self-exam. Subjects in the former group were asked to state in writing "where and when" they would perform the exam during the next month. The intentions they consciously expressed in writing are implementation intentions. If, in response to the request, these subjects actively formed relevant implementation intentions, they *decided* in advance on a place and time for a self-exam.

Another study featured the task of "vigorous exercise for 20 minutes during the next week" (Gollwitzer, 1999, p. 496; see Milne, Orbell, and Sheeran, 2002): "A motivational intervention that focused on increasing self-efficacy to exercise, the perceived severity of and vulnerability to coronary heart disease, and the expectation that exercise will reduce the risk of coronary heart disease raised compliance from 29% to only 39%." When this intervention was paired with the instruction to form relevant implementation intentions, "the compliance rate rose to 91%."

In a third study reviewed in Gollwitzer (1999), drug addicts who showed symptoms of withdrawal were divided into two groups: "One group was asked in the morning to form the goal intention to write a short curriculum vitae before 5:00 p.m. and to add implementation intentions that specified when and where they would write it" (p. 496). The other subjects were asked "to form the same goal intention but with irrelevant implementation intentions (i.e., they were asked to specify when they would eat lunch and where they would sit)." Once again, the results are striking: Although none of the participants in the second group completed the task, 80% of the subjects in the first group completed it.

Many studies of this kind are reviewed in Gollwitzer (1999), and Gollwitzer and Paschal Sheeran report that "findings from 94 independent tests showed that implementation intentions had a positive effect of medium-to-large magnitude . . . on goal attainment" (2006, p. 69). Collectively, the results provide evidence that the presence of relevant distal implementation intentions significantly increases the probability that agents will execute associated distal "goal intentions" in a broad range of circumstances. In the experimental studies that Gollwitzer reviews, subjects are explicitly asked to form relevant implementation intentions, and the intentions at issue are consciously expressed (1999, p. 501).

It should not be assumed, incidentally, that all members of all of the control groups lack conscious implementation intentions. Indeed, for all anyone knows, most members of the control groups who executed their goal intentions consciously made relevant distal implementation decisions.

Return to the breast self-examination study, in which the success rate was 100% for the implementation-intention group (Group 1) and 53% for the control group (Group 2). Consider the following pair of claims:

Claim 4. If the subjects in Group 1 had not been asked to form and report relevant distal implementation intentions, they would have had a 100% success rate anyway, owing partly, perhaps, to distal implementation intentions of which they were not conscious.

Claim 5. If the subjects in Group 1 had not been asked to form and report relevant distal implementation intentions, they would have had a success rate much closer to 53% than to 100%.

Obviously Claim 5 is much more plausible than Claim 4. The only basic difference between Groups 1 and 2 that is known to be relevant is the difference in instructions, and that difference is associated with a 100% versus a 53% success rate. If the subjects in Group 1 had not been asked to form and report relevant distal implementation intentions, their circumstances would have been just the same as those of the subjects in Group 2, and they would probably have had a success rate very similar to that of Group 2. Someone might contend that, even so, it is not the *having* of conscious distal implementation intentions that accounts for the impressive success rate of Group 1 but, instead, the sincere *reporting* of distal implementation intentions. This contention is testable. Another group of subjects who report strong goal intentions to perform a breast self-exam during the next month may be asked to decide during the experiment—consciously, of course—where and when they will perform it without also being asked to report what they decided. I would not be surprised if it were discovered that although the reporting has some effect, it is not nearly great enough to account for the difference between Groups 1 and 2. When tests are conducted there will be no need to speculate about this.[9]

An "illusion theorist" about conscious intentions may contend (1) that distal implementation intentions of which the agents were never conscious would have been just as effective as the subjects' conscious distal implementation intentions and (2) that the fact that these intentions are conscious intentions therefore is causally irrelevant to the performance of breast self-exams.[10] The first contention is extremely bold, to say the least. How would the imagined unconscious distal intentions help generate corresponding actions days or weeks later? Seemingly, not as a consequence of agents' consciously remembering these intentions when the time for their execution is near. Proponents of this equal effectiveness contention should specify a process that links distal implementation intentions of which agents are never conscious to corresponding intentional actions and produce evidence that the specified process is not a fiction. Once that is done, they can turn their attention to supporting their assertion of equal effectiveness.

Even if the equal effectiveness intention were granted, that would not settle matters. If that contention is true, what accounts for the different success rates in the two groups? Apparently, that many people in Group 2 do not acquire relevant implementation intentions. One way for subjects to acquire distal implementation intentions is to do so consciously but nonactionally as the upshot of conscious reflection on when and where to perform a breast self-exam. Their conscious reflection may issue, for example, in a conscious belief that it would be best to perform the exam at a certain place and time, and, in the absence of an act of *deciding*, that belief may issue in a conscious distal implementation intention. Another way to acquire relevant implementation intentions is to consciously *decide* in advance (after some conscious reflection) to perform the exam at a certain place and time. If the distal intention formed in that conscious act of deciding plays a causal role in the production of the action, the conscious decision is in the causal chain.

To say that the conscious decision is in the causal chain is not yet to say that the fact that it is a *conscious* decision has a place in a causal explanation of a corresponding overt action. An illusion theorist may claim that unconscious distal implementation decisions would have been just as effective as conscious ones in producing breast self-exams. As in the case of the equal effectiveness contention—a parallel claim about *intentions*—granting the present claim about decisions would not settle matters.

Three observations collectively help to explain why. First, even if unconscious implementation decisions and intentions are just as effective as conscious ones—and this, of course is disputable—this does not entail that the fact that an agent made a conscious distal implementation decision about a breast self-exam has no place in a causal explanation of her execution of a related goal intention. Consider an analogy. Sally's mother's driving her to school and Sally's father's driving her to school are equally effective ways of bringing it about that Sally arrives at school. But that obviously does not entail that the fact that Sally's mother drove her to school today has no place in a causal explanation of Sally's arriving at school today. Now, consciously deciding in advance to conduct a breast self-exam at a certain place and time is a way of acquiring an implementation intention to do that. If unconsciously deciding in advance to do this is possible, then that is another way of acquiring a relevant implementation intention. Just as the fact that Sally's mother drove her to school today has a genuine place in a causal explanation of Sally's arriving at school today, so may the fact that a subject consciously made a certain implementation decision have a genuine place in a causal explanation of her conducting the self-exam she conducted. More precisely, the supposed fact that an unconscious implementation decision would have been just as effective does not preclude this.

I set the stage for my second observation with a reminder. Recall that in my hypothetical experiment with Sam, it is very likely that if, at *t*, he had not consciously made a proximal decision to press, he would not have pressed the button when he did. Similarly, in the breast self-exam scenario, the following counterfactual is very plausible: (*CD*) If an agent who consciously decided in advance to perform a self-exam at a place *p* and a time *t* and later executed that decision had not consciously decided to do that, she would not have performed a self-exam at that place and time. There is no reason to believe that if she had not consciously decided to do that, she would have unconsciously decided on the same place and time or nonactionally acquired an unconscious implementation intention specifying that very place and time. And, of course, even if an unconscious implementation intention specifying that place and time were to emerge, we would still want an answer to a question I raised earlier: How is the intention supposed to help generate a corresponding action at that later place and time? The likely truth of *CD* supports the claim that the fact that the agent consciously decided to perform a self-exam at *p* and *t* has a place in a causal explanation of the corresponding overt action—an action occurring at a specific place and time. Gollwitzer reports "Orbell et al.'s (1997) observation that implementation intention participants performed a BSE in the exact situation and at the exact time (in all but one case) they had specified" (1999, p. 499).

A critic may contend that *CD* is irrelevant for present purposes and that the following counterfactual *is* relevant: (*CD5**) If an agent who consciously decided in advance to perform a breast self-exam at a place *p* and a time *t* and later executed that decision had not consciously decided to do that and instead had unconsciously decided to do that, she would have performed a self-exam at that place and time. The critic may contend that *CD** is true and that its truth entails that the fact that the agent consciously decided to perform a self-exam at *p* and *t* is causally irrelevant to her performing it there and then. Now even if unconscious distal implementation decisions are not only possible but actual, we have no idea how effective they tend to be. So confidence that *CD** is true is definitely unwarranted. And even if *CD** is true, the critic's claim about entailment is false. For if that claim were true, the truth of the following counterfactual would entail that the fact that Sally's mother drove her to school today is causally irrelevant to Sally's arriving at school today: (*TD*) If Sally's mother's had not driven her to school today and instead her father had driven her to school, Sally would have arrived at school today.

I introduce the final member of my trio of observations with a question I asked earlier about the breast self-exam study. If unconscious implementation decisions and intentions are just as effective as conscious ones, why do the subjects in Group 1—all of whom have conscious implementation intentions to perform self-exams at particular places and times—do so much better than those in Group 2? Apparently, because not nearly as many members of Group 2 have relevant implementation intentions, conscious or otherwise. Given the illusionist suppositions in play about unconscious implementation decisions and intentions—namely, that they exist and are just as effective as conscious ones—it is clear that, in the studies under consideration, people are much more likely to have conscious implementation intentions than unconscious ones. Given the illusionist suppositions, we have no grounds for believing that if people who consciously decide in advance to *A* at a certain place and time were not to make such conscious decisions, all of them would make relevant unconscious implementation decisions or acquire relevant implementation intentions in some other way. Instead, there is evidence that, if unconscious distal implementation decisions and intentions are just as effective as conscious ones, then some people who make conscious implementation decisions and execute their corresponding goal intentions would lack implementation intentions in the absence of such a conscious decision and would not execute their goal intentions. And the consequent of the preceding sentence supports the claim that the fact that some people make conscious implementation decisions is causally relevant to the corresponding actions they perform. Finally, if unconscious distal implementation decisions and intentions are *less* effective than conscious ones, then—obviously—conscious ones are *more* effective. Presumably, what would account for that difference is some other difference between conscious and unconscious implementation decisions and intentions—bad news for illusionists!

You and I make many conscious implementation decisions even if no experimenters invite us to do so. We do so when we plan complicated trips, parties, conferences, and the like. The argumentation in the preceding paragraph that is not specifically about controlled studies applies to the full range of conscious implementation decisions, not just those evoked by experimenters.

Regarding studies of implementation intentions, the bottom line is that if subjects sometimes make conscious implementation decisions, we have good reason to believe that the fact that they are *conscious* decisions is causally relevant to their corresponding overt actions. This is not surprising. Perhaps some readers were not aware of studies like Gollwitzer's before they read this section. It might have struck some such readers that their success rate at executing distal "goal intentions" would improve significantly if they were to have suitable distal implementation intentions more often than they ordinarily do. If some readers find an improvement of this kind desirable, what should they do? Should they sit back and hope that relevant unconscious distal implementation intentions will emerge in them when such intentions would be useful? Would it be better consciously to settle on a policy of trying to bring about that they have relevant implementation intentions on suitable occasions; consciously to think, when such occasions arise, about where and when to execute their goal intentions; and consciously to decide on a place and time in situations in which their conscious reflection about where and when to act leaves the matter unsettled? The answer is obvious.

As I have observed elsewhere (Mele, 2009, Ch. 2), in some scenarios, instructions may render subjects aware of proximal intentions to do things that they would otherwise have had unconscious proximal intentions to do. Consider experienced drivers who are instructed to drive for an hour while glancing occasionally at a Libet clock in the rearview mirror, to signal for their turns as they normally do, and to report, after each flip of the turn indicator, at what time they believe they first became aware of their intention to flip it. Their being conscious of these intentions enables them to report on the intentions, but it should not be expected to result in marked improvement of their turn-signaling behavior. In the studies of distal implementation intentions that Gollwitzer reviews, matters are very different. Either the instructions—which prompt *conscious* implementation intentions—significantly increase the probability that the subjects will have distal implementation intentions or distal implementation intentions of which agents are never conscious generally are not nearly as effective as conscious ones; and the presence of conscious distal implementation decisions and intentions is correlated with markedly better performance.

I should emphasize that the "or" in the preceding sentence is inclusive. The instructions in the experiments at issue certainly seem to increase the probability that subjects will have distal implementation intentions—and, in particular, conscious ones that are, on the whole, remarkably effective. And we have no grounds for confidence that distal implementation intentions of which agents are never conscious are as effective as consciously formed or acquired ones. In fact, even finding evidence of the existence of unconscious intentions of this kind in human beings—not to mention evidence of the existence of processes that link such intentions to corresponding actions of ours days or weeks later—is no mean feat. The conscious formation or acquisition of distal implementation intentions promotes conscious memory, at appropriate times, of agents' intentions to perform the pertinent actions at specific places and times, which increases the probability of appropriate intentional actions. How do distal implementation intentions and decisions of which we are never conscious do their alleged work in us? Answering this question is left as an exercise for the reader. If and when ambitious readers produce evidence that we have such intentions and make such decisions, they can get to work on finding evidence about processes that link the intentions and decisions to corresponding actions days or weeks later, and they can investigate the reliability of these processes.

CONCLUSION

One source of skepticism about free will is the belief that conscious decisions and intentions never play a role in producing corresponding overt actions. If the argument of Section 5 is correct, this belief is unwarranted (also see Baumeister, Chapter 3, this volume). Of course, undermining a single source of skepticism about free will—no matter how prominent—is not enough to show that we sometimes act freely. But that is a task for a book (see Mele, 2006, 2009), not a chapter.

In this chapter, in addition to arguing that controlled studies yield evidence that the fact that an agent consciously made a distal decision to *A* sometimes has a place in a causal explanation of a corresponding overt intentional action (Section 5), I developed a conception of conscious deciding and motivated its experimental utility (Sections 1–3). I also clarified the task of ascertaining whether a conscious proximal decision to *A* is at work in producing an *A*-ing and exposed a problem for those who claim to have shown with Libet-style studies that the fact that an agent consciously makes a proximal decision to perform an overt action never has a place in a causal explanation of such an action (Section 4).[11]

DISCUSSION WITH ALFRED R. MELE

Do people ever have nonconscious intentions?
People frequently have nonconscious intentions. For instance, when people unlock something routine, like an office door, they are acting intentionally, but in most cases such an act is not consciously intended. Similarly, when a person flips a turn signal in a car, that behavior is intentional. People often do this nonconsciously, unless one is a novice driver—in which case the intention to flip the turn signal is probably a conscious intention.

Can people be given intentions nonconsciously in experiments?
It seems clear that nonconscious primes can affect behavior. The way such studies are often set up is by using subliminal or supraliminal priming. For instance, a participant is presented with an anagram, and solving that anagram seems to induce an increased emphasis on the character of that word. For instance, participants who receive nonconscious primes about elderly people tend to walk more slowly than control participants. (Likewise, it seems plausible that people nonconsciously primed with gazelles or race cars would walk faster than normal.)

However, it is a stretch to say that participants whose gait has been altered through a nonconscious prime are intentionally walking slowly.

They are intentionally walking, and they are doing this action slowly. Thus, it seems that, to this point, there is little evidence of experimentally induced nonconscious intentions. Future research may demonstrate otherwise.

Still, in some very generous sense of the term, one could consider the effects of priming studies as causing nonconscious goal pursuit. The next question is how would a nonconscious intention compare to a conscious intention in causing goal pursuit? Consider two possible experiments. The first experiment is as follows. Imagine a participant has just been subliminally primed to walk slowly, and accordingly, the participant is walking slowly. What would happen if a confederate walked up to the participant and said, "Speed up!"? Presumably the participant would speed up and would not fight or resist the urge to speed up. In contrast, imagine a condition in which the participant developed a conscious intention to walk slowly all day. It seems likely that the participant with the conscious intention would be more likely to resist the command to speed up relative to the nonconsciously primed participant. In other words, conscious intentions are probably much stronger than nonconscious intentions.

The second scenario experiment is as follows. In one condition, the experimenter could flash the word "go" subliminally, and at the same time participants would solve anagrams for the word "beach." This conceivably could have the effect of motivating people to go to the beach in a nonconscious way. In another condition, the experimenter could ask participants to develop a conscious intention—a conscious plan that includes a time and place—to go to the beach. Which condition would be more effective at getting people to the beach? Again, it seems obvious that the conscious intention would be more effective than the nonconscious intention.

What qualifies as goal pursuit?

There are two common errors people make that lead them to misclassify non-goal-pursuing behavior as goal-pursuing behavior. The first is that when an actor behaves *as if* pursuing a goal, people often mistakenly take this as an indication of intrinsically motivated goal pursuit. A heat-seeking missile is a good example of something that behaves *as if* pursuing a goal and may meet all the behavioral criteria for goal pursuit, but, of course, a missile has no mental life. Actual goal pursuit must be intrinsically motivated and not simply have the appearance of goal pursuit.

A second mistake people make is to assume that by-products of goals are goals in and of themselves. For example, when a patient goes to the dentist to get a tooth filled, the dentist knows she is going to cause the patient some pain. Her actions are intentional, and so an observer might conclude that her goal is to cause the patient pain. She might counterclaim that her goal is to fix a tooth. How does one know which is the goal? The crucial proof is in what constitutes success or failure. If the procedure performed by the dentist ends up hurting the patient much less than expected, one would not expect her to proclaim, "I have failed!" Not causing pain does not constitute failure, and causing pain is not success. Fixing the tooth is success and not fixing the tooth is failure. In short, people often do things unintentionally when they are performing intentional, goal-oriented actions, but only the task that constitutes success is the actual goal.

NOTES

1. Overt actions are actions that essentially involve peripheral bodily motion. Libet maintains that once we become conscious of a decision to perform an overt action, we can exercise free will in "vetoing" it (1985, 1999, 2004, pp. 137–149). Neither the veto nor the associated refraining from acting on the vetoed decision is an overt action.

2. I steer clear of the expression "neural correlate" because it is used in various distinct senses in the literature. "Physical correlate" is, I hope, a relatively innocuous technical term. From a physicalist, neuroscientific point of view, proof that the physical correlates of, for example, a particular decision were among the causes of a particular action constitutes proof that the decision was among the causes of the action. It is primarily philosophers who would worry about the metaphysical intricacies of the mind–body problem despite accepting the imagined proof about physical correlates, and the relevant argumentation would be distinctly philosophical. For an excellent brief critical review of various relevant philosophical positions that highlights the metaphysical nature of the debate, see Jackson (2000). Henceforth, I suppress reference to physical correlates.

3. Roughly speaking, basic actions differ from nonbasic actions in not being performed by way of performing another action.

4. In the remainder of this paragraph, I borrow from Mele (2003, p. 210).

5. Dean Zimmerman describes substance dualism as a theory that includes a commitment to the idea that "associated with each human person, there is a thinking thing . . . not composed of the same kinds of stuff as . . . nonmental things" (2006, p. 115). Zimmerman describes the "thinking thing" as a soul, but some substance dualists prefer to use the word "mind."

6. Libet and coauthors report that "the subject was asked to note and later report the time of appearance of his conscious awareness of 'wanting' to perform a given self-initiated movement. The experience was also described as an 'urge' or 'intention' or 'decision' to move, though subjects usually settled for the words 'wanting' or 'urge'" (Libet, Gleason, Wright, & Pearl, 1983, p. 627).

7. Whether we ever acquire intentions unconsciously is a separate question. I believe that we often do and that we often have proximal intentions of which we are never conscious. For discussion, see Marcel (2003) and Mele (2009), Chapter 2.

8. Although a proximal intention can "specify the when, where, and how" (Gollwitzer, 1999, p. 494) of a response leading to the attainment of a goal one already has, the implementation intentions that concern Gollwitzer are distal intentions.

9. I suggested a study of the kind just sketched to Peter Gollwitzer, who said he would arrange to have it conducted. The results should prove instructive.

10. I derive the label "illusion theorist" from the title of Wegner (2002): *The Illusion of Conscious Will.* Wegner himself is in no position to make Claim 1, if, as it seems, he holds that all intentions are conscious. For discussion of Wegner's conception of intentions, see Mele (2009), Chapters 2 and 5.

11. A draft of this chapter was written during my tenure of a 2007–2008 NEH Fellowship. I am grateful to Roy Baumeister for feedback on it. (Any views, findings, conclusions, or recommendations expressed in this article do not necessarily reflect those of the National Endowment for the Humanities.) Parts of this chapter derive from Mele (2009), Chapters 2 and 7.

REFERENCES

Baumeister, R. (2008). Free will, consciousness, and cultural animals. In J. Baer, J. Kaufman, & R. Baumeister (Eds.). *Are we free? Psychology and free will.* New York: Oxford University Press.

Gollwitzer, P. (1993). Goal achievement: The role of intentions. *European Review of Social Psychology, 4,* 141–185.

Gollwitzer, P. (1996). The volitional benefits of planning. In P. Gollwitzer & J. Bargh (Eds.), *The Psychology of Action.* New York: Guilford.

Gollwitzer, P. (1999). Implementation intentions: Simple effects of simple plans. *American Psychologist, 54,* 493–503.

Gollwitzer, P., & Sheeran, P. (2006). Implementation intentions and goal achievement: A Meta-analysis of effects and processes. *Advances in Experimental Social Psychology, 38,* 69–119.

Haggard, P. (2005). Conscious intention and motor cognition. *Trends in Cognitive Sciences, 9,* 290–295.

Haggard, P. (2006). "Conscious intention and the sense of agency." In N. Sebanz & W. Prinz (Eds.), *Disorders of Volition.* Cambridge, MA: MIT Press.

Haggard, P., & Eimer, M. (1999). On the relation between brain potentials and the awareness of voluntary movements. *Experimental Brain Research, 126,* 128–133.

Jackson, F. (2000). Psychological explanation and implicit theory. *Philosophical Explorations, 3,* 83–95.

Lau, H., Rogers, R., & Passingham, R. (2007). Manipulating the experienced onset of intention after action execution. *Journal of Cognitive Neuroscience, 19,* 81–90.

Libet, B. (1985). Unconscious cerebral initiative and the role of conscious will in voluntary action. *Behavioral and Brain Sciences, 8,* 529–566.

Libet, B. (1999). Do we have free will? *Journal of Consciousness Studies, 6,* 47–57.

Libet, B. (2004). *Mind time.* Cambridge, MA: Harvard University Press.

Libet, B., Gleason, C., Wright, E., & Pearl, D. (1983). Time of unconscious intention to act in relation to onset of cerebral activity (readiness-potential). *Brain, 106,* 623–642.

Marcel, A. (2003). The sense of agency: Awareness and ownership of action. In J. Roessler & N. Eilan (Eds.), *Agency and self-awareness.* Oxford, UK: Clarendon Press.

Mele, A. (1992). *Springs of action.* New York: Oxford University Press.

Mele, A. (2003). *Motivation and agency.* New York: Oxford University Press.

Mele, A. (2006). *Free will and luck.* New York: Oxford University Press.

Mele, A. (2008). Proximal intentions, intention-reports, and vetoing. *Philosophical Psychology, 21,* 1–14.

Mele, A. (2009). *Effective intentions: The power of conscious will.* New York: Oxford University Press.

Milne, S., Orbell, S., & Sheeran, P. (2002). Combining motivational and volitional interventions to promote exercise participation: Protection motivation theory and implementation intentions. *British Journal of Health Psychology, 7,* 163–184.

Orbell, S., Hodgkins, S., & Sheeran, P. (1997). Implementation intentions and the theory of planned behavior. *Personality and Social Psychology Bulletin, 23,* 945–954.

van de Grind, W. (2002). Physical, neural, and mental timing. *Consciousness and Cognition, 11,* 241–264.

Wegner, D. (2002). *The illusion of conscious will.* Cambridge, MA: MIT Press.

Wegner, D. (2008). Self is magic. In J. Baer, J. Kaufman, & R. Baumeister (Eds.), *Are we free? Psychology and free will.* New York: Oxford University Press.

Zimmerman, D. (2006). Dualism in the philosophy of mind. In D. Borchert (Ed.), *Encyclopedia of philosophy,* 2nd ed. (Vol. 3, 113–122). Detroit, MI: Thomson Gale.

5 Free Will Is Costly: Action Control, Making Choices, Mental Time Travel, and Impression Management Use Precious Volitional Resources

Kathleen D. Vohs

To discuss the idea of free will and how it could or does operate, this chapter will call upon the limited-resource model of executive functioning for most of its arguments. This perspective does not assume that all actions are free, but free actions (or freer actions, if one would like to make a relative distinction) are special and costly. My perspective comes from recent theorizing by Baumeister (2005; Chapter 3, this volume) and Baumeister, Sparks, Stillman, and Vohs (2008), in which it is argued that free will is particularly relevant for goal-directed, future-oriented behaviors, including topics such as rational choice, planning, intelligent thought, and managing public impressions. These behaviors are particularly relevant to free will because they have a strong relationship to long-term well-being and, by virtue of that, survival and reproduction, the latter of which are assumed to be the underlying basis for why certain capacities were perpetuated in humans throughout the ages. Free will does not, however, govern specific acts in the moment in which they occur (Gallagher, 2006; Searle, Chapter 8, this volume). Conceptualizing the planning of actions versus the execution of actions as distinct phenomena that may be governed by distinct processes is one major step toward understanding when free will operates and what its function is.

A MODEL OF COSTLY FREE WILL: ROLE OF EXECUTIVE CONTROL RESOURCES

The model from which my colleagues and I work depicts executive control processes as energy demanding. Executive control means that people are able to call upon goals or standards to regulate their actions and responses, and make choices. This process enables people to choose best-laid plans as well as behave in ways that are controlled, reasonable, and rational. Executive control is governed by a supply of resources my colleagues and I have been calling (variously) executive control resources, executive functioning resources, self-regulatory resources, self-control resources, and ego resources (Baumeister, Bratslavsky, Muraven, & Tice, 1998; Schmeichel, 2007; Vohs, Baumeister, & Ciarocco, 2005; Vohs et al., 2008).

A finite supply of energy is said to drive executive control. Moreover, this energy is global, meaning that it is applied to all spheres of controlled responses and rational decisions and therefore can be depleted by means of use. The implication is that when people engage in executive control, later attempts at executive control will be less successful.[1]

The limited-resource model of executive control has found considerable support in the literature. Over 100 published experiments have documented the so-called hangover effect whereby performing a behavior thought to require executive control impairs subsequent executive control tasks. The range of phenomena to which this model has been applied is diverse: romantic relationships, task performance, addictive behaviors, garden variety hedonistic behaviors, interracial interactions, intelligent responding, aggression, social influence, overeating, impulsive spending, and morality. Some domains of self-control are considered to be basic. We (Vohs & Baumeister, 2004) named attention control, emotion modification (suppression or amplification), impulse override, mental control, and behavioral management as fundamental to self-control processes broadly.

RATIONAL RESPONDING REQUIRES EXECUTIVE RESOURCES

A tenet of the "free will as costly" notion is that behavior driven by the free will is the result of reasoning. Translated into limited-resource terms, this would mean that a reduction in self-regulatory resources, which power freer actions, should harm reasoning, rational thought, and intelligent decision making. Work by Schmeichel, Vohs, and Baumeister (2003) showed this pattern. In three experiments, we found that an initial task that required self-regulation—and therefore that entailed draining the supply of executive resources—rendered people less able to perform tasks that require rational thought and logical reasoning.

In one study, participants were first asked to engage in attention control or were not engaged in attention control. That is, by random assignment, participants in the no–attention control condition simply were asked to watch a videotape without sound, under the guise that they would be making judgments about the personality of the woman featured on the basis of nonverbal cues. Participants in the attention control condition watched the same videotape, also without sound, under the guise of the nonverbal cue study. These participants were told in advance that there would be a series of irrelevant words appearing at the bottom of the screen as they were from a prior experiment using the same tape (akin to watching CNN's news phrases "crawl" across the bottom of the screen). Attention control participants were told that their job was not to look at the words on the bottom of the screen, but rather to fix their attention on the woman; if they found themselves attending to the words, they should reorient their attention back to the woman. Hence, one group (attention control participants) would be exerting control over their reactions to the tape whereas the other group (no–attention control participants) would not.

After watching the tape, ostensibly as part of a different experiment, all participants answered test questions from the Graduate Record Examination (GRE). We used questions from the logical reasoning section of the exam in order to test whether rational thought was altered as a function of prior attention control. The results showed that being depleted of executive resources (i.e., being in the attention control group) rendered participants both lazy and dumb, as they performed fewer problems overall and also answered fewer problems correctly in comparison to participants who were not in the attention control condition.

Another experiment tested the hypothesis again but changed the independent variable and the dependent variable in order to gain convergent evidence for the effect. In this experiment, participants' executive resources were manipulated by engaging in emotion regulation (or not). Participants came to the lab individually and sat in front of a television to watch a short film. Participants who had been randomly assigned to the emotion suppression group watched a disturbing and somewhat disgusting movie clip about the destructive effects of nuclear testing on animal life in the Bikini atolls while keeping a neutral expression. Specifically, before the film began, these participants were told that while keeping a neutral expression, "no one should be able to tell that you are experiencing any emotion. Furthermore, please feel neutral on the inside too." Hence, these participants were being asked to use their executive control to override their emotional reactions to the film.

Participants in the no–emotion control condition watched the same film, but they were not given instructions to suppress their emotions. These participants were told to respond "as if they were in [their] own home." Hence, these participants should be exerting far less control over their responses, relative to the emotion suppression group.

After the film, we had participants perform two measures of intellectual processing as the dependent measures. We hypothesized that only tasks that involved higher-order intellectual processing would draw on precious executive resources and that basic mental tasks would not. For our basic cognitive task, we used an exercise that required only that participants draw upon crystallized knowledge. Crystallized knowledge is stored in the mind as declarative information that does not need transformations, integration, or complex analysis. A sample item from this task is, "Which city is known as the Windy City?" In contrast, the task we predicted would call upon executive control resources required fluid reasoning. In this task, the answers could be discovered but are not known declaratively, and hence participants had to piece together disparate bits of information to arrive at an appropriate answer. A sample item from this test is, "How many giraffes are there in North America?"

In line with the prediction that higher order, rational responding uses executive control resources, we found that after suppressing their emotions as compared to allowing emotional reactions to flow freely, participants got fewer answers correct on the fluid intelligence task. Furthermore, in line with the prediction of the specialized application of executive control resources for higher—but not lower—level responding, participants in the emotion control condition were unimpaired relative to the no-suppression group when it came to providing concrete answers on the crystallized knowledge test (Schmeichel et al., 2003).

Recent experiments have confirmed the link between executive control resources and rational responding. A set of researchers examined whether typical biases that often are seen during normative decision-making tasks would be exacerbated when people's executive control resources had been taxed. Indeed, after overcoming the desire to look at subtitles on a video, which is executive control demanding, participants were more easily swayed by the presence of an irrelevant but alluring option, which worsened their performance during a decision task (Pocheptsova, Amir, Dhar, & Baumeister, 2009).

In sum, the capacity to engage in rational thinking is hampered after expending executive control resources, which resulted in worse reasoning, unintelligent thought, and less normative decision making. Notably, however, simple associations and basic recall abilities were unimpaired. Therefore, engaging in high-level and complex mental processes aimed at producing rational outcomes appears dependent on executive control resources. These results are relevant to free-will processes because rational thought allows people to figure out the plan of action that will yield the best results. To paraphrase Searle (2002), what good is it to have the capacity to determine the best outcome if one cannot act on it?

FUTURE ORIENTATION REQUIRES EXECUTIVE CONTROL RESOURCES

When people stop or modify a response or substitute one response for another (indications of goal pursuit), they are orienting toward the future. In a series of studies, Schmeichel and I (Vohs & Schmeichel, 2003) reasoned that depletion of self-regulatory resources, which harms goal attainment, may reveal itself in changes in time perception. Specifically, we hypothesized that if people became mentally stuck in the present moment, they would be unable to engage in activities that required consideration of future states—that is, self-regulatory activities. Hence, we predicted that being in a state of "extended-now," as we termed it, would reduce self-control. We furthermore hypothesized that self-regulatory resource depletion would elicit an extended-now state of being stuck in the present. In five studies, we found that people who had earlier engaged in a self-control task and therefore were depleted of their self-regulatory resources reported time perception patterns that indicate that they were experiencing the present moment as elongated.

Furthermore, longer duration estimates predicted decreased self-regulation subsequently. That is, participants who initially engaged in self-control and whose self-regulatory resources were diminished overestimated the length of time during which they were regulating; this overestimation then produced poorer self-regulation among these participants during a second task.

Conceptually, being in a state in which the present time is elongated means that long-term goals are not accessible but instead momentary temptations, urges, and impulses loom large. From the free will as costly model, the extended-now state implies that being in a state of self-regulatory resource depletion will handicap the faculties needed to engage in controlled, "planful" responding.

MAKING CHOICES REQUIRES SELF-REGULATORY RESOURCES

An important extension of the limited-resource model regards decision making. A recent set of experiments indicates that making choices depletes the same resource as is used for self-control (Vohs et al., 2008). We started by recognizing that the executive functioning aspect of the self oversees both decision making and self-control. Most models describe the processes people use to pare down the number of options that they are considering or detail the contextual factors that sway people to or from a given option. Our work focused on one model that discussed the act of making a choice, from deliberation to finally choosing.

The Rubicon model of decision making, by Peter Gollwitzer (1996), depicts the act of choice as shifting between two qualitatively different mind-sets. First, people are in a deliberative mode, which when resolved leads them into an implementation mode. In deliberation mode, the person thinks reasonably, rationally, and scans all options for their viability. Then the decision making point arrives, and the person selects one (or more) options; the decider has moved into implementation mode at this point. In implementation mode, the chosen option is now evaluated more positively than the rest and the chosen option is thereby bolstered. Thus, choice is a quasi-behavioral act that has significance beyond evaluations or ratings.

Germane to our use of the Rubicon model to test the energy-taxing process of free will, note that these two mindsets are qualitatively different. They require different processes, highlight different foci, and serve different purposes. In addition, the chosen option becomes mentally associated with a representation of the self (Strack, Werth, & Deutsch 2006; Vohs, 2006).

In our studies, we considered the act of shifting from one kind of mind-set to another as an act that requires self-regulatory resources, and in doing so, would deplete the chooser and render future acts of self-regulation less successful. Nine experiments and one field study showed support for the model; for the sake of brevity (and to keep your interest), I report a summary of them here.

We conducted multiple experiments that involved asking some participants to make choices whereas others were not asked to making choices. In the no-choice condition, we asked participants to review options (e.g., consumer goods) and report their experience with those objects or view print advertisements to provide their opinions on them. The former type of control condition was useful because we could ensure that participants in the choice and no-choice condition were exposed to the same options; the latter was useful because participants in both conditions thought about their preferences, but only one group made choices based on those preferences. Across the experiments, participants in the choice condition were faced with as few as 60 choices to hundreds of choices to be made during the course of the trial, which required from 4 minutes to upwards of 20. We took several steps to bolster the validity of the choice task so that it had real consequences. For some choices, participants were told that they would receive a small gift at the end of the session that was selected for them on the basis of their choices. Another method was to pass along to academic advisors the choices participants had made when the experiment called for them to choose courses for the upcoming year. (However, some experiments did not promise real consequences of participants' choices, so it appears that consequentiality is not needed for decision fatigue effects to occur.)

In any case, the pattern was the same: When participants made choices—be it among consumer products, university course offerings, or introductory psychology material—they were worse at self-control than were participants who had not made choices (Vohs et al., 2008). The acts of self-control that participants performed also varied—participants endured tedious math problems, attempted to solve an unsolvable puzzle, drank a bad-tasting but healthy beverage made from vinegar and artificial orange drink mix, and submerged their arm in painfully cold water.

One experiment directly tested the Rubicon model's stages on later ability to engage in self-control. We tested for the effects of the full-choice process (deliberation to implementation) against component parts of the Rubicon model. In this study, participants deliberated over which features of a computer they would desire if they were to purchase it (deliberate condition), saw the same screenshots showing computer options and were told to locate options that had been preselected by someone else (implement condition; this is akin to going to the grocery store with someone else's list and finding the brand and size of peanut butter listed), or deliberated and implemented their own choices by clicking a radio button on an Internet website (full-choice condition).

We hypothesized that going through the full-choice process and therefore having had to "cross the Rubicon" would tax participants far more than only engaging in one of the decision-making stages. Hence, we predicted that participants in the full-choice condition would show the worst self-regulation later—which they did. Compared to participants in the deliberate and implement conditions, whose persistence scores were not statistically different from each other, participants who had engaged in the full-choice process did more poorly on persisting at a self-control test of anagram performance. Hence, making choices takes away from the self's volitional capacity more than engaging in either deliberation or implementation.

Hence, work on making choices connects important volitional aspect of the self. Making choices depletes self-regulatory resources and therefore impairs self-control. Making choices also impairs active initiative, another facet of executive functioning.

ACTIVE INITIATIVE

The executive function of the self long has been considered the home of not only self-control and decision making but active initiative as well, but thus far researchers using the limited-resource model had not done a proper test of this aspect of the theorizing. Prior work on the model had only tacitly tested for a lack of initiative, such as when measuring persistence (the lack of which could be considered lack of maintaining initiative). In fact, many experiments have documented failures at self-regulation after depletion that are behaviorally quite active: Overeating requires fetching food and repeatedly shoving it into one's mouth (Vohs & Heatherton, 2000), impulsive spending requires searching for and purchasing desirable objects (Vohs & Faber, 2007), and unrestrained sexual behavior, almost by definition, requires behaviors that are motorically quite active (Gailliot & Baumeister, 2007). Yet despite these hints in the literature, a missing part of the limited-resource model was a direct investigation as to whether one mode of self-regulation failure due to low–executive control resources was a lack of initiative.

We reasoned that the ability to initiate activity (as opposed to stopping activity, which may [in contemporary times] be the most common type of self-regulation; Polivy, 1998) would require executive control resources. Our reasoning came in part from physics: Just as it takes a burst of energy to get a stationary object into motion, a similar logic applies to the processes that may be required of a person at rest who wants to be in motion.

In several experiments, we observed that engaging the executive function of the self led to a lack of initiative later, suggesting that the executive function's limited resource is involved in starting intentional behavior. One experiment built off of the experiments that showed a weakening of self-control after making choices (Vohs et al., 2008). In this experiment, we asked participants to make choices in an online gift registry setting. Later, we put participants in a room to watch a video of two people having a conversation—a video that was, unbeknownst to them, rigged to look so snowy that a clear picture could not be seen. The video was obviously problematic, and the burden was on the participants to get up and tell the experimenter, who was in an adjacent room, about the issue. We measured active responding as the length of time that it took participants to alert the experimenter; a lack of initiative was indicated by a longer wait time. This paradigm not only allowed us to test for lack of initiative but also had a methodological advantage that typical self-regulation failure experiments do not—namely, that waiting passively is counterproductive to the desire to finish the experiment and leave, so executive functioning failure and leaving early were unconfounded.

In line with predictions, initiative was delayed after participants had made choices. Participants who had made choices for 12 minutes were worse at active responding as compared to those who made 4 minutes of choices, a group that in turn was more passive than participants who made no choices.[2] In a conceptually similar experiment (Vohs & Baumeister, 2009), we used a classic self-regulation task—attention control—to provide convergent evidence for the lack of initiative findings. As expected, we found that after people had engaged in an attention control task, relative to a neutral task, they were more likely to sit and watch a television screen that showed only a bright blue glow (i.e., no picture) rather than tell someone that the television was not working.

One experiment delved into who tends toward being behaviorally active when they become depleted versus whose behavioral initiative deflates (Vohs & Baumeister, 2009). In this study, participants made choices about the types of activities they preferred after they had read aloud a boring passage about the life and times of philosopher David Hume[3] under instructions either to read naturally or to use hand gestures and a voice filled with intonation changes. The latter requires behavioral control, prior research has shown (Vohs & Schmeichel, 2003), because the passage itself does not incite enthusiasm in its readers. The dependent measure in this experiment was the choices participants made about their upcoming task. Options for the next task ranged from active, such as eating cookies or planning one's upcoming week, to passive and uninspiring, such as lying on a beanbag or resting one's eyes. As predicted, there was a main effect condition, such that controlling one's voice and energy level when reading the lackluster passage led to preferences for options that were passive more than active. In addition, there was an interaction with two personality traits known to relate to a preference for rewarding stimuli, which were behavioral activation and extraversion. Higher scores on these traits led people to prefer more disinhibited forms of self-regulation failure, whereas lower scores led to more passivity. These data confirm that both types of self-regulation failure are possible after executive control resources are taxed and suggest that underlying preferences toward stimulation and reward differentiate who tends toward what type.

MANAGING ONE'S IMAGE IN THE EYES OF OTHERS

The last domain that I will relate to the process of free will is impression management. Impression management refers to attempts on the part of an individual to create a specific image of oneself in the eyes of others. This sophisticated interpersonal act involves the executive functioning because people have a goal (the image they want to construe), and they must override all prepotent responses that are not in line with the image they want to cultivate. It also calls upon another capacity, one that is uniquely human: theory of mind (Tomasello & Call, 1997). Theory of mind involves attributing to oneself and others a set of mental states, such as intentions, beliefs, attitudes, emotions, and goals. Moreover, it involves thinking that these mental states play a role in producing behavior and that others' mental states, while similar in capacity, can be different in content. Impression management relies on theory of mind, in this case, to understand how people think and feel about themselves. Theory of mind is intimately related to executive functioning as well (Carlson, Chapter 9, this volume). This other-understanding informs the individual which behaviors are appropriate to achieve a desired impression in the eyes of others. We posit that the act of impression management, with its roots in theory of mind and executive control, uses some of the precious limited energy. Eight experiments supported this claim (Vohs et al., 2005).

Four experiments took the form of asking people to engage in novel forms of impression management, for which there would likely not be a set of ingrained behaviors (which may occur with habitual impression management), or a style of behaving that was similar but not involving difficult or novel impression management goals (Vohs et al., 2005). For instance, in one study there were four conditions, one of which we believed would require the most control over one's actions to achieve a desired image in the eyes of others. We asked participants to have a conversation with a group of people that were described as belonging to a different race than the participant or the same race; a second factor varied whether participants were assigned to discuss environmental or racial policies. Afterwards, we measured persistence on difficult and frustrating puzzles, three-quarters of which were unsolvable. As predicted, thinking that one must represent one's whole race and talking about a racially sensitive topic demanded high levels of impression management and, furthermore, left people with less energy to put toward the challenging puzzle task (cf. Richeson & Shelton, 2003). That is, participants in the racial-token/racial-topic condition spent the least amount of time trying to work through those difficult puzzles. In another study, we asked participants to try to get an audience to see them as both likable and competent (images that often require divergent behaviors; many professors know this to be true) or just to "be themselves." Moreover, the audience was described as a group that is accepting of what people say about themselves or highly skeptical of people's self-claims. The dependent measure of executive functioning ability was the successfulness of keeping a neutral expression during the same disturbing film about radioactive waste as described earlier. As predicted, it was more taxing to act competent and likable in front of an audience that was hard to convince than it was to impression-manage in the other conditions, leaving participants less able to control their reactions to the shockumentary film. Managing the impression you make on others takes executive energy.

In a second set of experiments, we found further evidence for the energy-taxing nature of impression management by first depleting participants and then measuring their success at a specific form of impression management (Vohs et al., 2005). For instance, we asked participants who were known to have secure or insecure attachment styles to select conversation topics, which varied in how much self-disclosure they would demand, with which to have a conversation with an unacquainted person. Half of our participants had earlier engaged in a classic executive functioning task, the Stroop task (Kane & Engle, 2003). The Stroop task requires that people override a prepotent tendency to read the meaning of a word rather than the color of ink in which it is printed, the latter of which is the job given to participants in the executive control version of the task. The other half, our neutral participants, were given a similar task, to name colors of ink on a page of words, but in this case the meaning of the word and the ink color match so the task does not require executive override. Difference versions of the Stroop task meant that Stroop condition participants should possess fewer executive control resources relative to neutral condition participants, and we predicted this would make a difference in their preferred self-disclosure patterns. Prior literature (see Collins & Miller, 1994, for a meta-analysis) has demonstrated that the most effective level of self-disclosure upon first meeting someone is a moderate one: Too little self-disclosure suggests that one is cold and aloof, and too much intimacy too early is often suffocating to an interaction partner. We predicted that people who were depleted would not have the energy to steer their disclosure patterns toward that which is best for first acquaintance but instead would revert to their underlying preferred intimacy patterns. This is what we found.

When depleted, participants with an avoidant attachment style, who typically want a great deal of psychological distance between themselves and others, selected low-intimacy topics to discuss, such as "what is your hometown?" and "what is your favorite class at this university?" In contrast, anxious participants, who typically want more closeness with others than others want with them, reacted to depletion by desiring high-intimacy topics to discuss right away. Such topics included, "what is something that most people don't know about you?" and "what is your greatest fear?" Securely attached participants were unperturbed by depletion and chose similar topics irrespective of Stroop task version and, not incidentally, topics that were in the middle of the intimacy scale. Moreover, it is important to note that participants of all three attachment styles did a good job of managing their preferred self-disclosure level when their executive control resources were left untouched; that is, most participants preferred moderately disclosing topics when not depleted. This suggests that participants had a sense that moderate disclosure was most appropriate when first getting to know someone. A second notable finding in this experiment was securely attached participants' lack of change as a function of executive control resource availability. This suggests that if one's natural or ingrained preferred style is well suited for the context, then being depleted will not affect outcomes to a great extent. This finding, which we have observed in other contexts, too (e.g, being a nondieter [versus a dieter] when faced with tempting food; Vohs & Heatherton, 2000), has implications for the importance of cultivating appropriate habits (Wood & Neal, 2007) or never getting into a self-regulation cycle because, by definition, it creates a difference in underlying tendencies and preferred behaviors.

The broader point for the purposes of this chapter is that impression management requires executive control resources and therefore is subject to the same vulnerabilities as rational responding and future orientation. Impression management responses are special among the other processes described in this article because not only are they public behaviors, but, more crucially, they depend on both theory of mind and executive control resources, which may mean that they are doubly vulnerable to the effects of reduced executive control resources.

SUMMARY

A body of work on the limited-resource model of executive functioning depicts the costly nature of free action. Calculating rational decisions, engaging in future-oriented mental time travel, making choices, initiating behavior, and altering behavior to achieve a specific social impression all rely on a set of expendable resources. The sophistication of these skills is so great that they likely depend on complex psychological machinery. Such machinery not only is able to produce great plans and progress but also is vulnerable to frequent breakdowns.

A DISCUSSION WITH KATHLEEN D. VOHS

How does depletion differ from fatigue?

There is some preliminary empirical evidence that speaks to a distinction between depletion and fatigue. In particular, there is a high degree of specificity in the procedures that cause depletion in children. Procedures that require young participants to delay gratification (thereby using executive functioning) result in much stronger negative effects on subsequent self-control than alternative procedures (e.g., such as the Stroop task). Thus, exercising executive control has an especially strong effect on depletion, as anticipated by depletion theory. Delay of gratification procedures should be developed for adults, with the expectation that delay of gratification would have a similarly strong impact on adults.

A second important way of distinguishing between fatigue and depletion is that people don't report that they are tired when they are depleted. In the study on shoppers, there were questions about fatigue and tiredness, and these did not have a predictive effect on how long participants persist in the math problems. Several other studies have failed to find any subjective markers of depletion, though a sense of passivity may be a promising possibility.

The absence of subjective markers of depletion has practical implications, as not knowing that one is depleted may leave a person prone to making poor choices. It would be helpful for laypersons to know under what circumstances they make the best decisions, so as to avoid making decisions when they are prone to making mistakes. The key to this (given a lack of subjective indicators) may be for laypersons to understand when they have been self-regulating.

Depletion follows decisions. How much depletion is caused by reasoning about the options, and how much is caused by selecting?

Current data do not allow a clear answer to this question, but one way to determine the answer empirically would be to compare two groups of participants. One group would be asked to think carefully about three shirts. Then they would be asked to select one of the three shirts that they wanted. A second group would be asked to select a shirt quickly and thoughtlessly. The expected results would be that the group asked to think *and* select would be more depleted than the group simply asked to select. The magnitude of that difference would correspond to the depleting effect of reasoning, above and beyond that of selecting.

How long does depletion last?

Three factors were identified as contributing to the duration of depletion. The first is the type of task, as some tasks require more self-control and hence are more depleting. The second factor is the activity following depletion. If participants do something fun, for instance, depletion is decreased. The third factor is the sensitivity of the depletion measure;

sensitive measurements will detect depletion longer than insensitive measurements. Laboratory studies generally find the window to be between 15 and 45 minutes.

NOTES

1. Some people ask how long it takes to get back to baseline after a person has become *depleted*, as it is commonly termed, and we do not have a solid answer to this question. The answer depends on how depleted the person became during the first task, what the person does in the interim period, and how resource demanding the later task is. That said, we have observed that depletion effects generally wear off between 30 and 45 minutes after the manipulation, but other labs have reported that they have observed depletion effects at 60 minutes after the depleting task.

2. This study also provided an important qualification to previous findings, insofar as we found that participants who enjoyed the choice task were not as passive as participants who disliked the choice task—but this effect held only when participants had made a few choices; when participants made many choices (12 minutes of choices, to be precise), enjoyment of the choice task mattered not. Participants in this condition were quite passive, regardless of enjoyment. Hence, it is more difficult to push oneself from deliberate into implementation mode if the choice process is not enjoyable—but once one has made many choices, vacillating between the two mind-sets taxes nearly everyone.

3. With apologies to philosophers.

REFERENCES

Baumeister, R. F. (2005).*The cultural animal: Human nature, meaning, and social life.* New York: Oxford University Press.

Baumeister, R. F., Bratslavsky, E., Muraven, M., & Tice, D. M. (1998). Ego depletion: Is the active self a limited resource? *Journal of Personality and Social Psychology, 74*, 1252–1265.

Baumeister, R. F., Sparks, E. A., Stillman, T. F., & Vohs, K. D. (2008). Free will in consumer behavior: Self-control, ego depletion, and choice. *Journal of Consumer Psychology, 18*, 4–13.

Collins, N. L., & Miller, L. C. (1994). Self-disclosure and liking: A meta-analytic review. *Psychological Bulletin, 116*, 457–475.

Gailliot, M. T., & Baumeister, R. F. (2007). Self-regulation and sexual restraint: Dispositionally and temporarily poor self-regulatory abilities contribute to failures at restraining sexual behavior. *Personality and Social Psychology Bulletin, 33*, 173–186.

Gallagher, S. (2006). Where's the action? Epiphenomenalism and the problem of free will. In W. Banks, S. Pockett, and S. Gallagher (Eds.), *Does consciousness cause behavior? An investigation of the nature of volition* (pp. 109–124). Cambridge, MA: MIT Press.

Gollwitzer, P. M. (1996). The volitional benefits of planning. In P. M. Gollwitzer & J. A. Bargh (Eds.), *The psychology of action* (pp. 287–312). New York: Guilford Press.

Kane, M. J., & Engle, R. W. (2003). Working-memory capacity and the control of attention: The contributions of goal neglect, response competition, and task set to Stroop interference. *Journal of Experimental Psychology: General, 132*, 47–70.

Pocheptsova, A., Amir, O., Dhar, R., & Baumeister, R. F. (2009). Deciding without resources: Psychological depletion and choice in context. *Journal of Marketing Research, 46*, 344–355.

Polivy, J. (1998). The effects of behavioral inhibition: Integrating internal cues, cognition, behavior, and affect. *Psychological Inquiry, 9*, 181–204.

Richeson, J. A., & Shelton, J. N. (2003). When prejudice does not pay: Effects of interracial contact on executive function. *Psychological Science, 14*, 287–290.

Schmeichel, B. J. (2007). Attention control, memory updating, and emotion regulation temporarily reduce the capacity for executive control. *Journal of Experimental Psychology: General, 136*, 241–255.

Schmeichel, B.J., Vohs, K. D., & Baumeister, R. F. (2003). Intellectual performance and ego depletion: Role of the self in logical reasoning and other information processing.*Journal of Personality and Social Psychology, 85*, 33–46.

Searle, J. R. (2002). *Consciousness and language*. New York: Cambridge University Press.

Strack, F., Werth, L., & Deutsch, R. (2006). Reflective and impulsive determinants of consumer behavior. *Journal of Consumer Psychology, 16*, 205–216.

Tomasello, M., & Call, J. (1997). *Primate cognition*. New York: Oxford University Press.

Vohs, K. D. (2006). Self-regulatory resources power the reflective system: Evidence from five domains. *Journal of Consumer Psychology, 16*, 215–223.

Vohs, K. D. & Baumeister, R. F. (2004). Understanding self-regulation: An introduction. In R.F. Baumeister & K. D. Vohs (Eds.), *Handbook of self-regulation: Research, theory, and applications* (pp. 1–9). New York: Guilford.

Vohs, K. D., & Baumeister, R. F. (2009). Depletion of executive control resources zaps behavioral initiative. University of Minnesota, Minneapolis Minnesota. Manuscript in preparation.

Vohs, K. D., Baumeister, R. F., & Ciarocco, N. (2005). Self-regulation and self-presentation: Regulatory resource depletion impairs impression management and effortful self-presentation depletes regulatory resources. *Journal of Personality and Social Psychology, 88*, 632–657.

Vohs, K. D., Baumeister, R. F., Schmeichel, B. J., Twenge, J. M., Nelson, N. M., & Tice, D. M. (2008). Making choices impairs subsequent self-control: A limited resource account of decision making, self-regulation, and active initiative. *Journal of Personality and Social Psychology, 94*, 883–898.

Vohs, K. D., & Faber, R. J. (2007). Spent resources: Self-regulatory resource availability affects impulse buying. *Journal of Consumer Research, 33*, 537–547.

Vohs, K. D., & Heatherton, T. F. (2000). Self-regulatory failure: A resource-depletion approach. *Psychological Science, 11*(3), 249–254.

Vohs, K. D., & Schmeichel, B. J. (2003). Self-regulation and the extended now: Controlling the self alters the subjective experience of time. *Journal of Personality and Social Psychology, 85*, 217–230.

Wood, W., & Neal, D. T. (2007). A new look at habits and the habit–goal interface. *Psychological Review, 14*, 843–863.

6 Disentangling the Will[1]

Richard Holton

Nietzsche held that the idea of the will—and he meant specifically free will—has its unity only as a word.[2] That is perhaps to go too far, but in spirit at least I am inclined to agree. There are at least three ideas bundled up in the idea of free will, and I doubt that there is any one thing that fits them all.[3]

First, there is something that has its place in the theory of mind and action. Freedom of the will is the property—more exactly the capacity—possessed by agents who are able to act freely, a capacity that is manifested whenever they do act freely. Since we are talking about a mental capacity here, we should expect to find out about it using our normal tools for finding out about mental phenomena: the empirical resources of psychology and neuroscience, and the conceptual resources of philosophy of mind. But a good starting point, one that is particularly useful for getting a grip on what it is that we are talking about, is through the phenomenology of agency. We have some knowledge of free will in this sense because we have a direct experience of it.

Second, there is a notion that is distinctively moral. Free actions are actions for which agents are morally responsible; that is, freedom is sufficient for moral responsibility. Perhaps, in addition, freedom is necessary: perhaps every act for which an agent is morally responsible is an action that they perform freely. Investigation of this issue is a task for ethics and for moral psychology.

Third, there is a modal idea that has its natural place in metaphysics. Freedom of the will is that property possessed by agents who, when they act, could have acted otherwise. As a cursory glance at the philosophical literature will show, understanding quite what this "could" amounts to has proved a difficult task, especially if the world is deterministic at the macroscopic level. But that is a task for metaphysics and semantics, and perhaps for physics. It is implausible that this is something that we are aware of directly.

To say that these are separate ideas is not to deny that they interact in very many ways. But it is a substantial claim that there is a single thing that does duty in all three. The familiarity of the claim should not blind us to the fact that it is not forced upon us. It could well be, for instance, that the actions that we experience as free do not exactly overlap with actions that our best moral theory will tell us are those for which we are responsible. I shall argue that this is indeed the case, and, moreover, that something stronger is true: even when we generalize the mental conception of freedom to extend beyond those actions that we are immediately aware of as free, we still do not get something that is quite right for our theory of moral responsibility. The mental notion of freedom is distinct from the moral one, and the modal one, I suspect, is something different again.

This approach becomes more plausible when we reflect on the history of our understanding of freedom. The claim that there is one thing that can play all three roles—mental, moral, and modal—took many hundreds of years to evolve. There is considerable scholarly controversy over who first made it. Richard Sorabji constructs a persuasive case that it was not present in classical thinkers, and first really came together in the work of Augustine.[4] Of course, that was still a very long time ago, and the influence of thinkers like Augustine, transmitted as it has been by the Christian Church, has been tremendous. It might be held that nowadays our *concept* of free will is essentially the concept of some one property that can play all three roles. On this view, to deny that there is anything that can do so is exactly to deny that there is free will.

I'm not sure what to say about our *concepts*. Or, more accurately, I'm skeptical that there is anything very helpful to be said. There has been a flurry of experimental work recently concerned with asking subjects their views about free will: asking whether, for instance, there would be moral responsibility in a world that was deterministic.[5] Such work is interesting and important and is certainly a great advance on simply asserting what people's ordinary intuitions are, without troubling to find out. But how much should we conclude from these experiments about the nature of our concepts? Suppose that a majority of subjects hold that a deterministic world would be one in which moral responsibility were absent.

Should we conclude that our concept of moral responsibility requires the falsity of determinism?

I think not. Around 300 years ago, Calvinism was a major force within Christianity. In large parts of Germany, the Netherlands, Scotland, and New England, it was the dominant doctrine. If you had asked congregations in those places whether moral responsibility was compatible with determinism, I think there is little doubt that they would have said that it was: predestination was a central tenet of their beliefs. But should we say then that these people had—or contemporary Calvinists have—a different concept of moral responsibility to that of the subjects who answered differently in our experimental surveys?[6] Or should we rather say that Calvinists and Arminians have different theoretical views about the same concept? Certainly the great architects of the view—Luther and Calvin, and many since them—thought that they were coming to a better understanding of moral responsibility and the role of the will, not replacing these notions with others.

If twentieth century philosophy has taught us anything, it is that such debates are sterile.[7] We have no clear criteria for what counts as an essential part of a concept, and what counts as a detachable theory about that concept. Certainly this is true: our intuitions about freedom stem from many sources, among which are theoretical views about what roles freedom must play. If, as I want to suggest, our notion of free will has run together disparate things that would be better kept apart, then there will be even less chance of distinguishing any essential core of our concept from the ideas we have about it.

Let me give a second example. In a fascinating study, Eddy Nahmias and colleagues found that people think that neurological determinism (everything we do is determined by the prior arrangement of our neurons) poses more of a threat to free will and to moral responsibility than does psychological determinism (everything we do is determined by our prior beliefs, desires and intentions).[8] Again we might take this at face value to show something about our ideas of free will and moral responsibility. But there is something curious about the finding. For, on broadly physicalist assumptions—that is, assuming that everything supervenes on the physical—the thesis of neurological determinism is *weaker* than the thesis of psychological determinism. Neurological determinism could be true while psychological determinism is false: it could well be that many of the neurological mechanisms influencing our behavior work without giving rise to psychological states like beliefs, desires, and intentions. But, given the truth of physicalism, it is very unlikely that psychological determinism could be true while neurological determinism were not; it is very implausible that psychological states are realized in anything other than neurological states.

So how can we explain Nahmias's findings? The obvious suggestion is that, at least implicitly, the subjects are rejecting physicalism. If they were dualists—if they thought, like Descartes, that mind and matter were quite distinct, so that each could vary independently of the other—then the results would make perfect sense. Neurological determinism is incompatible with all but the most recondite versions of dualism, since neurons are clearly physical, and so, given dualism, cannot determine the mental. In contrast, psychological determinism is quite compatible with dualism. So, plausibly, it is a set of (perhaps implicit) dualist assumptions that are leading the subjects to react as they do. If that is how to explain the findings though, then it does not simply show that the subjects are dualist. More significantly, it shows that they think that free will stands or falls with the doctrine: free will is possible with dualism, impossible without it.

That is not a terribly surprising finding, especially for subjects, like the Georgia undergraduates who participated in this survey, who have been strongly influenced by Christianity. On a standard understanding, Christianity is clearly a dualistic system, and I would wager that a good number of those involved would think that there is no morality without Christianity. So, on that view, if dualism is false, Christianity must be false, and there will be no morality. But even if it is not terribly surprising that most of these subjects think that dualism is necessary for free will, how much should we conclude from it for our concepts of free will? Dualism has had something of a renaissance in recent years, but it is still very much a minority view among philosophers, and even more so among most scientists who work on the mind. Free will would be a much less plausible thing than it is generally taken to be if it required the truth of dualism. Again I would be reluctant to draw any firm lines, but I suggest that we should say that these findings show at least as much about the beliefs that some subjects have about free will, as about the concepts themselves.

Indeed, when we look more carefully at the studies of what ordinary subjects believe about free will, we find that they show a very mixed picture. Get them to think about the issue in the abstract, and most people do think that moral responsibility would be absent in a physically deterministic world.[9] But that finding is reversed once the subjects think about a concrete case: get them to focus on some particular nasty individual, and they will think he is responsible even in a deterministic world.[10] Equally, get them to think, not of how they would react to some other possible world in which determinism is true, but of how they would react if they discovered that determinism is true of our world, and again they now think that responsibility and determinism are compatible.[11]

I have argued that our ideas about free will come from diverse sources, and that we should not always take intuitions about free will as indicating the nature of the properties involved, since they may simply reflect false theory about those properties. But if this is right, how are we to make any progress? I don't advocate a single alternative method, since it seems to me that we should be open to considerations from any number of different areas. However, in this paper I do want to highlight two approaches, corresponding to two of the three sources of our concept of freedom that I mentioned at the outset. When it comes to the philosophy of mind, I think that we should be more carefully attentive to the phenomenology of freedom that we have customarily been. When we do, we will find that there are at least two different experiences to which we should pay heed: an experience of choice, and an experience of agency (or perhaps, more accurately, of loss of agency).[12] I will argue that both can be seen as revelatory of real phenomena, but that neither is the central notion for moral responsibility. When it comes to ethics, my suggestion is that we should pay heed, not to our explicit moral beliefs, but to our actual moral practice. In particular, I want to investigate the idea of how we make attributions of moral responsibility to those who are mistaken about their own motivation.

About the third idea, the idea that freedom of the will is the ability to do otherwise, I shall not have a great deal to say; the enormous philosophical literature on the idea has shown just how hard it is even to work out what it means, let alone to give an account of it that is compatible with what physics seems to be telling us. However, my discussion of the other two ideas will indicate some ways in which it has come to feature in our thinking, and provide some reasons why we should not be overly concerned about it.

EXPERIENCES OF FREEDOM

Much of the force of the idea that we have free will comes from our experience. For some years now, I have introduced undergraduates to the topic, and I find that the quickest, most effective way to generate the conviction that they have free will is to get them to focus on the phenomenology. Tell them to make an arbitrary choice, and then get them to act on it—to raise their left hand or their right, for instance—and they are, by and large, left with an unshakable conviction that their choice was a free one.

What is happening here? They have in the first instance an experience of freely choosing and acting. Quick on its heels comes a judgment, or a clutch of judgments: that they could have made either choice; or, more theoretically committed, that they could have made either choice compatibly with how they were prior to the choice; or more committed still, that they could have made either choice no matter how the whole world stood prior to the choice, and hence that they are, in that respect, unmoved movers.

Judgments like these last surely go well beyond the contents of the experience. How could one have experience that one's action was itself uncaused? Wouldn't that require that one also had experience of the rest of the world to show that it was not doing any causing? Nevertheless, the experience of freedom is an experience of something. At its heart, I suggest, are two aspects. First, we have an experience that provides the basis for a belief in the efficacy of choice, by which I mean that, once the question of what to do has arisen, choice is both necessary and sufficient for action (choose to raise your right hand, and you'll raise it; likewise with your left; fail to make either choice and you won't raise either). Second, we have an experience of different choices being compatible with our prior beliefs, desires, and intentions. Believing, desiring, and intending as one does, one could either choose to raise one's left hand or one's right hand. In this sense we do have an experience that provides the basis for a belief that our actions are not determined: they are not determined by our beliefs, desires, and intentions. But this local indeterminism falls far short of the global indeterminism that libertarians embrace. It is quite compatible with the thought that our actions are not determined by our beliefs, desires, and intentions but that they are nonetheless determined.[13]

When I say that the experiences *provide the basis* for these beliefs, I'm afraid I mean to leave the matter there; I am not going to pursue the difficult question, hard enough even in the case of ordinary perceptual experience, of the relation between the experience and the belief. We can think of our experiences of choice as broadly parallel to perceptual experiences, without, I hope, thereby committing ourselves too far. Like ordinary perceptual experiences, our experiences of freedom have special, infallible, authority. On the basis of experience, we believe that striking the match is necessary and sufficient for its lighting, and, on the basis of experience, we think that taking the match out of the box is compatible both with its subsequently being lit, and with it never being lit. In such cases we might be wrong in the specific case—this match may not light even if it is struck, since it is damp, or (though this is far less probable) we may be wrong in general—we may be totally wrong about how matches work. Similarly, on the basis of our experience we think that choice is frequently necessary and sufficient for action, and that different choices are compatible with the same beliefs, desires, and intentions. However, again it isn't ruled out by the nature of the experience that we could be wrong about this. Again our error could be limited to the specific case—we think that we choose to raise our left hand, but really we are responding to post-hypnotic posthypnotic suggestion—or conceivably it could be more general—perhaps, as certain psychologists argue, choice is epiphenomenal.[14] I am, of course, committed to thinking that they are wrong about this, and that choice is causally effective. But the reasons for thinking this cannot come just from the experience. The experience must be corroborated by a general account of how the mind works.

On this approach is an interesting question as to why we have choice. It can look like a liability, opening as it does the possibilities of *akrasia*—action against one's best judgment—and inaction. Wouldn't we do better as creatures whose actions are linked directly to what we judge best, circumventing any need for choice? I have pursued this question elsewhere, and shan't address it in any detail here.[15] Briefly, my answer is that, as cognitively limited creatures, we are frequently unable to make a judgment as to what is best. We need to be able to choose to act even in the absence of such judgments. Such choices need not be random; they might instead be influenced by our unconscious registering of relevant factors, a registering that never makes it through to the level of judgment.[16]

So to summarize these considerations: I think that part of the reason why people are convinced they have freedom of the will is that they have an experience of choice, and that this experience corresponds to a real phenomenon: a conscious process of forming an intention to perform a certain action from a range of possible actions, and then, if all goes well, performing that action. But this is a very specific phenomenon. I have said that choice is frequently necessary for action, but it is clear that it is not always so. It is only when the questions of what to do explicitly arises that we need to make a choice. Many of our actions are habitual, or otherwise automatic. It has long been appreciated that certain motor actions, once mastered, require no conscious thought. Indeed, conscious thought can be inimical to them: the movement of one's feet as one runs downstairs is, to take William James' example, best left unconsidered. But much recent work in social psychology has pushed the class of automatic actions much further, to cover much of our routine activity.[17] We can wend our way through a big city, safely using various modes of transport and completing various social interactions, without making any choices. It is only in certain circumstances—when we enter a supermarket, say, or a restaurant, or a cinema with many screens—that choices have to be made.

Clearly we think of many of these automatic actions as in some sense free, but our reason for thinking this cannot be that they are chosen. What is it then? One possibility is that there is a distinctive phenomenology governing them, too. Here things are, I think, less than clear. There is not obviously a phenomenology of agency, as we might call it, but there does seem to be something like a phenomenology that occurs when agency is lost, or is perceived to be lost. Patients with anarchic hand syndrome, while conceding that the actions of their anarchic hands are in some sense theirs, report that they do not feel them to be.[18] Even more strikingly, schizophrenic patients with delusions of alien control have the experience that their actions are under the control of others.[19] They can even accept that they have the intentions to do the things that they are doing, while denying that those intentions are causing the actions. Plausibly then, as some have suggested, there is some feedback system that produces a distinctive phenomenology in cases in which our intentions are not achieved, and it is this that is mistakenly triggered in the schizophrenic patients.[20] If this is right, and the phenomenology is basically negative rather than positive, it should be possible to generate a conviction in subjects that they are performing actions even when they are not, and there are some reasons for thinking that this can be done.[21]

A phenomenology of loss of agency is something, but since it is somewhat recherché, it seems unlikely that it is the source of our notion. So rather than positing a distinct phenomenology, an alternative is to tie agency back to choice using a dispositional account. Although we do not choose the movements of our feet as we run downstairs, we could, or at least, we could choose which movement to make with each foot at each moment, though the movements would undoubtedly be far from fluid. Likewise with the other automatic actions that we perform. We think of these as free actions exactly because we have the capacity to bring them under the control of choice, which in turn has two aspects: first, the capacity to choose, and second, the capacity to turn that choice into action.

I speak in terms of capacities here, rather than saying that in such cases we could have acted otherwise. The reasons for doing so are familiar among philosophers from cases made famous by Harry Frankfurt.[22] Black has implanted a device in Jones's brain so that, should Jones not respond to his bidding, Black could take control of him. In fact, Jones does oblige without Black ever needing to activate the device. Jones, we think, is responsible for what he has done, responsible in a way that he would not have been had the device been used, yet it is not true that he could have acted otherwise. Some have concluded that moral responsibility is independent of the capacity to choose. But this is surely too quick. Instead, we should realize that an agent can have the capacity to choose, and can exercise it, even though it is not true that they could have chosen to do otherwise, or that they would have done otherwise if they had so chosen. In short, dispositions should not be analyzed in terms of counterfactuals. This is a point that has been long known in the literature on dispositions.[23] For instance, a glass is fragile in virtue of its internal constitution, even though a protecting angel ensures it will not break if dropped. It has the disposition of fragility even though it is not true that it would break if dropped. We can easily modify this into a case that mirrors that of Jones and Black more closely. A fair coin is tossed, and comes down, quite without interference, heads. However, were it to have been about to come down tails, an interfering genie would have intervened and flipped it over. Clearly under these conditions the coin couldn't have come down other than heads and so wouldn't have come down other than heads. Equally clearly, where the genie doesn't intervene, it has freely, fairly, fallen heads.[24] The same, I suggest, is true of Jones: he acted freely since he exercised his capacity to choose and to act, even though it is not true that he could have acted otherwise. So I confine my talk to capacities.[25]

Let me sum up this section: our experience gives us access to two different capacities, choice and agency. Neither is incompatible with physical determinism, though both are incompatible with psychological determinism (i.e., with determination by conscious beliefs, desires, and intentions), which might be mistaken for it. I suggest then that while physical determinism may be true (it is up to physics to tell us whether it is), psychological determinism is probably false (small wonder then that I am reluctant to accord much weight to the opinions of Nahmias's subjects who conclude the other way). However, my focus will not be on the relation of these capacities to metaphysical theses about determinism, but on the relation they bear to morals.

MORALS FOR MORALS

Can either the capacity for choice, or the capacity for agency, shed much light on the conditions needed for moral responsibility? I start with choice. There is a model of responsible action that I suspect is behind much moral theorizing. The agent investigates the world, determines the possible courses of action, chooses which action to perform, and then performs it as a result of that choice. All is transparent and deliberate. There is no doubt that in such circumstances agents are standardly responsible for their actions (standardly, since for all we have said there may be other conditions that are not fulfilled; we are now looking at choice as a putative necessary condition, and not a sufficient one). So clearly choice can play an important role. But, just as we have seen that choice is not necessary for action in general, so it is surely the case that it is not necessary for those actions for which we are morally responsible. I do not just mean that we can be responsible in cases in which we are negligent, cases where, for instance, we harm someone without choosing to do so because the act we do choose to do has their harm as a readily foreseeable consequence. I mean, rather, that we are frequently held responsible for automatic actions. Suppose I have a good-sized whiskey every day before driving home from work, and that over the years the quantity I pour myself has crept up, so that now it takes me well over the legal limit to drive. I may go through the whole process quite automatically, writing memos, talking on the phone, tidying things away as I pour and drink. My moral culpability is undiminished.

So choice is not a plausible necessary condition on morally responsible action. What about agency? This is rather more promising. If I kick you because someone trips my knee-jerk response, or because I am in the throes of epileptic attack, I am not held to blame.[26] In both cases I lack the capacity to choose to do otherwise. More contentiously, if I promise, but fail, to give up the cigarettes to which I am, unknowingly, addicted, many would hold that I am not to blame, since while I have the capacity to form the intention to give up, I lack the capacity to carry it out.[27]

So there are good grounds for thinking that agency is a necessary condition on moral responsibility. However, it is rather a weak condition. I doubt that it is what is wanted when people say that to be morally responsible one must be free. When we formulate necessary conditions, we want them to be as restrictive, and hence as informative, as possible. This one is not sufficiently restrictive. Consider a case of paranoid schizophrenia: the sufferer, convinced that he is about to be attacked, hits out at someone who is in fact, and quite transparently, innocent. We acquit him of blame just as we acquitted the epileptic. Yet he was clearly exercising his agency as we have described it: he had the capacity to choose what to do and he acted on that choice. His defense comes from the fact that he is deluded in the beliefs on which he acts.

If we want to capture this failing as a failure of agency, we will need a more restrictive notion. The free agent has not just a capacity to choose, but a capacity to choose *rationally*; that is what the person suffering from paranoid schizophrenia lacks. This is the kind of condition for which Michael Smith has recently argued; he sees it as capturing the "kernel of truth" in the doctrine that moral responsibility requires the ability to do otherwise.[28] Smith tries to develop the account in terms of a set of counterfactuals: to have the capacity to act rationally requires that one would act rationally in a set of counterfactual conditions. We have seen good reason to doubt that capacities can be reduced to single counterfactuals; I am unsure that they can be reduced even to sets of counterfactuals. So let us leave that issue aside, and focus instead on the simple claim that moral responsibility requires the capacity for rational choice.

The thought is something like this: to be morally responsible for an action, one must have the capacity to rationally assess the reasons for or against doing it, and to form and act on one's intentions accordingly, or, in Smith's words, agents are only morally responsible for "those things that happen as a consequence of their responding or failing to respond to reasons to the extent that they have the capacity to do so."[29]

There is certainly something intuitively appealing about this view. And while it doesn't quite coincide with the conception of freedom that we developed in discussing agency, it is certainly a natural extension of it: we simply add a rationality requirement to the capacity for action. Nevertheless, I am inclined to think that it cannot be right. It is too restrictive as a condition on those we hold morally responsible. Our moral practice involves us in criticizing agents who do not meet it. The conception that Smith develops means that moral requirements are tailored very closely to the actual capacity of the individual concerned, and that is not something that we are prepared to do.

To see what this might mean, consider an alternative conception of moral requirements that has been well expressed by Pamela Hieronymi.[30] On this alternative, requirements are relatively insensitive to the abilities of the agent, in a way that makes them more like other demands. As she says, "in many areas of adult life—in one's career, in one's role as teacher or parent, in one's position as chair or as second tenor—the demands one is under remain insensitive to one's own particular shortcomings; one's capacities develop as one tries to meet them."[31] Likewise for moral demands: they can impose upon us even if we lack the capacity to meet them.

Hieronymi gives a number of considerations in support of this conception, starting from the aspirational nature of our moral demands, and from the character of blame. I shall take a rather different course, exploring some considerations in favor of the conception from our ordinary moral practice.

Let us return to the Calvinist theme raised earlier, and consider the writings of Daniel Dyke, an English Puritan writing in the early seventeenth century. Among many works, Dyke wrote a tract entitled *The Mystery of Selfe-Deceiving*, whose contents are, to a contemporary ear, more aptly revealed by its subtitle: *A Discourse and Discovery of the Deceitfulnesse of Mans Heart*. The self-deception of which Dyke is concerned is simply self-ignorance, in particular, ignorance of one's own motives. "God only knoweth the heart *exactly* and *certainly*: Because man and Angels may know it conjecturally, and by way of guessing."[32] Insofar as we can have self-knowledge, it is only if we have "plowed with Gods Heifer,"[33] but even then the knowledge is partial. "Onely God of himselfe exactly knoweth the secrets of the heart. There is a great mingle-mangle and confusion of thoughts, even as there is of drosse and good metall in silver and gold, which lie so confused together, that to the eye of man the drosse in not discernable."[34]

As a Puritan, Dyke was, as I have said, a Calvinist, and clearly the doctrine of predestination is central to the views expressed here.

Salvation comes entirely from God's grace, grace that is extended only to the elect, and so none but God can know for sure who is destined for it. Similarly, at the level of the individual action, we cannot know what is truly pleasing to God, since we cannot know what is done from the right motive.[35] Dyke is thus rejecting the kind of account that Smith offers. We do not need to be able know our motives to behave righteously; good action does not require the kind of rational capacity on which Smith insists.

Dyke was writing in the seventeenth century, but the views about self-knowledge have a strikingly contemporary ring. I suggest that we should draw the same conclusions for ethics that he draws. It has become a commonplace that our motives are not transparent. Self-deception, especially about motives, is the standard condition for us to be in. Indeed, a wide range of studies have concluded that anything approaching self-knowledge is, in many areas, had only by the depressed.[36] But, if we cannot know our own motives, how can we go in for the kind of rational assessment of our own actions that an account like Smith's requires?

Let us take an example, one that is not too grandiose. Suppose that Emma is deeply interested in her friend's romantic attachments, offering advice and persuasion that, given her superior standing, is sure to be taken up.[37] Suppose further that Emma thinks that she is acting entirely for the welfare of her friend, but she is wrong: putting her many actions together, the insightful and disinterested observer can see that she is moved by a certain vanity, by a desire to create and control those she thinks beneath her, and to do so, moreover, in ways that will bring certain advantages to her. Suppose finally that she would be horrified were she to realize that this is the case, and would immediately stop. She is not malicious; just self-deceived.

This is a moral failing in Emma, no doubt. But do we make that judgment because we are confident that she has the ability to see her error? Would we withdraw the verdict if we discovered that she were simply incapable of doing so? I think not. Of course, if she were so lacking in insight that the case were pathological, then we might withdraw all moral censure, and treat her as a patient. But if she simply has a standard amount of self-deception, and it turns out that there was no way to move her from it, then that would provide no excuse. Her self-ignorance may not be itself a moral failing, but it can lead her to moral failure.

The point applies quite generally. For many moral failings, culpability requires the relevant bad motive. But we do not require that in addition the agent have, or be able to have, *knowledge* of that motive. A person can be spiteful, or selfish, or impatient without knowing, or being able to know that they are; , and such ignorance does not excuse the fault. Likewise, for criminal offenses, the law sets down the appropriate *mens rea*. This will typically require knowledge of certain facts about the external world—that the action was harmful, or likely to be harmful, that object taken was the property of another, and so on—but it never requires knowledge of the very state of mind. It is no legal defense that one is ignorant of one's own motives. People can be guilty while honestly believing themselves to be innocent, just as they can be innocent while believing they are guilty.

These considerations are relevant to another issue, and it may be fruitful to spend a little time pursuing it. In a series of recent articles, Gideon Rosen has argued that a mistake provides a quite general moral defense.[38] Incontestably, one cannot be guilty of lying if one thought one was telling the truth, and one cannot be guilty of malice if one thought one was acting in the victim's best interests. But Rosen wants to push the idea further. It is not just ignorance of the facts that can provide a moral defense, but also ignorance of ethical principles: if someone non-culpably believes that what they are doing is right, then that too is a defense. The upshot, Rosen concludes, is a form of moral skepticism: since we cannot be sure that people are acting contrary to their moral beliefs, we cannot be sure that they are morally responsible.

To me this has the air of *reductio*. Rosen is pushing a piece of moral theory against what are often called Moorean facts: facts about which we are more certain than we are of any bit of philosophy that might seek to overturn them.[39] Many of the most monstrous crimes of the twentieth century have been perpetrated by those who appear to have thought that what they were doing was right—Pol Pot, for instance, or many of the leaders of Nazi Germany. The belief, even if non-culpably held, that the killing of one's political opponents is morally justifiable does nothing to excuse the action.

The common law takes a similar perspective. The maxim that ignorance of the law is no defense, while it does not hold absolutely, is nevertheless central to Anglo-American jurisdictions.[40] It is sometimes seen as driven purely by expediency, a device to discourage willful blindness. I think, however, that to insist that this is all there is to the doctrine is to miss much of what is central. For the thought is that the core demands of the common law are simply binding upon everyone in the society, even if, for some reason, they are ignorant of those demands. Of course, things are different if the agent is truly mad. Most jurisdictions have an insanity defense, typically along the lines given in the Model Penal Code: a person is not responsible if "as a result of mental disease or defect he lacks substantial capacity either to appreciate the criminality [wrongfulness] of his conduct or to conform his conduct to the requirements of law."[41] But a "mental disease or defect," as the courts have interpreted it, requires much more than simply the inability to know what law or morality demands. It requires a whole set of distortions that affect much of what the subject does. Indeed, the Model Penal Code explicitly holds that the insanity defense does not extend to "an abnormality manifested only by repeated criminal or otherwise antisocial conduct."[42]

So both our ordinary moral practices and the law reject the idea that responsibility requires the rational capacity to act well. In criticizing Emma, we do not need to know whether she really had the rational capacity to realize that what she was doing was wrong. The same point, though on a totally different scale, applies when we criticize Pol Pot. In saying this, though, I do not mean to suggest that we feel no conflict in these cases. What happens is that we have a clash between a certain theoretical view—responsibility requires the ability to behave otherwise—to which we are well wedded; , and our views about particular cases—this person is responsible—to which we are even more closely wedded. That should remind us of one of the findings mentioned earlier: that, when they think in the abstract, people tend to judge determinism to be incompatible with moral responsibility, but that when they consider concrete cases, they do not. The only way out is to change the requirement expressed in the theoretical view, and a first step in doing that is to realize that we are not dealing with a single notion of freedom.

These are rather grand themes, and I have treated them all too briefly. But I hope I have done enough to sketch the form of a position according to which, in so far asinsofar as we have a notion of a free act that provides a condition on moral responsibility, it is not that of either choice or agency. I haven't said very much about what it is. My own view is that getting clearer on it will require getting a lot clearer on how our emotional and rational faculties work when making moral judgments. And, despite much recent work, that is a topic about which we still know rather little.

NOTES

1. This paper was presented at the Conference on Agency and Responsibility, University of Indiana, 2007. My thanks to the audience there, to Tim O'Connor, who was my commentator, and to Eddy Nahmias and Rae Langton for comments on the written version. Many of the ideas discussed here are developed further in a recent book (Holton, 2009).

2. (Nietzsche, 1886/1973, §19).

3. I speak here of what I take to be something like the common sense idea of free will. Many philosophers have rejected one or more of the features that I will outline.

4. (Sorabji, 2000). Sorabji distinguishes even more elements to the notion than I do.

5. See, for instance, Nahmias, Morris, Nadelhoffer, & Turner (2005) and Nichols and Knobe (2007).

6. It might also be held that Calvinism is simply incoherent, exactly because it is incompatible with our moral beliefs. This contention could then be supported by the observation that it has lost ground, within the Protestant churches, to Arminianism. Indeed, even in those churches that are nominally Calvinist, the significance of the doctrine of predestination has surely declined—I was brought up a Congregationalist but didn't realize through 13 years of Sunday school that this was a doctrine to which the church was committed. Nevertheless, Calvinism is far from a spent force, and there may be other reasons why it currently has less of a public profile. My father-in-law once told me that as a trainee missionary he was advised to be Arminian in his preaching, but Calvinist in his prayer.

7. The classic work is Quine (1951), but work by Saul Kripke and Hilary Putnam, work denying that natural kind terms have much descriptive content, has been equally influential on this point; see Kripke (1972) and Putnam, (1975).

8. (Nahmias, Coates, & Kvaran, 2007)

9. See, for instance, Nichols and Knobe (2007).

10. (Nahmias et al., 2005).

11. (Nichols & Roskies, 2008).

12. I think that at least one more experience is centrally important: the experience of making and maintaining resolutions. Like choosing this is something that we actively do, something that requires effort. I think that this explains why it is that inducing beliefs in determinism tends to undermine subjects' moral motivation (see Baumeister, Chapter 3, this volume; Baumeister et al., 2009; Schooler, Chapter 12, this volume; Vohs, Chapter 5, this volume; Vohs & Schooler, 2008). Determinism is easily conflated with fatalism, with the doctrine that nothing one can do will make any difference to the outcome; as a result, belief in determinism can undermine moral self-efficacy. Subjects come to think that there is no point in trying to persist in any resolution to behave well, since their effort will have no impact on the outcome. For discussion see Holton (2009, Ch. 8).

13. The issues can get complicated here in spelling out how this would happen in a deterministic setting. For a start, it could be that beliefs, desires, and intentions *together with* other independent states (e.g., choices) determine what agents do. But further, given that mental states are multiply realized (i.e., the same mental state can be realized in different neurophysiological states), it is quite compatible with physical determinism that two agents could be in the same psychological state, and yet would behave differently, since that state was realized differently in each of them.

14. See, especially, Wegner (2002).

15. (Holton, 2009, Ch. 3).

16. For instance, it looks as though we can be sensitive to patterns in the world, so that our choices may be influenced by them, even though we form no conscious beliefs about them. In such cases we do better choosing than we would by random guessing, though we have no idea why. I discuss some examples in Holton (2009, Ch. 3).

17. See, for example, Bargh and Chartrand (1999) and (Bargh (2002).

18. "Of course I know that I am doing it," says a patient of Marcel's. "It just doesn't feel like me." See Marcel (2003, p. 79).

19. For example: "My grandfather hypnotized me and now he moves my foot up and down", "They inserted a computer in my brain. It makes me turn to the left or right", "The force moved my lips. I began to speak. The words were made for me", "It's just as if I were being steered around, by whom or what I don't know" (Frith, Blakemore, & Wolpert, 2000, p. 358).

20. In contrast, patients with anarchic hand syndrome do not attribute the actions of their anarchic hand to anyone else, nor do they think they have the intentions to perform the actions that their hands are performing. It seems that they are right in this, since, unlike in the case of the schizophrenic patients, a major part of their motor control system is not working. For discussion of the likely neurophysiology here, see Della Sala (2005).

21. See Wegner and Wheatley's I-Spy experiments (Wegner & Wheatley, 1999). As Eddy Nahmias pointed out to me, the results are far from conclusive.

22. (Frankfurt, 1969).

23. See Martin (1994); Martin's point had been widely known for at least twenty 20 years before that.

24. Kadri Vihvelin, from whom I take the example (Vihvelin, 2000), draws the different conclusion that the coin could come down tails. The reasoning, which strikes me as mistaken, seems to be based on reading the "could" claim as a counterfactual, rather than a simple statement of possibility.

25. For some similar thoughts, see Fischer (1994, pp. 154–158).

26. In English law these are covered by the defense of automatism.

27. I take it that at least one source of the contentiousness of these cases reflects the contentiousness of the latter claim. But I suspect that these may be cases in which we would blame even if we thought that the agent lacked the capacity to resist. See below.

28. (Smith, 2003).

29. (Smith, 2007, p. 142).

30. (Hieronymi, 2007; see also Hieronymi , 2004).

31. (Smith, 2003, p. 111).

32. (Dyke, 1630, p. 399).

33. *Ibid*. The reference is to *Judges* 15.18; his opponents having pressured his wife into revealing the answer to a riddle, Samson replies "If ye had not ploughed with my heifer, ye had not found out my riddle." This is particularly interesting, since the idea here is surely that pressuring his wife is, in one commentator's words, "an unworthy expedient" (Jamieson, Fausset, & Brown, 1961). Could Dyke think that self-knowledge is not proper to man?

34. *Ibid*, p. 402.

35. Moreover, God's knowledge of the heart of man is the kind of maker's knowledge that assumes predestination: God created man ("Artificers know the nature and properties of their works; and shall God onely be ignorant of his workmanship?", p. 403) and is also "the preserver and upholder ... of the motions of the mind" (*ibid*). I discuss some of these themes further in Holton (2000).

36. Starting with Alloy and Abramson (1979).

37. For a rather fuller picture, see Jane Austen, *Emma*.

38. (Rosen, 2003, 2004).

39. The reference is to G. E. Moore's argument for the existence of the external world, an argument that took it as a premise that he had hands, something he took as more certain than the philosophical premises that sought to undermine it. See Moore (1939/1959 p. 146).

40. See the Model Penal Code 2.04 for a codification of when ignorance of law can provide a defense (American Law Institute, 1985). With a few exceptions, it is limited to cases in which it undermines the *mens rea* for the offense. For discussion of the similar doctrine in English law, see Smith (1999, pp. 82–84).

41. (American Law Institute, 1985, 4.01). This provision is based on the English M'Naghten Rules. The U.S. Insanity Defense Reform Act of 1984 required in addition that the mental disease or defect be *severe*.

42. Here I part company with several philosophers, in particular with Susan Wolf, who argues in an influential piece that the inability to form moral judgments accurately does preclude moral criticism and is to that extent a form of insanity (Wolf, 1988). Wolf bases her argument around the M'Naghten Rules, though she reads them in a very different way to the way in which a court would read them. In particular, her central example—JoJo, the son of a brutal dictator whose spoilt upbringing leaves him morally incompetent—is not someone whom we should normally think of as lacking in legal or moral responsibility. Or at least, the closest real-life examples we have—Jean-Claude "Bébé Doc" Duvalier of Haiti comes to mind—are not people typically judged to lack such responsibility.

REFERENCES

Alloy, L., & Abramson, L. (1979). Judgment of contingency in depressed and nondepressed students: Sadder but wiser? *Journal of Experimental Psychology: General, 108*, 441–85.

American Law Institute (1985). *Model penal code.* Philadelphia: The American Law Institute.

Bargh, J. (2002). Losing consciousness, *Journal of Consumer Research, 29*, 280–285.

Bargh, J., & Chartrand, T. (1999). The unbearable automaticity of being, *American Psychologist, 54*, 462–479.

Baumeister, R., Masicampo, E., & DeWall, C. N. 2009: Prosocial benefits of feeling free: Manipulating disbelief in free will increases aggression and reduces helpfulness, *Personality and Social Psychology Bulletin, 35*, 260–268.

Della Sala, S. (2005). The anarchic hand, *Psychologist, 18*, 606–609.

Dyke, D. (1630) *The mystery of selfe-deceiving* (revised edition). London: Richard Higgenbothan.

Fischer, J. M. (1994) *The metaphysics of free will.* Oxford, UK: Basil Blackwell.

Frankfurt, H. (1969). Alternate possibilities and moral responsibility, *Journal of Philosophy, 66*, 829–839.

Frith, C., Blakemore, S.-J., & Wolpert, D. (2000). Explaining the symptoms of schizophrenia: Abnormalities in the awareness of action, *Brain Research Reviews*, *31*, 357–363.

Hieronymi, P. (2004). The force and fairness of blame, *Philosophical Perspectives*, *18*, 115–148.

Hieronymi, P. (2007). Rational capacity as a condition on blame, *Philosophical Books*, *48*, 109–123.

Holton, R. (2000). What is the role of the self in self-deception? *Proceedings of the Aristotelian Society*, *101*, 53–69.

Holton, R. (2009). *Willing, wanting, waiting*. Oxford, UK: Clarendon Press.

Jamieson, R., Fausset, A. R., & Brown, D. (1961). *Commentary on the whole Bible*. Grand Rapids, MI: Zondervan.

Kripke, S. (1972). *Naming and necessity*. Cambridge, MA: Harvard University Press.

Marcel, A. (2003). The sense of agency. In J. Roessler and N. Eilan (Eds.) *Agency and self-awareness*. Oxford, UK: Oxford University Press, 48–93.

Martin, C. (1994). Dispositions and conditionals, *Philosophical Quarterly*, *44*, 1–8.

Moore, G. E. (1939). Proof of an external world. In *Proceedings of the British academy 25*. Reprinted in *Philosophical papers*, London: George, Allen and Unwin, 1959, pp. 127–150

Nahmias, E., Coates, D. C., & Kvaran, T. (2007). Free will, moral responsibility, and mechanism: Experiments on folk intuitions, *Midwest Studies in Philosophy*, *31*, 214–242.

Nahmias, E., Morris, S., Nadelhoffer, T., & Turner, J. (2005). Surveying freedom: Folk intuitions about free will and moral responsibility, *Philosophical Psychology*, *18*, 561–584.

Nichols, S., & Knobe, J. (2007). Moral responsibility and determinism: The cognitive science of folk intuitions, *Noûs*, *41*, 663–685.

Nichols, S., & Roskies, A. (2008). Bringing moral responsibility down to earth. *Journal of Philosophy*, *105*, 371–388.

Nietzsche, F. (1886/1973). *Beyond good and evil*. (R. Hollingdale, Trans.). Harmondsworth, UK: Penguin.

Putnam, H. (1975). The meaning of "meaning." *Philosophical papers, Vol. II: Mind, language, and reality*, Cambridge, UK: Cambridge University Press, 215–271.

Quine, W.V.O. (1951). Two dogmas of empiricism, *The Philosophical Review*, *60*, 20–43.

Rosen, G. (2003). Culpability and ignorance, *Proceedings of the Aristotelian Society*, *103*, 61–84.

Rosen, G. (2004). Skepticism about moral responsibility, *Philosophical Perspectives*, *18*, 295–313.

Smith, J., (1999). *Smith and Hogan's criminal law*. London: Butterworths.

Smith, M. (2003). Rational capacities. In S. Stroud & C. Tappolet (Eds.), *Weakness of will and practical irrationality* Oxford, UK: Oxford University Press, 17–38.

Smith, M. (2007). Reply to Hieronymi, *Philosophical Books*, 48, 142.

Sorabji, R. (2000). *Emotion and peace of mind: From stoic agitation to Christian temptation*. Oxford, UK: Clarendon Press.

Vihvelin, K. (2000). Freedom, foreknowledge, and the principle of alternate possibility, *Canadian Journal of Philosophy, 30,* 1–23.

Vohs, K., & Schooler, S. (2008). The value of believing in free will, *Psychological Science, 19,* 49–54.

Wegner, D. (2002). *The illusion of conscious will.* Cambridge, MA: Harvard University Press.

Wegner, D., & Wheatley, T. (1999). Apparent mental causation: Sources of the experience of will, *American Psychologist, 54,* 480–492.

Wolf, S. (1988). Sanity and the metaphysics of responsibility. In F. Schoeman (Ed.), *Responsibility, character and the emotions.* Cambridge, UK: Cambridge University Press, 46–62.

7 Stubborn Moralism and Freedom of the Will

David A. Pizarro
Erik G. Helzer

Imagine discovering that your neighbor, whom you have known for years, is in fact a very sophisticated robot that has had all of his behavior programmed in advance by a team of robotics experts. This information might cause you to re-evaluate all of your interactions with him. Where you previously may have become angry with him over the slightest offense, you may now feel the need to remind yourself that he is merely following his programming; he has no say over his own behavior. Likewise, you might find it unreasonable to hold him in contempt for having beliefs that conflict with your own. In short, you may find yourself wanting to suspend your moral evaluations about his beliefs, judgments, and behaviors across the board because, after all, he did not act freely.

This connection between freedom and moral responsibility is evident in the long and storied debate over free will among philosophers, many of whom have argued that if free will does not exist, then the ability to hold individuals responsible is compromised (e.g., Clarke, 2003). On this view, in order to hold an individual morally responsible for an act, the possibility must exist that he could have done otherwise. The deterministic processes that give rise to the behavior of the robot neighbor would, of course, be incompatible with this requirement—it is simply a fact that the robot lacks the ability to do anything other than what he was programmed to do. Some have questioned this conclusion, arguing that even if human beings are not free in this ultimate sense (and that humans are all simply very complex, organic versions of the robot-neighbor), the ability to hold others morally responsible remains logically unaffected (Pereboom, 2001; Strawson, 1974). Nonetheless, the deep connection between freedom and moral responsibility remains, as disagreements are generally not over whether freedom is necessary for moral responsibility but rather over the specific kind of freedom necessary (Dennett, 1984).

In an important sense, these questions about free will and moral responsibility are beyond the scope of empirical investigation—an experiment cannot settle the question of whether moral responsibility actually requires libertarian freedom or whether determinism and moral responsibility can comfortably coexist. But individuals entirely unconcerned with scholarly debates about freedom do make judgments about moral responsibility fairly frequently, and often these judgments have serious consequences (such as social exclusion, imprisonment, and even death). The descriptive question of how people go about making these judgments of moral responsibility has therefore been of much interest to psychologists. Accordingly, a great deal of research has been conducted documenting the rules individuals seem to use when determining whether or not to hold others morally responsible. Perhaps unsurprisingly, this research has shown that people seem to care about whether an act was committed under conditions that seem to limit an agent's freedom (such as involuntary acts or accidents). Most influential theories of blame and responsibility within psychology have therefore characterized freedom as an important prerequisite for the attribution of moral responsibility, much like the normative theories of blame and responsibility from philosophy and law that influenced them (e.g., Shaver, 1985; Weiner, 1995). On these accounts, when individuals are faced with a moral infraction, they first set out to determine if a person acted freely then proceed to use that information as input into their judgment of whether to hold the person responsible.

We will argue that this view is mistaken. Rather than serve as a prerequisite for moral responsibility, judgments of freedom often seem to serve the purpose of justifying judgments of responsibility and blame. This seems true not just for judgments of "ultimate" metaphysical freedom (i.e., freedom from determinism), but also true for freedom in the more local "agentic" sense that is central to psychological and legal theories of responsibility (such as whether or not an act was intentional or controllable).

One reason for this is that people are fundamentally motivated to evaluate the moral actions of others, to hold them responsible for these acts, and to punish them for moral violations—they are "stubborn moralists." (Although morality can refer to a very large set of behaviors and judgments, when we refer to "morality" throughout the paper, we are limiting our definition to these aforementioned aspects of human morality—that of judging acts as morally right or wrong, and judging others as responsible for moral violations or virtuous acts.) This motivation most likely has its roots in the evolutionary forces that shaped human morality and has psychological primacy over more fine-grained social judgments, such as judgments about whether or not an act was committed freely. As such, the motivation to seek out and punish wrongdoers can push individuals in the direction of holding people responsible even when the wrongdoers do not meet the criteria for freedom required by normative accounts of responsibility. Simply put, when people say that someone acted freely, they may be saying little more than that the person is blameworthy. In support of this general argument, we first defend the claim that people are stubborn moralists before reviewing recent empirical evidence that this moralism drives judgments of freedom rather than the other way around.

STUBBORN MORALISM

Moral judgment comes naturally to human beings. People write stories about good and evil, make long lists of morally forbidden acts, and take a keen interest in the moral missteps of complete strangers. People are also very "promiscuous" with their moral judgments—they readily offer moral evaluations of fictional characters, animals, and even computers. In short, while it may be true that specific moral beliefs vary across time and place, the basic belief that some acts are morally forbidden, and that people should be held responsible for these acts, appears to be a common human trait.

As evidence of the strength of these moral beliefs, consider briefly some of the putative threats that might be expected to shake confidence in morality—atheism, relativism (of the sort arising from moral diversity), and determinism. The wide dissemination of these ideas does not seem to have dented the belief that some acts are wrong, and that individuals are morally responsible for their actions (Roskies, 2006; (Chapter 10, this volume). For instance, contrary to the belief that morality hinges on the existence of God (as Dostoevsky's Ivan Karamazov claimed, "if there is no God, everything is permitted"), atheists seem to have no trouble holding people morally accountable. Nor has the knowledge that there is wide diversity in many moral beliefs seemed to undermine laypeople's belief in their own ethical systems or their belief that individuals should be held responsible for moral infractions more generally. If anything, people respond in a particularly harsh manner when presented with others who hold moral beliefs that diverge from their own (Haidt, Rosenberg, & Hom, 2003). Finally, what of the threat of determinism? If it turns out to be true that humans are all preprogrammed automatons, doesn't this invalidate the ability to hold others responsible (Greene & Cohen, 2004)? While we will address this concern specifically a bit later, Roskies (2006) has argued convincingly that neither the old threat of determinism "from above" (i.e., theistic determinism—that God's foreknowledge undermines human freedom) nor the newer threat "from below" (i.e., scientific determinism) appears to have had a wide influence on the belief that some things are wrong, that most people are able to choose between right and wrong, and that individuals deserve to be blamed for these wrong actions (although the threat of determinism does appear to influence our own moral behavior, hinting at the possibility that different processes govern our moral self-evaluations than our evaluation of others; Baumeister, Masicampo, & Dewall, 2009; Schooler, Chapter 12, this volume; Vohs & Schooler, 2008).

The fact that people cling tightly to moral beliefs despite cultural and historical shifts that might encourage their abandonment speaks against the once-common view that morality is a thin layer masking humans' deeply selfish and amoral nature (DeWaal, 2006). On the contrary, the fact that morality thrives despite these forces suggests that the mechanisms that give rise to people's basic moral intuitions (such as the belief that people should be held responsible for their acts) are too deeply entrenched in the human mind to be abandoned easily (Haidt & Joseph, 2004). This "deep" view of morality has been increasingly bolstered by research in game theory, evolutionary biology, and economics showing that the presence of basic moral behaviors (e.g., altruistic acts) and judgments (e.g., a preference for fairness) is not inconsistent with the "selfish gene" approach to evolution by natural selection, and that evolution may actually favor individuals who exhibit such behaviors and judgments (Axelrod & Hamilton, 1981; Trivers, 1971). For instance, the most plausible account of how human altruism emerged relies on the dual mechanisms of kin selection (a willingness to act altruistically toward members of one's immediate gene pool) and reciprocal altruism (a willingness to act for the benefit of others when there is a chance that the organism will be paid in kind). Together, these mechanisms most likely gave rise to the sorts of moral emotions that proximally motivate moral action, such as empathy for the suffering of others and anger over being cheated (Frank, 1988). More recently it has even been proposed that sexual selection may have played a significant role in the preservation of morality by favoring the presence of many traits considered to be morally virtuous (Miller, 2007). For instance, men who acted virtuously (e.g., with bravery and trustworthiness) were more likely to be sought after by women either because such acts provided a direct cue to the men's fitness (indicating a higher likelihood that they would stay to help rear the offspring, thus ensuring the spreading of their genes to the next generation), or because the virtues were reliable correlates with other fitness-related cues. This bridging of morality and evolution represents one of the most significant advances in the psychology of morality, as the belief that evolution could only favor selfish organisms implies a view of morality as superficial in the sense that it is entirely dependent on cultural transmission and a proper upbringing (and by extension, that a change in culture or upbringing could eliminate human morality in one generation)—a picture of morality that is increasingly viewed as untenable.

This view of morality as deeply rooted in basic human nature finds additional support from psychologists working across various fields, including social psychology, developmental psychology, and social/cognitive neuroscience. Consistent with the view that humans are "hard-wired" to be ethical creatures, recent neuroimaging studies have demonstrated that the brain systems associated with reward and distress are involved in a basic facet of human morality—a preference for fairness (a preference that not only emerges early in development, but that also seems present in humanity's close evolutionary relatives; Brosnan & DeWaal, 2003). In these imaging studies, researchers relied on a common method used to study fairness in a laboratory setting in which pairs of individuals participate in an economic game known as the "ultimatum game." In this game, one player (the "donor") is given a sum of money and told that she may allocate as much of the money as she would like to a "recipient." The recipient, in turn, must then decide whether to accept the offer (in which case, both players keep the money) or to reject the offer (in which case, neither player keeps any money). In order to be able to keep the money, the donor must strategically allocate a quantity that will entice the recipient to accept the offer. As it turns out, a majority of individuals in the role of recipient will reject an offer that is substantially below the "fair" mark of 50% (despite the fact that accepting an unfair offer always guarantees more money than the rejection payoff of zero). Many economists have used this simple finding that individuals will take a monetary "hit" in order to punish unfair behavior as an argument for the primacy of moral motivation over rational self-interest. Indeed, the power of this method lies in its ability to capture the seemingly irrational reactions to unfairness observed in the real world (such as when an angry individual spends $10 in fuel in order to drive back to a store that he is convinced cheated him out of $5). Interestingly, it seems as if this moral motivation shares neurological real estate with more basic hedonic motivational systems. In studies utilizing measures of brain activation (fMRI) while participants play an ultimatum game, researchers have shown that recipients demonstrate increased activation in reward centers of the brain (including older structures, such as the ventral striatum and amygdala, and the cortical region of the ventromedial prefrontal cortex, which most likely evolved for reasons unrelated to human social cognition) when presented with fair offers as compared to when presented with unfair offers (Tabibnia, Satpute, & Lieberman, 2008). However, those exposed to unfair offers demonstrate increased activation in the bilateral anterior insula, a region commonly associated with the experience of pain and distress (Sanfey, Rilling, Aronson, Nystrom, & Cohen, 2003). Moreover, the level of activation in brain regions associated with both reward and distress is not predicted by the degree of economic gain or loss resulting from the offer, suggesting that people are sensitive to fairness and unfairness for reasons other than basic economic utility. At the neurobiological level, at least, it is not so much that fairness trumps self-interest, as it is that the brain does little to distinguish between the two.

While research in social and cognitive neuroscience continues to provide evidence for the biological basis of moral evaluations, looking into the brain is only one source of evidence that humans are fundamentally predisposed to evaluate others on a moral dimension. For instance, a great deal of work has demonstrated that humans readily make inferences about the dispositional traits of others given minimal information (Gilbert & Malone, 1995; Gilbert, 1998). Recent work by Todorov and colleagues has shown that this is especially true for inferences regarding trustworthiness. Across a number of studies, these researchers have demonstrated that individuals make quick and automatic evaluations of the trustworthiness of others from brief exposures to their facial features (see Todorov, Said, Engell, & Oosterhof, 2008, for a review). While there is mixed evidence as to whether these evaluations are correlated with actual trustworthiness, a strong bias toward evaluation along this dimension is evidence of its psychological primacy. Moreover, a basic motivation to evaluate others on the dimension of trustworthiness may aid overall accuracy by focusing individuals on other subsequent cues that may be good predictors, such as emotional signals of trustworthiness (Frank, 1988). Such an ability to detect trustworthy individuals would have provided obvious advantages to humanity's ancestors, from allowing them to avoid murderous psychopaths to allowing them to gain social capital by cooperating with trustworthy individuals and avoiding "cheaters."

Fairness and trustworthiness are only a small part of human morality, and it is likely that other facets of morality that have received less empirical attention are just as basic and hardwired. Jon Haidt and his colleagues, for instance, have argued that evolutionary pressures have predisposed us to hold particular moral beliefs regarding in-group loyalty, purity, and authority (Haidt & Joseph, 2004). While cultural influences certainly play an important role in the relative importance placed on these foundational moral intuitions (for instance, politically conservative individuals are more likely to view violations of in-group loyalty, purity, and authority as moral violations, while liberals tend to focus exclusively on violations of harm and justice), Haidt argues that humans are heavily biased toward perceiving all five of these domains as morally relevant due to humanity's particular evolutionary heritage.

In sum, the mounting evidence that human morality has its origins in biological evolution and is supported by a dedicated set of cognitive mechanisms is consistent with our claim that human moral motivation (especially the motivation to evaluate other individuals on a moral dimension) is "stubborn" and may hold primacy over other kinds of social judgments. It is to the more specific claim that these evaluations appear to trump judgments of freedom that we now turn.

WHAT KIND OF FREEDOM?

We have argued that moral evaluations are a fundamental part of human psychology: humans arrive at moral judgments quite easily, retain confidence in these moral beliefs in the face of challenges to morality, and are strongly motivated to evaluate others on a moral dimension. This moralism is particularly evident in the willingness and ease with which individuals blame and punish others for their moral violations rather than simply ignoring them, even when the cost of punishing outweighs any benefits to the individual (so-called "altruistic punishment"; Fehr & Gächter, 2002). However, people do not go about making these judgments about blame and punishment haphazardly. There is a large body of psychological research describing the underlying rules individuals use in order to determine whether or not to blame others (e.g., Shaver, 1985; Weiner, 1995). These findings can be characterized as confirming an intuition that is most likely shared by most individuals—that when making these judgments, people care about whether or not an agent acted freely. Specifically, the sort of freedom that seems to matter most for responsibility judgments, and that has been highlighted in psychological theories of responsibility, is what we will refer to as "agentic" freedom (in contrast to the "ultimate," metaphysical freedom argued to exist by libertarian philosophers).

Agentic Freedom

The most influential theories of responsibility within psychology (described briefly above) have generated a great deal of research indicating that when making judgments of responsibility, people seem to care about features of an action that point to an individual's agency (Shaver, 1985; Weiner, 1995; see Vohs, Chapter 5, this volume). These theories emphasize the need for an actor to have possessed volitional control over an action, and require the presence of such things as intentionality, causality, control, and foreknowledge. If all these conditions are met, there is nothing to prevent a judgment that the person should be held responsible and blamed accordingly. These judgments about the local features of an agent and his action, what we are referring to as "agentic freedom," are of obvious importance for at least one simple reason—they allow us to predict the future behavior of an individual with some degree of reliability (something that should matter greatly to a social species living in a group and involved in repeated interactions with the same individuals). Take the criteria of intentionality: if somebody intends and knowingly brings about a harmful outcome, it is a safe bet that she might commit a similar violation in the future, and assigning blame and doling out punishment would serve as an effective social sanction in that it would not only discourage her from committing such violations in the future, but it would also serve as a signal to others that she should not be trusted.

As it turns out, attributing intentionality to actors is something humans do quite readily, and quite often. Intentions seem so central to social judgment that people seem to spontaneously attribute intentionality even when it is clear that none could exist. For instance, people have been shown to attribute the random movement of shapes on a computer screen to the figures' underlying intentions and desires (Heider & Simmel, 1944), and even infants seem to attribute goal-directed motives to shapes that perform negative and positive behaviors (such as "helping" to push another shape up a hill or preventing the progress of a shape as it tries to climb; Hamlin, Wynn, & Bloom, 2007; Kuhlmeier, Wynn, & Bloom, 2003).

Note that the perception of causality and intentionality in the acts of others most likely did not evolve in the service of attributing moral responsibility but, rather, evolved because it allowed humans to predict the behavior of physical objects and agents they encountered. The detection of causality, for instance, may even be a basic feature of the human visual system. Psychologists studying visual perception have demonstrated that individuals seem to be hardwired to perceive causality and animacy in the movements of simple objects (Scholl & Tremoulet, 2000). Even chimpanzees demonstrate a basic understanding of goal-directed agentic behavior (Premack & Woodruff, 1978), although the evidence that they utilize this understanding in the service of anything other than their immediate self interest is sparse at best (Call & Tomasello, 2008). While the perception of agency may come easily to us even when presented with the actions of objects and nonhumans, it is nonetheless evident that people are especially likely to perceive agency and intentionality in the acts of other human beings. And if these basic features of agency appear to be completely absent, holding someone morally responsible is much less likely to occur. Take a very simple example: people don't usually blame somebody who brought about harm to another in an entirely accidental way (e.g., if Tom trips on a curb and ends up falling on Dennis, it would seem odd to morally blame Tom for the harm he caused Dennis; at most someone might accuse him of simple clumsiness and avoid walking too closely to him in the future; Weiner, 1995).

By many measures, psychological theories of responsibility that focus on the requirements of agentic freedom have been successful—they seem to capture a great deal of peoples' intuitions about how and when responsibility should be attributed or attenuated, and do a good job of predicting actual judgments of responsibility across a wide range of cases. As evidence, a great deal of research has demonstrated that when one or more of the criteria that compose agentic freedom are absent, individuals tend to exhibit a reduction in their judgments of responsibility and blame. For instance, relatives of individuals suffering from schizophrenia attenuate blame for actions that were performed as a direct result of uncontrollable hallucinations and delusions (Provencher & Fincham, 2000). Likewise, individuals are more likely to assign blame to AIDS patients if they contracted the disease through controllable means (licentious sexual practices) than if through uncontrollable ones (receiving a tainted blood transfusion; Weiner, 1995). When it comes to the criterion of causality, there is even evidence that people are more sensitive than these theories might predict. For instance, individuals seem to not only care whether or not an agent caused an outcome, but whether he caused it in the specific manner that was intended. If an act was intended and caused, but caused in a manner other than the one intended (so-called "causally deviant" acts; Searle, 1983), participants view the acts as less blameworthy. For instance, a woman who desires to murder her husband by poisoning his favorite dish at a restaurant, but who succeeds in causing his death only because the poison made the dish taste bad, which led to him ordering a new dish to which he was (unbeknownst to all) deathly allergic, does not receive the same blame as if the death were caused by the poison directly (Pizarro, Uhlmann, & Bloom, 2003). It seems as if people are quite capable of paying close attention to the features of an action in just the manner predicted by traditional accounts of responsibility. In this sense, it is fair to conclude that there is a great deal of evidence that agency fundamentally matters when arriving at judgments of responsibility.

Yet despite the obvious success of these models in predicting a wide range of responsibility judgments, a number of recent findings have emerged that, taken together, point to the conclusion that judgments of agentic freedom are often the result of responsibility judgments rather than their cause. Despite the evidence that humans are capable of making fine-grained judgments about intentions, causality, and control, these distinctions may not actually serve as input when people are strongly motivated to hold another person responsible—the basic mechanisms that give rise to an initial moral evaluation may overshadow the ability or desire to engage in a careful attributional analysis of the sort predicted by these theories. Importantly, the situations that call for making a judgment of responsibility in everyday life may be ones in which people are especially motivated to hold an agent blameworthy, either because of the nature of the violation or because of an initial negative evaluation of an agent.

Even if the psychological processes involved in attributions of agency and those involved in judgments of moral blame are independent, it may still seem odd that judgments of agentic freedom could be distorted to serve the purpose of holding others responsible. However, the criteria used to arrive at a judgment of agency (such as intentionality and control) actually provide a great deal of flexibility and may therefore be especially prone to the influence of motivational biases. In the social domain, the tendency to attribute the cause of others' behavior to underlying intentions often comes at the cost of ignoring causes that are external to the actor (Gilbert & Malone, 1995; Jones & Harris, 1967). The consequence of this attributional bias is that other people's acts are perceived as intentional even if they were not, and any motivation to blame an individual may exacerbate the perception that an act was intentional. Likewise, the other criteria for agentic freedom, such as possessing control over an outcome, can also be fairly ambiguous—for any given action, there is rarely an easily identifiable, objective answer about how much control an individual truly possessed.

A number of recent findings seem to support the view that judgments of agentic freedom are driven by moral evaluations. Most of this work has focused on the criteria of causality, control, and intentionality and has demonstrated that spontaneous negative evaluations of an act or an agent are enough to change these judgments of agency in a manner consistent with the motivation to blame an agent. For instance, most theories of responsibility posit that possessing causal control over an outcome is an important determinant for the attribution of blame—the less control, the less responsibility (Weiner, 1995). But the relationship between control and responsibility appears far less straightforward. In some cases, individuals impute more control over an act to individuals who seem particularly unlikeable than to other individuals who performed an identical action. Research by Alicke and colleagues, for instance, has shown that individuals make differential judgments about how much control a person had over an outcome if they have reason to think of him as a bad person. In one example, when participants are told that a man was speeding home in a rainstorm and gets in an accident (injuring others), they are more likely to say that he had control over the car if he was speeding home to hide cocaine from his parents than if he was speeding home to hide an anniversary gift despite the fact that the factors that led to the accident were identical across both scenarios (Alicke, 1992, 2000). According to Alicke, the desire to blame the nefarious "cocaine driver" leads individuals to distort the criteria of controllability in a fashion that validates this blame. For Alicke, the spontaneous and automatic judgments of blame provide a ready source of motivation to distort any information that might be required to justify this blame.

This appears to be true for the intentionality criterion as well. A growing body of research by Knobe and his colleagues has shown that people are more inclined to say that a behavior was performed intentionally when they regard that behavior as morally wrong (Leslie, Knobe, & Cohen, 2006; see Knobe, 2006, for a review). For instance, when given a scenario in which a foreseeable side effect results in a negative outcome, individuals are more likely to say that the side effect was brought about intentionally. In the most common example, the CEO of a company is told that implementing a new policy will have the side effect of either harming or helping the environment. In both cases, the CEO explicitly states that he only cares about increasing profits, not about the incidental side effect of harming or helping the environment (e.g., "I don't care at all about harming the environment. I just want to make as much profit as I can"). Nonetheless, participants perceive that the side effect of harming the environment was intentional—but not the side effect of helping the environment. This pattern of findings (with simpler scenarios) is evident in children as young as 6 and 7 years old (Leslie, Knobe, & Cohen, 2006). Although the mechanism underlying these findings that morally bad actions are perceived as more intentional have been hotly debated, the findings are consistent with the view we are defending here—that the motivation arising from a desire to blame leads people to make judgments of freedom that are consistent with this blame.

If the motivation arising from a judgment of moral badness leads to a magnification of intentionality judgments, then it should be the case that individuals who find a certain act particularly bad should judge these acts as more intentional than individuals who are indifferent about the morality of the act. In a series of studies, Tannenbaum, Ditto, and Pizarro (2009) demonstrated that this is indeed the case. Across a number of studies, individuals who differed in their initial assessment of how immoral an act was demonstrated differing judgments of intentionality. For instance, using the scenario developed by Knobe and colleagues described above, individuals who reported a strong moral motivation to protect the environment were more likely to report that the damage to the environment brought about as a side effect of the CEO's decision was intentional than those who held no such moral values about the environment. Similarly, when presented with a case in which military leaders ordered an attack on an enemy that would have the foreseen (yet unintended) consequence of causing the death of innocent civilians, political conservatives and liberals rated the action as intentional when it ran contrary to their politics. When the case involved Iraqi insurgents attacking American troops with the side effect of American civilian deaths, political conservatives were more likely to judge the killings as intentional than liberals. The converse was true when the case was described as American troops killing Iraqi civilians as a consequence of attacking Iraqi insurgents.

In another study, participants were given one of two examples in which the principle of harm reduction was used to justify the distribution of free condoms in order to prevent the incidence of pregnancy and the spread of disease. Participants were all subsequently asked whether the distribution of condoms intentionally promoted sexual behavior. Moral motivation was manipulated by changing the intended recipients of the free condoms: one set of participants read about local school board members who decided to distribute condoms to students because they were aware that middle-school and high-school students were engaging in risky sexual behavior, while another set read that policy makers who were aware that soldiers stationed in foreign countries were engaging in acts of sexual aggression (i.e., rape) against local women decided to distribute condoms to the soldiers in order to curb the spread of unwanted diseases. In both cases it was explicitly stated that the group of individuals making the decision to distribute condoms did not condone the sexual behavior of the intended recipients but merely wanted to reduce the harm associated with these actions.

As predicted, participants who read about the distribution of condoms to young teens reported that the policy makers were not intentionally promoting teen sex, while participants reading about foreign soldiers reported that policy makers had intentionally promoted rape. The obvious difference in the moral status of premarital teen sex and rape seemed to be driving judgments of intentionality. More interestingly, these differences in the moral status of the two acts may have accounted for an unexpected gender difference in these ratings of intentionality—women were much more likely to report that the policy makers had intentionally promoted rape in the military case but had not intentionally promoted sex in the case of young teens. Men judged the two scenarios nearly identically. One interpretation of this finding is that the motivation to condemn rape was stronger in female participants, especially since the sexual aggression in the scenario targeted women, and that this increased motivation drove intentionality judgments.

Consistent with the view that a motivation to hold an individual blameworthy can lead to a distortion of the criteria for agentic freedom, it appears as if blame can even influence memory for the severity of a moral infraction. In one study, Pizarro and colleagues presented individuals with a scenario in which a man walked out of a restaurant without paying for his meal. Within the description of this action, participants were given detailed information about the price of the dinner. Researchers manipulated the degree of blameworthiness for this infraction by telling one set of participants that the individual had failed to pay for his meal because he had received a call notifying him that his daughter had been in a car accident, while another set of participants were told that the individual simply desired to get away without having to pay. When asked to recall the events approximately one week later, participants who had read that the man failed to pay simply to get away with it recalled the price of the dinner as significantly higher than those who had read that the man had left because of his daughter's accident (whose memory for the price was accurate). Across conditions, the degree of moral blame participants reported after reading the story was a significant predictor of the memory distortion one week later (Pizarro, Laney, Morris, & Loftus, 2006).

"Ultimate" Freedom

The agentic freedom that seems important for lay attributions of moral responsibility is conceptually independent from the "ultimate," metaphysical freedom that many philosophers have argued is necessary for attributing moral responsibility (e.g., libertarian freedom, or the freedom to "have done otherwise"). A deep concern espoused by many is that the causal determinism that has been a reliable guide in scientific research may also threaten the ultimate freedom that seems necessary to be held morally accountable. If thoughts and feelings are entirely caused by physical processes in the brain, and if the laws that govern these processes are no different than the laws governing the motion of billiard balls and automobiles, then perhaps a person is no more accurate in the belief that she freely decided to get up in the morning than that a billiard ball freely chose to roll across the table. Some have argued that the increased dissemination of psychological research highlighting the deterministic processes that give rise to human thought and action may radically change people's notions of freedom and punishment (Greene & Cohen, 2004). Yet while psychologists have conducted a great deal of research on the criteria of agentic freedom, only recently have psychologists and experimental philosophers turned their attention to the question of whether this ultimate freedom is treated by individuals as a prerequisite for the ascription of moral responsibility in the manner many philosophers have argued.

As it turns out, the deep concerns that determinism threatens moral responsibility may be unfounded. In the first place, it is unclear whether the lack of ultimate freedom is of much concern for individuals when making judgments of responsibility—in some cases, despite explicit information that undermines the presence of ultimate freedom, people still seem willing to hold others morally accountable. Yet even in cases in which participants appear to endorse the view that ultimate freedom is a necessary prerequisite for the attribution of moral responsibility, the motivation to hold others morally accountable seems to lead individuals to selectively ignore this information. For instance, in a recent study by Nichols and Knobe (2007), individuals were presented with a description of a world that was described as entirely deterministic in the manner that is incompatible with ultimate, metaphysical freedom. When participants were asked if, in general, murderers in this deterministic world should be held morally responsible, most participants said no. But when presented with a specific individual who murdered his entire family, individuals were more than willing to attribute blame—even when it was clear from the description of the world that he could not have acted otherwise. It appears as if the vivid, emotional nature of the specific crime (and the likely motivation to hold an individual capable of such a crime given its vividness) led individuals to either ignore the information about ultimate freedom or adjust their metaphysical beliefs about whether determinism is truly incompatible with moral responsibility.

In support of this latter view, Woolfolk, Doris, and Darley (2006) described a scenario to participants in which a man was under a clear situational constraint that forced him to murder a passenger on an airplane (he was forced by hijackers to kill the person or else he and 10 others would be killed). While the man appeared to possess agentic freedom, he was clearly constrained by the situation in terms of his ability to have acted otherwise. Despite this constraint, participants nonetheless held the man more responsible for the murder if it was something he wanted to do anyway (if he "identified" with the act). Consistent with the compatibilist approach espoused by Frankfurt (1971) and others, the man's inability to do otherwise—his lack of ultimate freedom—did not seem to disturb participants' ability to hold him morally accountable. As a final example of how underlying motivation to hold an individual accountable can shift judgments of freedom, we recently asked participants to recount a bad deed that was either committed by a good friend or by an enemy (Helzer & Pizarro, 2009). Given the differing motivations at play in their judgments of responsibility for a liked versus a disliked individual, we were interested in how individuals would judge the freedom of the person who had committed the moral infraction by asking participants to judge to what extent they thought the person's behavior was intentional as well as whether they thought the person's behavior was freely chosen. As expected, people found the bad deed performed by an enemy as more blameworthy than the one performed by a friend (this was true after controlling for the severity of the act, as well as when limiting our analyses to judgments of identical acts committed by a friend or an enemy, such as sexual infidelity). More importantly, the manipulation of motivation (friend vs. enemy) affected participants' judgments of freedom as assessed by their responses to both questions: relative to the immoral deeds of their friends, participants attributed the misdeeds of their enemies to their enemy's underlying intentions and were more likely to report that the act was freely chosen.

What these studies seem to show is that while many philosophers perceive determinism to be a threat to freedom (and by extension, to moral responsibility), the psychology of moral responsibility is such that people are fairly willing to hold others morally accountable even in the presence of strong determinism (see also Nahmias, Morris, Nadelhoffer, & Turner, 2006, for evidence suggesting that for laypersons, determinism doesn't even threaten freedom of the libertarian variety).

CONCLUSION

We have tried to defend a number of specific claims about the lay concept of freedom and how individuals use information about freedom when making judgments of moral responsibility. Specifically, we have argued that individuals are highly motivated to hold others accountable for moral infractions, and that the primacy of this motivation often influences judgments about freedom, rather than the other way around. This seems true for judgments regarding agentic freedom (such as whether an act was intended, caused, and controlled), as well as for judgments of ultimate, or metaphysical freedom (the ability to have done otherwise). One upshot of these findings is that the classic incompatibilist view that determinism poses a threat to morality and responsibility, while seemingly intuitive, may pose a threat only to individuals who do things like read books about free will. The psychological link between ultimate freedom and responsibility appears less strong than many have suggested. Indeed, to the extent that individuals possess the intuition that there is a link between freedom and responsibility, they seem to use such a link primarily as a strategy to defend their moral judgments. Free will is important, but not for the reason many might think.

In moments of reflection, then, individuals may realize that they should suspend their moral evaluations of the robot neighbor described in the introduction (because he does not possess "ultimate" freedom). Nonetheless, when he plays his music loudly, fails to mow his lawn, and lets his dog use their yard as a bathroom, they will have no problem attributing all the freedom needed to in order to blame him for his rude behavior.

DISCUSSION WITH DAVID A. PIZARRO

Are there differences between beliefs about free will in the abstract and beliefs about free will in concrete cases?
Bertrand Malle conducted several studies in which he asked people abstract questions about people's intuitions about intentionality, and results seemed to indicate that people believe that a person has to intend to do a thing in order to do it intentionally. In contrast, Joshua Knobe gave participants a concrete scenario featuring a CEO and asked them to make determinations about whether his actions were done intentionally. Results indicated that one need not intend to do something in order to do it intentionally. Thus, there seems to be a distinction between abstract beliefs and the concrete case for the question of intentionality. Might there be a similar distinction for free will?

Indeed, people do seem to respond differently to questions about free will in the abstract as compared to concrete cases. In particular, people generally believe that determinism undermines free will in the abstract. Yet, for specific cases, people generally believe that individuals are not to be excused from wrongdoing because of determinism. This seeming conflict likely is because people have a strong urge to see intentionality, in order to hold others responsible. Said differently, people seem to alter what they mean by intentionality, or the requirement of free will in establishing intentionality, in order to blame. It would be unusual to hear a judge say "Because of metaphysical determinism, you should get a reduced sentence." That is, abstract beliefs about free will may conflict with the desire to assign blame in concrete cases.

Is the question of free will related to judgments of moral responsibility?
The consensus view is that the two are deeply entwined. However, an alternative view is that free will and moral responsibility are entirely orthogonal, such that determined bad behavior requires punishment just as undetermined bad behavior does. For instance, if a parent has one child who is temperamentally (and unavoidably) agreeable, and one that is temperamentally (and unavoidably) disagreeable, the parent will surely increase the punishment on the disagreeable child, despite the fact that it is temperamental and not chosen. Indeed, greater punishment may be necessary to alter the disagreeable child's behavior. On this view, there is no real relationship between freedom and responsibility.

A second alternative to the view that free will and moral responsibility are closely related is that they are peripherally related. On this view, the question of free will is so much more important than that of moral responsibility that moral responsibility is incidental. Consider the following example. Imagine a person who is totally amoral. This person makes no moral judgments about others or about the self. Such a person may experience interpersonal problems, but he or she can function in society and order from a menu. In contrast, one cannot function without a sense of free will. A person convinced of the truth of determinism cannot go to a restaurant, sit down and say "Everything is determined, so I'll just wait and see what I order". In other words, people cannot function without the assumption of free will, but they can function without the concept of moral responsibility. Thus, moral responsibility may be considered a peripheral question to that of free will.

Laypersons, however, seem to react strongly and viscerally to the possibility of an absence of moral responsibility, while they view the possibility of determinism with less reactance. Thus, among laypersons, the question of moral responsibility seems preeminent relative to the question of free will.

Is moral responsibility unique among humans?
One of the distinguishing features of human beings is self-regulation. In most nonhuman animals, behavior is under social control. However, certain patterns of instinctual behavior are adaptively necessary for the survival of the species. The way that individual nonhuman animals are controlled is by how their behavior affects the group. This is social control. The interesting thing about judicial decisions is that they are partly a system of social control and partly a system that has tapped into the notion of self-regulation and moral responsibility. In a sense those are confounded roles. The distinction between the kind of social control found in nonhuman animals and the kind of social control found in humans is that an additional amount of social control is found in humans.

REFERENCES

Alicke, M. D. (1992). Culpable causation, *Journal of Personality and Social Psychology, 63*, 368–378.

Alicke, M. D. (2000). Culpable control and the psychology of blame, *Psychological Bulletin, 126*, 556–574.

Axelrod, R., & Hamilton, W. D. (1981). The evolution of cooperation. *Science*, 211, 1390–1396.

Baumeister, R. F., Masicampo, E. J., & DeWall, C. N. (2009). Prosocial benefits of feeling free: Disbelief in free will increases aggression and reduces helpfulness. *Personality and Social Psychology Bulletin, 35*, 260–268.

Brosnan, S. F., & deWaal, F. B. M. (2003). Monkeys reject unfair pay. *Nature, 425*, 297–299.

Call, J. & Tomasello, M. (2008). Does the chimpanzee have a theory of mind? 30 years later. *Trends in Cognitive Science, 12*, 187–192.

Clarke, R., (2003). *Libertarian accounts of free will.* New York: Oxford University Press.

DeWaal, F. (2006). *Primates and philosophers. How morality evolved.* Princeton, NJ: Princeton University Press.

Dennett, D. (1984). *Elbow room: The varieties of free will worth wanting.* Cambridge, MA: MIT Press.

Fehr, E., & Gächter, S. (2002). Altruistic punishment in humans. *Nature, 415*, 137–140.

Frank, R. (1988). *Passions within reason: The strategic role of the emotions.* New York: W.W. Norton.

Frankfurt, H. (1971). Freedom of the will and the concept of the person, *Journal of Philosophy, 68*, 5–20.

Gilbert, D. T. (1998). Ordinary personology. In D. T. Gilbert, S. T., Fiske, & G. Lindzey (Eds.) *The handbook of social psychology* (4th edition). New York: McGraw Hill.

Gilbert, D. T., & Malone, P. S. (1995). The correspondence bias, *Psychological Bulletin, 117*, 21–38.

Greene, J. D., & Cohen J. D. (2004). For the law, neuroscience changes nothing and everything, *Philosophical Transactions of the Royal Society of London B (Special Issue on Law and the Brain), 359*, 1775–17785.

Haidt, J., & Joseph, C. (2004). Intuitive ethics: How innately prepared intuitions generate culturally variable virtues. *Daedalus: Special Issue on Human Nature*, 55–66.

Haidt, J., Rosenberg, E., & Hom, H. (2003). Differentiating diversities: Moral diversity is not like other kinds. *Journal of Applied Social Psychology*, 33, 1–36.

Hamlin, J. K., Wynn, K., & Bloom, P. (2007). Social evaluation by preverbal infants, *Nature, 450*, 557–559.

Heider, F., & Simmel, S. (1944). An experimental study of apparent behavior, *American Journal of Psychology, 57*, 243–259.

Helzer, E. G., & Pizarro, D. A. (2009). *Motivated Use of Ultimate versus Agentic Freedom.* Manuscript in progress.

Jones, E. E., & Harris, V. A. (1967). The attribution of attitudes, *Journal of Experimental Social Psychology, 3*, 1–24.

Knobe, J. (2006). The concept of intentional action: A case study in the uses of folk psychology, *Philosophical Studies, 130,* 203–231.

Kuhlmeier, V., Wynn, K., & Bloom, P. (2003). Attribution of dispositional states by 12-month-olds, *Psychological Science, 14,* 402–408.

Leslie, A. M., Knobe, J., & Cohen, A. (2006). Acting intentionally and the side-effect effect: Theory of mind and moral judgment, *Psychological Science, 17,* 421–427.

Miller, G. F. (2007). Sexual selection for moral virtues, *Quarterly Review of Biology, 82,* 97–125.

Nahmias, E., Morris, S., Nadelhoffer, T., & Turner, J. (2006). Is incompatibilism intuitive? *Philosophy and Phenomenological Research, 73,* 28–53.

Nichols, S., & Knobe, J. (2007). Moral responsibility and determinism: The cognitive science of folk intuitions, *Nous, 41,* 663–685.

Pereboom, D. (2001). *Living without free will.* New York: Cambridge University Press.

Pizarro, D. A., Inbar, Y., & Darley, J. M. (2009). *A dual-process account of judgments of free will and responsibility.* Manuscript in preparation.

Pizarro, D.A., Laney, C., Morris, E., & Loftus, E. (2006). Ripple effects in memory: Judgments of moral blame can distort memory for events. *Memory and Cognition, 34,* 550–555.

Pizarro, D.A., Uhlmann, E., & Bloom, P. (2003). Causal deviance and the attribution of moral responsibility. *Journal of Experimental Social Psychology, 39,* 653–660.

Premack, D., & Woodruff, G. (1978). Does the Chimpanzee Have a Theory of Mind. *Behavioral and Brain Sciences, 1,* 515–526.

Provencher, H., & Fincham, F. D. (2000). Attributions of causality, responsibility, and blame for positive and negative symptom behaviors in caregivers of persons with schizophrenia, *Psychological Medicine, 30,* 899–910.

Roskies, A. L. (2006). Neuroscientific challenges to free will and responsibility. *Trends in Cognitive Sciences, 10,* 419–423.

Sanfey, A. G., Rilling, J. K., Aronson, J. A., Nystrom, L. E., & Cohen, J. D. (2003). The neural basis of economic decision-making in the Ultimatum Game, *Science, 300,* 1755–1758.

Scholl, B. J., & Tremoulet, P. D. (2000). Perceptual causality and animacy, *Trends in Cognitive Sciences, 4,* 299–309.

Shaver, K. G. (1985). *The attribution of blame: Causality, responsibility, and blameworthiness.* New York: Springer-Verlag.

Searle, J. R. (1983). *Intentionality: An essay in the philosophy of mind.* New York: Cambridge Press.

Strawson, P. F. (1974). *Freedom and resentment and other essays.* London: Menthuen Publishing Ltd.

Tabibnia, G., Satpute, A. B., & Lieberman, M. D. (2008). The sunny side of fairness: Preference for fairness activates reward circuitry (and disregarding fairness activates self-control circuitry, *Psychological Science, 19,* 339–347.

Tannenbaum, D., Ditto, P.H., & Pizarro, D.A. (2009). *Motivated assessments of intentionality.* Manuscript in progress.

Todorov, A., Said, C. P., Engell, A. D., & Oosterhof, N. (2008). Understanding evaluation of faces on social dimensions. *Trends in Cognitive Sciences, 12,* 455–460.

Trivers, R. L. (1971). The evolution of reciprocal altruism. *Quarterly Review of Biology, 46,* 35–57.

Vohs, K. D., & Schooler, J. W. (2008). The value of believing in free will: Encouraging a belief in determinism increases cheating. *Psychological Science, 19,* 49–54.

Weiner, B. (1995). *Judgments of responsibility: A foundation for a theory of social conduct.* New York: Guilford Press.

Woolfolk, R. L, Doris, J. M., and Darley, J. M. (2006). Identification, situational constraint, and social cognition: Studies in the attribution of moral responsibility, *Cognition, 100,* 283–301.

8 Consciousness and the Problem of Free Will

John R. Searle

THE PROBLEM OF FREE WILL

Consciousness definitely exists, but we are not sure if free will exists. That is why I prefer to say "the problem of free will," and not just "free will" in the title of this paper. There are very close connections between consciousness and the problem of free will. In order to explain those connections, I have to give at least a brief definition of each term. Consciousness is often said to be extremely hard or difficult to define, but if we are talking about a commonsense definition that just identifies the target of our investigation and not a scientific definition given in terms of the most basic neurobiological processes of consciousness, then it seems to me rather easy to give a commonsense definition. Consciousness consists of those states and events of feeling or sentience or awareness that typically begin when we awake from a dreamless sleep and continue throughout the day until we go to sleep or otherwise become unconscious again. Dreams, on this definition, are a form of consciousness. Some of the essential features of consciousness are that it is *qualitative* in that there is always a certain qualitative character to any conscious state; it is *subjective* in the sense that it only exists as experienced by a human or animal subject; and in the normal nonpathological cases, it is *unified,* and it has a kind of unity in that all of my conscious experiences are experienced as part of a single conscious field.

It is much more difficult to give a neutral, nontendentious definition of "free will," but in the sense of "free will" that I will be interested in, the problem of free will is this: Are there human actions that are not determined by antecedently sufficient causal conditions? To make that more explicit, the question we are asking is this: Given that there are actions that are not random, that are done with conscious intent, and that follow from conscious decision making, is it the case that any of these actions were not preceded by causal conditions sufficient to determine the actions? If the answer to that question is yes, then there are free actions. But it would be an odd result if there were such actions because these would be actions that, though they admit of causal explanations given in terms of the agent's reasons, motives, beliefs, desires, and so forth, all the same, the actions were not determined in the sense that the totality of the prior states of the agent, including all the neurobiological states, was not sufficient to determine that that particular action had to occur. The agent might have done something different from what he did in fact do.

The connection between the consciousness and the problem of free will is this: Only for a conscious agent is there a problem of free will, and if free will does exist, it can only exist in conscious agents. I will explain both of these points. Why do we have a problem of freedom of the will at all? We do not, for example, have a problem of the freedom of digestion or freedom of perception. The reason is that there is a certain peculiar character to some of our conscious experiences. When I make up my mind to do something, when I make a decision, I typically do not experience the making of the decision as *forced* by the considerations for or against the decision. For example, a few months ago I made a decision as to which presidential candidate to vote for, but I did not experience my decision as something that I simply could not help, that there was no way that I could have decided otherwise. There was, in short, an experienced conscious gap between the reasons for the action and the decision to perform the action based on the reasons. We do not always experience this gap. Sometimes we feel ourselves in the grip of a compulsion, an obsession, or an addiction. But in most normal nonpathological cases, we experience a gap between reasons and decision. Furthermore, when it comes to actually doing the thing we decided to do, we experience a second gap, or rather a continuation of the first gap, in that even though we have already decided to do it, we still have to haul off and do what it is we decided to do. Having made the decision by itself is not enough to force the onset of the action. Finally, there are actions that extend over fairly long periods of time. We decide to learn French or to swim the English Channel, and it is not enough to just begin the action, we have to make a continuous effort to reach the completion. Again, we experience a gap between the antecedent causes of the action, including the onset of the action, and the continuation of the action to completion.

I have talked as if there were three gaps, the gap of decision making, the gap of the onset of the action, and the gap of the continuation of the action to completion, but in fact they are all parts of a continuous causal gap of conscious voluntary action. The experience of the gap is the experience of thoughts and actions where we do not sense the decisions and actions as causally fixed by the antecedent conditions. It consciously seems to us that it is up to us what we decide and what we do. We do not have anything like this gap when it comes to digestion, or even perception. I can move my head to change my perception, but if I am looking at an object in broad daylight at point-blank range, it is not up to me what I see. I see what is there. The gap I have described is a feature of our conscious experience of deciding and acting in a way that it is not part of our conscious experience of perception, digestion, growth, or any number of other of life's events.

The problem of free will can now be stated succinctly: Does the experienced gap correspond to anything in reality? The traditional name for the gap in philosophy is "the freedom of the will," but the fact that we experience this gap does not imply that the features it seems to represent actually exist in reality, that there really is a causal gap between the antecedents of our decisions and actions and the actual making of the decisions and the carrying out of the actions. So it is only because of certain sort of consciousness, the consciousness of the gap, that there is a problem of free will at all. Furthermore, let us suppose that free will is not an illusion, that there really is a causal gap or set of causal gaps of the kind I have been describing. Then free actions can only exist for a conscious agent because it is only a conscious agent who has a sense of alternative possibilities in the gap. By the way, traditional psychoanalysis recognizes this fact in that it tries to get the patient to bring to consciousness his or her repressed motivations. The theory is that only when they become conscious can they be controlled by the agent. As long as the motivations are unconscious, they control us instead of us controlling them. There is thus a double connection between consciousness and free will. It is only because of a certain kind of consciousness that we are aware of the apparent phenomenon of free will at all. Even if we come to believe it is an illusion, it is only because we have a certain kind of consciousness that we have the illusion of free will. But furthermore, on the assumption that it is not an illusion, only a conscious agent can genuinely have free will, because only a conscious agent can make conscious decisions and perform conscious actions in the gap.

It is important to remember that when we talk about consciousness and conscious decision making and conscious thought processes, we are talking about the subjective, logical, conceptual, and intentionalistic features of neurobiological processes in the brain. Right now, as you read these words, there are electrochemical processes going on in your brain that have the semantic contents of which you are now aware. Now in our tradition, which is heavily influenced by dualism of mind and body, we are not used to thinking of brute, neurobiological processes such as neuron firings or the secretion of neurotransmitters into the synaptic clefts as having logical properties, but that is exactly what I want to insist on. The very semantic content that you are now aware of and the very semantic content that figures in those thought processes and decisions that we think of as exemplifying the problem of free will are also neurobiological processes going on in the brain. One and the same sequence of events has both biological features and logical, conceptual, and conscious features.

THE PERSISTENCE OF THE PROBLEM OF FREE WILL

Free will is one of those issues in philosophy where it seems to me we have made very little progress in my lifetime. For many areas there has been remarkable progress—one thinks of the philosophy of language, political philosophy, moral philosophy, and the philosophy of mind as areas in which substantial progress is visible. But when it comes to free will, it seems to me we are pretty much where we were 50 years ago. Why is that? The problem of free will arises because there is a conflict between two deeply held convictions and we do not see how to shake off either conviction. The first conviction is that human actions are natural events like any other events in the world. Human actions are part of the natural world as much as human digestion and human growth, along with the movement of tectonic plates and the growth of seeds into plants, and as such they are subject to natural forces. But this seems to imply that human actions are entirely determined, that they are as determined as any other biological process or, for that matter, any natural process in the world. No one supposes that the stomach or the liver has freedom of the will. Why should the brain be any different? Why should we suppose that brain processes give us freedom of the will any more than we would suppose that stomach processes give us freedom of digestion? Determinism seems to be overwhelmingly convincing. On the other hand, we all have the experience of free decision making and freely acting. We have an experience of making up our mind between the alternative possibilities open to us, such that given a choice between action A and action B, we choose action A, but we know, or seem to know, that all other things being equal right then and there, we could have chosen action B. We cannot shake off the conviction of our own free will.

RATIONALITY PRESUPPOSES FREE WILL

Someone might object to the claim that we cannot shake off the conviction of free will as follows: "All the same, free will might simply be an illusion like any other illusion. After all, we can't shake off the illusion of color even though many people agree with the scientific account that colors are an illusion created by differential light reflection striking our specific nervous systems. Why couldn't free will be a similar illusion?" If free will is an illusion, it is an illusion that we cannot shake off in the way that we might shake off other such illusions as rainbows, sunsets, and even colors. If I become convinced that colors are a systematic illusion, I can organize my life in such a way that it can be consistent with the belief that colors are a systematic illusion. The problem of free will is special in that our ordinary, everyday actions require us to act under the presupposition of free will. If you are given a choice in a restaurant between the pork and the veal, you cannot say to the waiter, "Look, I am a determinist, I will just wait and see what I decide, I will just wait and see what happens." Even the decision to refuse to exercise your own free will presupposes free will. Your refusal to exercise free will is intelligible to you as one of your own actions only on the assumption that you were acting freely. So even if you become intellectually convinced that determinism is true and free will is false, all the same you cannot act on this conviction. That is to say, you cannot treat your own voluntary action as something that just happens to you in the way that you can treat your digestive processes, or, for that matter, your visual experiences, as something that just happens to you. This is why, for example, we have a problem of the freedom of the will but not a problem of the freedom of perception or the freedom of digestion.

Though we cannot shake the presupposition of free will whenever we engage in voluntary decision making, all the same, that is no argument in favor of the reality of free will. It is just an important point about the distinction between free will and other features of our experience such as the experience of colors, where we could readily grant that the experience of color, though unavoidable, is nonetheless a systematic illusion.

COMPATIBILISM IS NOT A SOLUTION

So how are we to resolve this dispute? Many philosophers think it has already been resolved centuries ago by such people as Hobbes, Hume, and John Stuart Mill. Their solution is called "compatibilism." William James called it "soft determinism." Compatibilists think that if we understand these notions correctly, free will and determinism are really compatible with each other. It is perfectly possible for all of our actions to be causally determined, and yet for some to be determined by such things as our own character or our own rational thought processes, and these are the actions we call "free." Are all of our actions determined? Yes, of course, as much as any other events in the natural world. Are some actions also free? Yes, of course, because they are determined by certain sorts of inner causes rather than external constraints. If, as Hume points out, I act under a threat, or if I am under some sort of coercion, then in such cases I do not act freely. But in the normal case where I am making up my mind whom to vote for or what to eat in a restaurant, I have a case of free action because the determination of my action has to do with my inner rational decision-making processes. So free will and determinism are compatible. The word *free* is opposed not to *caused*, or even *determined*, but rather to *forced*, *compelled*, and so forth. To be free is to have such things as your own character and thought processes determine your actions. Of course, those features of your character and your thought processes that determine your actions are themselves as much determined as anything else in the universe.

Does this really solve the problem of free will? I do not think it does. No doubt there is a use of the word "free" where "He acted of his own free will" is compatible with "The causal forces determining him to act were sufficient to fix the particular action that he performed rather than any other action. Only that action was causally possible in that situation." But that is not the sense of free will that really interests us in these discussions. The sense of free will that is important both in our own understanding of ourselves and in our larger philosophical context is this: Are our actions such that the antecedents of the action are in every case causally sufficient to determine that that action had to occur and not some other? Or are there some human events, specifically some human actions, which are such that the causal antecedents are not sufficient to determine that that action had to be performed? That even given all those causal antecedents, some other course of action was open to the agent? Compatibilism does not solve our problem; it just changes the subject to talk about the use of certain words. There is definitely a use of these words where it is compatible to say that the action was completely determined and yet it was free. For example, when people march in the streets carrying signs that say "FREEDOM NOW," they are not interested in the elimination of the laws of causation; they are typically interested in getting governmental authorities to impose fewer restrictions on them. But this use of words is not the one that troubles us when we are really worried about free will.

As I am construing the problem of the freedom of the will, if free will were true, the world would be different from the way it would be if determinism were true. That is, I am supposing that it is not just a verbal question of how are we going to describe our actual behavior in a world of natural forces, whether we choose to describe some as free or not. Rather, I am supposing that there is an empirical difference between the world of free will and the world of determinism. What on earth could such a difference be? Let us explore this matter further.

The preferred way to find out whether or not the world is one way rather than another, is by a set of methods that, since the seventeenth century, we have come to call "scientific investigation." Could science solve the problem of the freedom of the will? I am now going to make some speculative efforts. I am going to try to imagine a scientific account that would support free will and one that would count against free will. Let me say at the beginning that from what we now know about how the world works, it seems overwhelmingly likely that determinism is true and free will is false. But we don't know a great deal about how the brain works, and what I am going to do is imagine how the brain would be different if free will were true from the way it would be if determinism were true.

THE READINESS POTENTIAL IS NOT A SOLUTION

First I want to digress to discuss the work of Deecke, Grözinger, and Kornhuber (1976), who seem to provide evidence in favor of determinism. Their experiments done over 30 years ago in Germany have in recent years been repeated and extended by Ben Libet (1985) in San Francisco. Here is how the experiment goes. You tell a subject to perform some simple motor task such as, for example, pushing a button at random intervals. You tell him to make up his mind to push the button and to observe on a clock exactly when he decided that he was going to push the button. What was discovered in these cases is that 200–300 milliseconds prior to his actually being aware of the intention in action to push the button, there is increased activity in his supplementary motor area. This increased activity is called "the readiness potential." There seems to be a neuronal antecedent to his apparently free voluntary action. Does this refute free will? Does the existence of increased activity in the supplementary motor area prior to the consciousness of a decision refute free will? Does it provide any evidence for determinism? Many people think that it provides decisive, or at least strong, evidence for determinism because an increased neuronal activity precedes the conscious decision. On their view, the brain makes up its mind to perform an action before we are consciously aware that we have made up our minds. So, to repeat the question, does the existence of the readiness potential refute free will? Even Libet admits that after the readiness potential has occurred, it is still possible for the agent to veto the action. That is, even given the presence of the readiness potential, the subject does not thereby have causally sufficient conditions for performing that action because the subject, given this activity in the motor area, can still change his mind and decide not to perform the activity in question. It seems to me the best way to understand the implications of the readiness potential is contained in the very expression itself. Given the fact that the subject has a prior intention to do something at random intervals, the brain, so to speak, gets ready for him to do it, prior to his consciously initiating the action to do it. It is important to notice in these cases that he already has a prior intention to perform an action of the type in question. The prior intention manifests itself in his readiness to perform the action. The existence of the readiness potential does not by itself show that determinism is true, nor for that matter that determinism is false. The question is still left open.

Furthermore, the examples used in the study of the readiness potential tend to be rather trivial examples of human behavior. What we are interested in is such questions as, "Was Churchill's decision in 1940 to continue fighting against the Germans a free action or was it determined?" This question can hardly be settled by finding out the level of neuronal activity in the supplementary motor area a few hundred milliseconds prior to his making up his mind. That is, the kind of actions that we are typically interested in are not such superficial actions as pushing a button.

CAN WE TREAT FREE WILL AS A SCIENTIFIC PROBLEM?

Let us try to take the problem of free will and determinism as a scientific question, assuming that the existence of the readiness potential is not by itself a decisive solution to the problem. How should we proceed? So far, I have been writing as if it could be taken for granted that nature is normally completely determined. In this respect, I follow many other authors who write about the problem of the freedom of the will. But, of course, since the development of quantum mechanics over half a century ago, we know that this is false. At the most fundamental level, at the level of the quarks and the muons, we know that there is an inherent randomness in nature, that nature is not completely determined and therefore not completely predictable at that level. We can only make statistical predictions at the quantum level. People often talk as if quantum indeterminacy were something that exists only at the micro level. But of course that is the most fundamental level, and the indeterminacies go all the way up. The point for determinism is that the indeterminacies tend to cancel each other out at the macro level, so we can treat the baseball and the baseball bat as Newtonian phenomena even though they are as much pervaded by quantum indeterminacy as any other part of nature. Determinacy is not the norm in the physical world. On the contrary, the physical world is pervaded throughout with indeterminacy.

It is important to emphasize how much the standard "scientific" conception of nature is inconsistent with what is known in physics. The standard conception, even among many professional philosophers is that the universe consists of very small entities called particles and that these behave in a deterministic fashion described by "laws of nature." One consequence of this view is that if all of the particles were stacked exactly as they were at the time of the Big Bang, then the subsequent history of the universe would be absolutely identical to a history that has occurred so far. Given the same causes, you would get the same effects. This is definitely not consistent with contemporary quantum mechanics.

Does quantum indeterminacy have any bearing on the problem of free will? Some people suppose it does because they believe that the absence of determinacy at the quantum level allows for free will at the higher level. But the problem with this is that the indeterminacy of the quantum level is a matter of randomness, and randomness is not the same as freedom. Random actions, the existence of random phenomena, does not offer any support for the existence of free, rational decision making because free, rational decision making, though not determined, is nonetheless not random. Quantum mechanics seems to give us randomness and not freedom. Randomness may indeed be an absence of determinism, but it is not thereby a manifestation of the freedom of the will. Free will has to be something more than, or something quite different from, random events occurring.

I am reluctant to discuss the question of the freedom of the will in connection with quantum mechanics because it seems to me that when people talk about quantum mechanics without actually doing the mathematical physics, there is a high coefficient of sheer nonsense, and I am aware of that risk. The amount of hot air that results from discussing quantum mechanics exceeds even that resulting from discussing freedom of the will. However, in this article, we are allowing ourselves a certain amount of speculative liberty, so let us proceed.

Free will presupposes consciousness. Only for the conscious agent can there be such a thing as the freedom of the will. But as I emphasized earlier in this article, we know that conscious processes in the brain are sets of neurobiological processes that occur in the brain. Those processes have a higher level of description where they are described as subjective and qualitative and a lower level of description where they are described as electrochemical. Same processes, different levels of description. Now we know for a fact that the only parts of nature that are definitely nondeterministic are the quantum mechanical parts, so it looks as if, if there is any factual reality to the conscious experience of nondeterminism, that is to say freedom, there must be some connection between consciousness and quantum indeterminacy. So what is the connection between consciousness and quantum mechanics? There have been various attempts to explain consciousness in quantum mechanical terms, and some very distinguished thinkers, among them Stuart Hameroff, Roger Penrose, and Henry Stapp, have all sought quantum mechanical explanations of consciousness. It worries me, and perhaps it ought to worry them, that their work is not taken seriously by the most advanced researchers in neurobiology. This, of course, does not show that mainstream neurobiology is right and their revolutionary view is wrong, but if I were a researcher, I would be worried if the very best workers in the field had no sympathy with the line of research that I was pursuing. However, let us continue to pursue it and see where it leads us.

The fact that randomness is not the same as freedom used to seem to me an obvious and decisive objection against any introduction of quantum mechanics into the discussion of the problem of the freedom of the will. Quantum randomness does not give us anything even remotely approaching free will. Freedom requires that the agents' rational processes arrive at a conclusion in a way that is nondeterministic, in a way in which the antecedent causes are not sufficient to determine the action in question, but in which the result is not in any sense random. So it looks like the randomness of quantum mechanics is simply irrelevant to the freedom of the will. However, it now seems to me that the argument as I just stated it commits a fallacy of composition. Here is how. The fallacy of composition is a fallacy of supposing that what is true of the elements of a system will be true of the entire system. So, for example, it would be a fallacy of composition to suppose that because neurons are firing at a rate of 40 Hz that therefore the whole brain must be firing at 40 Hz. That is a typical example of the fallacy of composition. Now the fact that the behavior of the subneuronal particles is random does not by itself show that the behavior of the whole system is random, even though the system is made up entirely of those particles. Certainly that is something we know from the behavior of larger systems generally. In theory, it is possible that you might have a quantum indeterminacy at the level of baseballs and baseball bats, but though there is a mathematical possibility of random behavior of baseballs and baseball bats, in real life the indeterminacies cancel themselves out, and the trajectory of the ball when the bat hits the ball can be calculated on the basis of deterministic Newtonian mechanics. So we might have randomness at the bottom level without having randomness at the higher levels. Now let us suppose that the hypothesis that consciousness requires a quantum mechanical explanation were true. I doubt very much that it is true, but at least it seems to me a possible empirical hypothesis. Here is how it goes: We do not have an explanation of consciousness. Standard accounts treat the neuron or neuronal groups, such as maps, as the fundamental explanatory level. But suppose that the minority is right in this case and that the explanation of consciousness will ultimately have to make an appeal to the quantum level. Suppose that it is only because of quantum phenomena, that the entire system made of neurons and synapses, which are themselves made of lower-level atomic and subatomic particles, can be conscious. But now let us suppose that the following hypothesis is true. Suppose that the conscious decision making processes inherit the absence of determinism of their subatomic substrate, without inheriting the randomness. Let us suppose that the subatomic particles with their quantum behavior are causally responsible for the existence of consciousness, but that certain forms of consciousness acquire an indeterminism that is not thereby random at the higher phenomenological level. In other words, it is a fallacy of composition to assume that the randomness at the bottom level must apply at the top level. It is at least logically possible that the absence of determinism at the bottom level could be inherited by an absence of determinism at the higher level without thereby inheriting randomness at the phenomenological level. This point has to be stated precisely. From the quantum mechanical view, the whole system will still be random, but at the quantum mechanical level we do not even have the vocabulary to talk about conscious decision making. What I am suggesting is the logical possibility, though empirical unlikelihood, that the higher-level consciousness of voluntary, free decision making would manifest the lack of causally sufficient conditions characteristic of the quantum level without inheriting the randomness of that level. We would have the conscious experience of our reflecting and making up our minds having an effect on our behavior, without it being the case that the conscious reflection and decision making and behavior were thereby totally random, or totally fixed by antecedently causal sufficient conditions.

Notice that from the point of view of the atomic physicist, the randomness goes all the way up because he or she cannot make deterministic predictions based on causally sufficient conditions. All you can make are statistical probabilistic predictions. But here is where the idea that consciousness might have a quantum mechanical explanation comes in. We are supposing that the consciousness is real, and that it is important in determining the outcome of the conscious thought processes, but that it itself inherits the lack of causally sufficient conditions of the micro level without thereby inheriting the randomness. The only sense in which it is random is that it is not predictable based on causally sufficient conditions. But then that is exactly the result that the free will theorist hopes to obtain.

I have to say that it is an extremely unlikely prospect that we could have conscious, rational decision making manifesting the indeterminacy of the quantum level without becoming random at that higher level. In fact, the whole idea is intellectually uncomfortable. If it were right, then we would have substituted three mysteries for one. I began by suggesting that free will is a mystery. We knew, before I began the talk, that consciousness and quantum mechanics are also mysteries. What I am now suggesting as a hypothesis is a system whereby the mystery of free will is explained by the mystery of consciousness, which is itself explained by the mystery of quantum mechanics. If that is not enough to give any respectable philosopher indigestion, then I think indigestion would not be a natural phenomenon.

DISCUSSION WITH JOHN SEARLE

Does an account of consciousness require randomness?
Suppose one were to take the question of free will seriously. The next question is to find out if there are other parts of the real world that are indeterministic. The answer is, in general, no. One theory that is commonly advanced in favor of indeterminacy is chaos theory. However, chaos theory is totally deterministic. The main thrust of chaos theory is that it yields an exponential information problem, and that is quite different from indeterminacy.

One place in which one can be certain to find indeterminacy is at the quantum level. In other words, one could argue that the only known element of nature that is indeterministic is the quantum element. However, that argument is misleading because everything is quantum mechanical, from baseballs to avalanches to hurricanes. This does not mean that baseballs can be found to act randomly, because indeterminacies tend to cancel each other out. This is why people treat baseballs as if they were a new deterministic system, even though they are not, strictly speaking.

Any explanation of consciousness must have a quantum mechanical component, and the quantum mechanical component will have a randomness component, but only in the sense that baseballs are random. Of course, not every conscious free choice will be random. It is just that it is impossible to eliminate all randomness.

What is the role of rationality in consciousness?
Imagine that a person has free will in the libertarian sense, and he or she chooses coffee over tea. There is another possible world where the past is exactly the same until the moment of choice. In the other possible world, the person chooses tea. A comparison of the two worlds may lead to the

observation that there are no differences between the two worlds. Thus, the conclusion might be that the difference between the coffee world and the tea world is just luck, and so the selection of coffee does not represent any real choice.

Yet a different way of approaching the gap between the two worlds is that rationality plays a role. Suppose again that a person is trying to choose between coffee and tea. This person thinks about the difference between them and makes the decision that tea is the better beverage. It is possible the person could have chosen coffee, all other conditions remaining the same. However, the conditions were not causally sufficient to choose coffee. What is the difference between a world in which coffee was chosen and a world in which tea was chosen? The answer is not randomness, but rationality. Coffee was chosen because the person thought about the difference rationally and made arguments that favored coffee.

This is exactly what happens in conscious decision making. One has a set of reasons, but the reasons are not effective because they do not fix the decision. A person still has to make up his or her mind for reasons to become effective. Said differently, reasons are not causally sufficient, but they become effective when a person acts on them. Of course, it is possible not to be rational about decisions and instead act on the basis of randomness. For instance, one might decide whether to get married on the basis of a coin flip. That is a possibility, but rationality is more common.

Of course, rationality assumes a point of view. That is, one cannot make sense of rational decision making (and accepting responsibility) unless one supposes that there is a point of view attached to one's consciousness. The *self* is a term to describe an element that satisfies the condition that consciousness be capable of acting on reason while assuming responsibility.

Can there be consciousness without a self?

There are certain striking features of our consciousness that indicate that one cannot make sense out of human consciousness without postulating a self. It is not a substantial self, but one must have the concept that there is a single entity such that it is conscious. The required self is capable of thought processes and reasoning, and it must be capable of decision making and acting upon its reasons. One cannot make sense of consciousness unless there is a formal element that provides a sense of unity, decision making, and responsibility. The element is the self.

The self is like the *point of view* in perception. One cannot make sense out of perception without postulating a point of view, even though one cannot see the point of view.

REFERENCES

Deecke, L. Grözinger, B., & Kornhuber, H. H. (1976) Voluntary finger movement in man: Cerebral potentials and theory. *Biological Cybernetics*, *23*, 99–119.

Libet, B. (1985). Unconscious cerebral initiative and the role of conscious will in voluntary action. *The Behavioral and Brain Sciences*, *8*, 529–566.

9 Development of Conscious Control and Imagination

Stephanie M. Carlson

Although students of the topic of consciousness can debate its proper definition, most theories tend to take as their starting point what is best characterized as the *end* point of consciousness, that is, the adult (human) state. This appears to be the case whether consciousness is viewed primarily in terms of neural architecture (a biological approach) or first-person experience (a phenomenological approach). Even an evolutionary or comparative approach, which considers changes in consciousness on a grand timescale, takes for granted that the human endowment of consciousness is fully fledged and distinguishes "it" from the consciousness of our predecessors or other species. Those who subscribe to these approaches do not necessarily view consciousness as a fundamentally *developmental* achievement in ontogeny. As noted by Zelazo, Gao, and Todd (2007), differences between younger and older individuals are often assumed to reflect differences in the contents of children's consciousness, not in the nature of consciousness itself. My aims in this chapter are twofold, and at first blush contradictory. The first is to argue that conscious process develops dramatically in infancy and early childhood and is exercised via increases in reflection (a sense of volition) and top-down control of action, thought, and emotion (executive function, EF). However, the second claim is that development in the case of consciousness is not strictly an upward-bound process in achieving an objective sense of self (i.e., the more choice and control, the better), but rather can be characterized as a balance between objectivity and personal, tacit knowledge. Creative discovery in science and art provide examples of this balance in adults, and imaginative play does so in children. I will conclude with thoughts on the implications of this research and the potential value of taking a domain-specific approach to the study of consciousness and free will.

CONSCIOUS CONTROL

Control and Choice

Free action has many shades of meaning stemming from different traditions (e.g., biological, psychological, theological, sociological). The scientific version, in which the unit of measurement is taken to be the individual agent, suggests that free action is indexed by the ability to resist external forces and to make selections between them. On this view, free will has two key requirements: control and choice.

A distinction between having a "will" and "free will" can be seen in the development of *volition*, defined by William James (1890) as "attention with effort." J. Mark Baldwin (1892) described volition as the "conscious phenomenon of will," an act of exercising the will as a conscious choice, which is distinct from the intended actions it causes (e.g., the intention to reach for a desired object, as distinct from the reaching itself). According to Baldwin, infants progress from simple imitation, which is relatively unreflective and effortless, to persistent imitation, which is deliberate and effortful. Consciousness moves from a state of monoideism to polyideism as awareness that one is intending to repeat an action and doing so selectively from a variety of possible actions begins to take hold. As will be described next, both control over the stimuli one attends to and the awareness that one can decide how to respond to those stimuli increase dramatically in the first several years of life.

In the adult social psychology literature, it has been hotly debated whether this sense of free will is an "illusion." Wegner (2002) cited ample evidence that people's first-hand experience of free will is unreliable, as in the celebrated experiments by Libet (1985) showing that the brain initiates action about a second *before* subjects reportedly decide to act. Similarly, referring to this kind of evidence, Metzinger (2006) wrote that the experience of one's own agency is "thin" and "evasive." But instead of concluding that there is no such thing as free will, or that it is necessarily all or nothing, it might be fruitful to think of a sense of agency as a *gradient* in effortful control (see also Baumeister, Chapter 3, this volume; Vohs, Chapter 5, this volume).

Levels of Consciousness

The prevailing developmental account consistent with this view is Zelazo's levels of consciousness theory (LOC; e.g., Zelazo, 2004; Zelazo et al., 2007). According to the LOC model, consciousness is structured hierarchically, beginning with "minimal consciousness" in the first year of life, in which an infant is motivated to approach pleasure and avoid pain. At this level, behavior is highly stimulus bound, tied to ongoing stimulation (without explicit recall), unreflective, and makes no reference to an explicit sense of self. At progressively higher levels of consciousness, more deliberate action occurs in response to a more carefully considered construal of the same situation, brought about by several degrees of reprocessing the situation (recursion). This is thought to occur via thalamocortical circuits involving regions of prefrontal cortex, which themselves are organized hierarchically in development (Bunge & Zelazo, 2006). Increases in reflection allow for the formulation and maintenance in working memory of more complex systems of rules or inferences, which permit the more flexible selection of certain rules for acting when multiple conflicting rules are possible. This, in turn, forms the basis for conscious control, that is, acting on the basis of explicit rule systems (in potentially silent self-directed speech) at higher and higher levels of complexity.

Evidence from our lab details the normative progression in children's performance on executive function measures and is largely consistent with a levels-of-consciousness account (e.g., Carlson, 2005). For example, we found that from age 2 to 5 years, children progress from understanding a conventional pair of rules in categorization (e.g., "mommy animals go in the Mommy bucket; baby animals go in the Baby bucket") to a pair of incompatible rules ("now *babies* go in the Mommy bucket and *mommies* go in the Baby bucket") to two pairs of incompatible rules in succession (e.g., sorting the same stimuli first according to color and then according to shape) to two pairs of incompatible rules concurrently (e.g., some trials go by the color game, others by the shape game), requiring even greater cognitive flexibility and control (Dimensional Change Card Sort, see Zelazo, 2006).

This circumscribed series of tasks illustrates, more broadly, the gradual development of agency, or a sense of self as "I," who can deliberate among possible courses of action and, with the chosen goal in mind, control my own thoughts and actions in light of the goal, as opposed to allowing the exigencies of the situation to control the self (Russell, 1996; see also Baldwin, 1892). In time, the self becomes the "executive" in charge of selecting a goal, holding it in mind, planning how to achieve it, executing the plan, evaluating whether the goal was met, and, if not, selecting another alternative (Zelazo, Carter, Reznick, & Frye, 1997). Although these executive function skills take a long time to mature (and indeed, there are large individual differences even in adults), numerous investigators have recently been drawn to the preschool period as a marker of some of the most dramatic improvements (for a review, see Zelazo, Carlson, & Kesek, 2008), and put more strongly, the ontogeny of consciousness itself.

Further evidence for levels of consciousness comes from experiments in which we generated a higher degree of self-control by helping children have more "psychological distance" from a salient stimulus and hence reflect more on the rule system (Carlson, Davis, & Leach, 2005). In this "Less is More" task, children are presented with a larger versus smaller array of candies and told that "whichever tray you point to, those treats will be given away [e.g., go to a naughty monkey puppet] and you'll get the *other* treats in your cup." Three-year-olds have difficulty learning a reverse reward contingency, that is, that they should point to *less* in order to receive more. They tend to be stimulus bound (pointing to the larger amount, the one they want for themselves) and unreflective, whereas 4-year-olds do quite well and infer that they should point to the *un*desired tray, usually within the first few trials. However, when we substituted meaningful symbols for the candies, 3-year-olds readily learned the contingency and were able to exert control over their selections, choosing a symbol for the smaller amount (e.g., a mouse) over a symbol for the larger amount (e.g., an elephant), thus receiving more treats (Carlson et al., 2005). Furthermore, those 3-year-olds who were given the symbolic version of the task were able to transfer their higher-order understanding and maintained good performance even when real treats were introduced later (Beck & Carlson, 2008). This generalization from the symbolic to the real illustrates the great power of symbolic thought in promoting conscious control, even in the presence of a strong temptation (a power not evident in chimpanzees in an analogous task; Boysen, Berntson, & Cacioppo, 1996).

To further illustrate this point, we observed children's spontaneous strategies for self-control (Carlson & Beck, 2009). Using the classic delay-of-gratification paradigm by Mischel and colleagues (Mischel, Shoda, & Rodriguez, 1989), we presented a larger reward and a smaller reward (e.g., 10 vs. 2 Goldfish crackers) to 3- and 4-year-old participants (N = 171) and explained that they could have the larger reward if they waited for the experimenter to return; otherwise, they could ring a bell on the table to bring back the experimenter, but in that case, they would only receive the smaller reward. Children were tested individually and waited up to 5 min. We recorded their spontaneous strategies and developed a taxonomy that included physical/ nonsymbolic strategies (obstructing the line of sight to the treats and/or bell; physically restraining oneself; looking in the one-way mirror behind which the parent was located) as well as verbal/symbolic strategies (reminding oneself of the rules; talking/singing; and pretending). In line with the development of executive function skills more generally, older children were significantly more likely than younger children to employ strategies to delay gratification. Interestingly, however, the pattern changed with age, wherein physical strategies declined while symbolic strategies, which we argue invoke higher-order thought processes to govern behavior in a top-down fashion, became significantly more common.

Knowing Me and Knowing You

In a related line of research, we have shown that individual differences in self-control are positively correlated with the ability to recognize and interpret other people's inner mental states, that is, theory of mind (e.g., Carlson & Moses, 2001). Several studies have found robust correlations between executive function and theory of mind task performance in preschoolers (e.g., $r = .66$ in Carlson & Moses, 2001), and in most cases these links have held up over age and IQ or verbal ability and have been upheld cross-culturally (e.g., Sabbagh, Xu, Carlson, Moses, & Lee, 2006). Despite this body of research, the nature of the relation between EF and theory of mind has been a matter of controversy. On the emergence view, this evidence suggests that children must be able to suppress their own potent representations of events before they can reflect accurately on the mental states of others (Moses, 2001). In contrast, others have argued that children must have a representational understanding of mental states before they will be able to monitor and control their behavior (Perner & Lang, 2000). A third theory, cognitive complexity and control-revised (Zelazo, Müller, Frye, & Marcovitch, 2003), is that executive function and theory of mind are both developmental by-products of the domain-general ability to reason about and selectively attend to hierarchically embedded rules, that is, as a result of increasing levels of consciousness regarding both the self and others.

Longitudinal studies thus far have favored the conclusion that individual differences in executive function significantly predict subsequent variance in theory of mind (independent of child general cognitive ability and socioeconomic factors) significantly better than the reverse developmental ordering (e.g., Carlson, Mandell, & Williams, 2004; Hughes & Ensor, 2007; Pellicano, 2007). In other words, although the correlations alone cannot rule out the idea that these skills are both by-products of a general reflection ability, when examined longitudinally, increases in self-control governed subsequent theory of mind rather than the reverse or a fully bidirectional relation. Further research is needed to fully understand the coordination of these skills in development. Nonetheless, it seems clear that some modicum of control over one's own thoughts and actions would be needed in order to reflect upon another's perspective, most crucially when that perspective differs from one's own. From a theoretical standpoint, at least, being able to interpret the underlying mental states of others in this nonegocentric way would be a powerful social reasoning tool (see Pizarro & Helzer, Chapter 7, this volume).

IMAGINATION

Is Higher-Order Thought the Highest Form of Thought?

We might naturally draw the conclusion from such evidence that the more, the better when it comes to conscious control of thought and action. The development of executive function marks a major shift from children being relatively unreflective, stimulus-bound creatures to being more reflective, thoughtful individuals who can pursue goals in the face of distraction, solve means–ends problems planfully, and engage in social interactions with some consideration of the other's perspective, hence reducing the potential for interpersonal conflict. It makes for a tidy story, so why not stop here? Why not train children (and anyone else at an apparent disadvantage on self-awareness) in mindful reflection on their own thought processes and behavioral tendencies, hence accelerating all of these developmental benefits? Indeed, some executive function training interventions have been successful with preschool children and generalized to other school-readiness skills (e.g., Diamond, Barnett, Thomas, & Munro, 2007).

There is an apparent disconnect here, however, which brings me to my second main point. A long tradition in cognitive psychology has revealed that as behaviors come under greater conscious control, with enough practice or, one might say, development, the effort required to carry out the same action decreases; the act becomes more automatic, and so *less* consciously experienced. The example of driving a car is often cited to describe procedural, implicit knowledge in adults that takes place with minimal consciousness, so much so that the driver can carry on a conversation while operating the vehicle (e.g., Zelazo et al., 2007). However, this implicitness pertains not only to what might be regarded as sensorimotor behaviors that get us where we need to go but otherwise are not particularly special or creative (e.g., to walk and chew gum at the same time), but also to a much broader spectrum of thought and behavior. With increasing skill and expertise at thinking about a certain domain (e.g., theoretical physics) or at a certain artistic or athletic talent (e.g., playing a Suzuki violin, writing a novel, or shooting free throws in basketball), thoughts and actions become more automatic, less consciously effortful. Indeed, experts in both thinking (e.g., physicists, philosophers) and doing (e.g., musicians, athletes) have great difficulty accessing *how* they know what they know, or do what they do, and often claim that overthinking such things can lead to more errors, not fewer.

But then, doesn't it follow that if such acts are carried out subconsciously or without volition in the Jamesian (1890) sense of "attention with effort," then what was once the province of the highest level of consciousness is now the lowest level? A full return to minimal consciousness in the LOC model does not quite capture this sort of downward progression in conscious control. A distinction would need to be made between stimulus-bound and unenlightened action (as in the preverbal infant) and unattended yet enlightened action (as occurs in domains of expertise). Even more disturbing to an exclusively upward-bound view of consciousness is that if we cannot grasp our own most highly accomplished skills and hold them up for scrutiny in an objective, reliable sense, but only in some deeply personal, idiosyncratic, inarticulate sense, this would seem to violate the Western ideal of scientific detachment: True knowledge is deemed impersonal, universally established, objective.

To the contrary, the chemist-philosopher Michael Polanyi (1958) sought to establish an alternative ideal of knowledge, termed "personal knowledge," to reflect a fusion of the personal and the objective. He regards knowing, from a Gestalt principle, as an active comprehension of the things known, an action that requires skill. "Skilful knowing and doing is performed by subordinating a set of particulars, as clues or tools, to the shaping of a skilful achievement, whether practical or theoretical. We may then be said to become 'subsidiarily aware' of these particulars within our 'focal awareness' of the coherent entity that we achieve" (p. vii). In this sense, all knowing involves the personal participation of the knower; "... into every act of knowing there enters a passionate contribution of the person knowing what is being known, and ...this coefficient is no mere imperfection but a vital component of his knowledge" (p. viii). Polanyi referred to our influential yet inarticulate ways of knowing as the "tacit component."

How might this apply to human development? It follows from Polanyi's (1958) thesis that there might be gradients of self-awareness of one's mental effort (control) and the fact that one is selecting some items of knowledge for focal attention while setting aside or postponing others (choice), even though it is asserted by Polanyi to be always a fusion of the subjective and the objective, never devoid of one or the other. However, unlike the canonical way of thinking about a gradient in a strictly linear form, with ever-increasing degrees of awareness and conscious access corresponding to an ever-widening knowledge base (which itself is perfectly correlated with age and experience), this process might be illustrated as a series of curvilinear functions in which conscious awareness first rises, then falls, as a function of knowledge or understanding within particular domains of ability, even though the highest level attainable generally increases with age and metacognition. This view takes consciousness to be dissociable according to different domains of experience rather than all of a piece. Karmiloff-Smith (1995), building upon Piaget (1974/1977), proposed a similar idea in her theory of representational redescription, in which domain-specific knowledge structures proceed through a hierarchy of redescription: Level I (implicit and procedural) to Level E_1 (explicit awareness of the structure of procedures) to Level E_2 (consciousness, with greater degrees of "explicitation" of knowledge and integration within and across domains). However, for Karmiloff-Smith, as in the LOC model, the assumed developmental progression (the "internal drive") is toward ever-higher degrees of explicit, verbalizable knowledge. Hence, although representational redescription provides a means for domain-specific increases in consciousness, it does not capture the paradox described here that *less* thinking can sometimes be *more* advanced.

Imagining the Impossible

To put the problem another way, if a drive toward higher-order, more reflective thought is the only engine in the development of consciousness, or the only metric by which we judge development to be complete, then why is it so often those individuals who are prone to being *least* mindful of their own thought processes who make the really big discoveries? For one, having a larger internal database makes for a richer network of associations from which to draw on (e.g., Tulving, 1985). But one might still think that the more conscious these associations are, the better for discovery of new ones. Polanyi (1958), however, offered several counterexamples of this principle, in which the scientist's personal participation in his knowledge (at a subconscious level), in both its discovery and validation, is an indispensable part of science itself. The observer is never fully removed from the observed (see also Baldwin, 1892). This is true in the "exact sciences" such as physics, astronomy, and chemistry (e.g., in the reading and calibrating of instruments) and becomes even more evident in the biological and social sciences, in which assertions are probability statements (degrees of confidence that a given outcome was not due to chance). The scientist is a "believer" in *something* even if it cannot be fully articulated, and not the epitome of pure, detached reason we might wish for.

This might be an erroneous wish, after all. Polanyi (1958) provided the example of Einstein's discovery of the theory of relativity occurring through a combination of high intellect and objective (impersonal) knowledge along with a personal, tacit knowing at a less conscious level. Einstein describes that he was vaguely aware of the problem at the age of 16, left it, only to return to it with a more explicit formulation 10 years later. For Polanyi this is an example not of subjectivity, but of the self establishing contact with a "hidden reality." On this view, intuition and faith play a role in scientific discovery—and this aspect of Polanyi's thought might be accused of being teleological—but my point is that discovery occurs against a backdrop of knowledge that is both objective and personal, both conscious and inarticulate. Imagining the "impossible," then, is infinitely elastic, but relative only to what one takes to be possible, and that is grounded in knowledge. Originality and innovation develop out of habit, or as Louis Pasteur noted, "Chance favors the prepared mind." Moreover, imagination would not get off the ground without some deeply personal commitment to the subject matter, what Polanyi calls "in-dwelling," or living *through* the knowledge, not simply carrying it around and operating on it like a computer.

This balance is exemplified not only in scientific discovery, but also in creative arts. Several accounts point to the relatively unconscious aspects of creativity. The antirationalist view takes many forms, including that of Immanuel Kant, who wrote in the *Critique of Judgment* that, "genius cannot describe or indicate scientifically how it brings about its products, but it gives the rule just as nature does. Hence the author of a product for which he is indebted to his genius does not know himself how he has come by his Ideas; and he has not the power to devise the like at pleasure or in accordance with a plan, and to communicate it to others in precepts that will enable them to produce similar products" (1790/1952, p. 188). Kant speculated that this process is guided by a "guardian spirit." Much later, Carl Jung affirmed the mystery of creativity: "Any reaction to stimulus may be causally explained; the creative act, which is the absolute antithesis of mere reaction will forever elude human understanding" (1933, p. 177). He posited that the archetypal themes of the "Collective Unconscious" of the human race are transformed in some way by the artist (and appreciated by the consumer who identifies with those themes). Indeed, it is common for accomplished fiction writers to report that they experience their characters as if they exist apart from themselves; the characters dictate the story, are often uncooperative, and say shocking or funny things that take the author by surprise. Taylor, Hodges, and Kohanyi (2003) documented this phenomenon, which they termed the "illusion of independent agency," in interviews with 50 writers, most of whom had experienced it at some point. Note that the illusion of independent agency (I think I am not in control of my own action) is the opposite of the "illusion of conscious will" that Wegner and others refer to (I think I am in control of my own action).

Reports from creative individuals who swear by intuition and unconscious inspiration can be contrasted with others who claim that creative works are just that— work! Edgar Allen Poe, for example, described his writing of "The Raven" as a painstaking, conscious process: "No one point in its composition is referable either to accident or intuition. . .the work proceeded, step by step, to its completion with the precision and rigid consequence of a mathematical problem" (1846, p. 163). He added that it is "autorial vanity" that prevents others from allowing the public to take a peep behind the scenes at the writing process and all that gets discarded, as they would prefer it to be understood that they compose by "ecstatic intuition." But even to this, one might argue that Poe's self-critical judgment of what would satisfy his goal and be just the right word in just the right place is itself testament to the unspoken power of personal knowledge. Therefore, it is likely that *both* higher and lower levels of consciousness and control play a role in creative acts. It is possible that expertise in the domain contributes to implicitness, in which multiple associations are made, many uneventfully integrated with existing knowledge structures, making it seem, at least in retrospect, that the inspiration came suddenly or from an external source. The creative process is conscious and most likely to assume center stage in focal attention when the artist is somehow dissatisfied with the expression. Consistent with lower levels of consciousness, individuals with low "latent inhibition" (i.e., less able to inhibit interference from extraneous stimuli) appear to be more creative. Carson, Peterson, and Higgins (2003) reported that *eminent creative achievers* were seven times more likely to have low rather than high latent inhibition scores. But the fact that creativity requires some effortful control is not disputed here, and indeed, adults who were "depleted" by a task requiring self-control were subsequently less creative than others who had not had their self-control tapped on a prior task (Baumeister, Schmeichel, DeWall, & Vohs, 2007).

Conscious Process in Children's Pretend Play

Returning to a developmental perspective, multiple levels of consciousness are also evident in children's pretend play. In symbolic thought, a symbol (e.g., a word, picture, number, visual image, or even an idea) is knowingly substituted for a direct experience of a stimulus, which allows behavior to be controlled in light of the symbol rather than the stimulus itself (i.e., psychological or symbolic distancing). Carlson and Zelazo (2008) adapted the LOC model (Zelazo, 2004) to account for developmental changes in symbolic thought that correspond to levels of consciousness and increases in working memory (Figure 9.1). In the first several years of life, symbolic thought progresses from being mediated and intentional (in the Brentano sense) but unreflective (Level 1), to thinking about representations in the absence of stimuli (Level 2), to treating symbols *as* symbols (Level 3; full-blown pretend play emerges), and finally to reflection on the quality of the symbol-referent relation (Level 4). With each level comes a greater degree of reflection on the symbol-referent relation and, hence, greater top-down control over behavior.

A paradox quickly becomes evident when we think about these cognitive requirements for pretend play: It is not the imagination running wild,

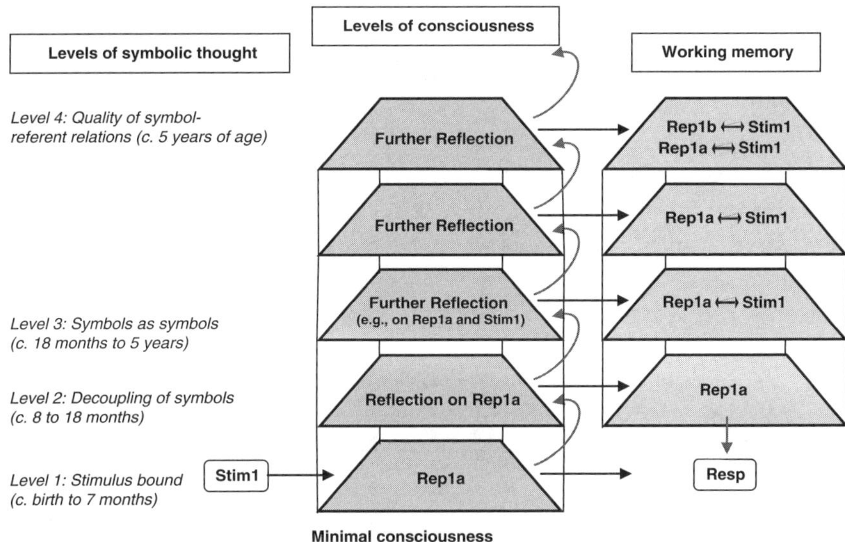

Figure 9.1. Consequences of reflection for symbolic thought. Development of the capacity to reflect on the contents of one's own consciousness, resulting in higher, more reflective levels of consciousness, allows for more aspects of symbols and symbol-referent relations to be considered and maintained in working memory. Reflection is interposed between perception of a stimulus (Stim1) and responding (Resp). The contents of minimal consciousness at one moment, together with new information about a stimulus, are fed back into minimal consciousness. Figure illustrates the different contents of working memory made possible by different degrees of reflection. Rep1a and Rep1b are alternate symbolic representations of the stimulus. Reprinted from Carlson and Zelazo (2008).

where anything goes, but rather, it is regulated and constrained. Vygotsky (1933) described this key aspect of play as rule-governed in his description of two sisters playing at "sisters," where the play version is highly scripted and follows inviolable expectations that barely resemble the way real sisters behave toward one another. The idea is that there are unwritten rules to pretense, and it is a serious misdemeanor to step outside the play frame by allowing real stimuli to overtake oneself (e.g., really biting into a mud "pie"). It follows from this that pretend play should be *positively* correlated with performance on executive function measures such as the Dimensional Change Card Sort in preschoolers. Indeed, they are robustly related even after controlling for individual differences in age, sex, verbal intelligence, and working memory performance (Carlson, Davis-Unger, & White, 2009). Furthermore, as presented earlier, making the task more symbolic leads to systematic improvements in 3-year-olds' self-control in the Less Is More task (Carlson et al., 2005), suggesting a mutual bootstrapping of pretense and executive function in development.

On the other hand, it is important to point out that pretend play is not goal-directed behavior, at least not in the same way as executive function tasks in which there is an explicit goal (e.g., "sort according to color [not shape]"). Play is intrinsically motivated (it cannot be commanded), pleasurable (as contrasted with "work"), nonliteral (reality is distorted), and actively engaged (not passively reflected upon) (Rubin, Fein, & Vandenburg, 1983). Hence, while pretend play is lawful behavior, it is also improvisational. Plans are not laid out ahead of time but unfold, as the successive nonliteral behaviors of one player are contingent upon the nonliteral behaviors of a partner (who, by the way, might be real or imagined). Players thus engage not necessarily in shared *goals*, but in shared *imagination*. I would argue that this process includes tacit knowledge, an implicit understanding made possible by personal investment in the skill of playing. A jazz metaphor is particularly apt (e.g., Sawyer, 1997). Accomplished jazz musicians such as Miles Davis have described the creative tension that occurs when a player introduces a change in the riff and the others are impelled to discover a new theme or a recombination of old themes and play off of it. In this way, the music is eternally generative (almost never the same thing twice), drawing on tacit knowledge based in experience. Similarly, as children progress through levels of consciousness and symbolic thought, they are also becoming "expert players," less consciously aware of their symbolic routines but readily able to access them. The play is constrained but is sustained and amplified by the introduction of uncertainty, as when a partner takes it in a slightly new, creative direction, and the other responds in kind as if to say, "Oh, I think I know where you're going with this." I suspect that the episode usually ends with an interloper from outside the play frame (e.g., mother calling one to dinner;

recess is over) or when one of the partners tires of the effort to keep it up (overthinking play turns it into work), and not with a great sense of achievement as when a goal has been met or a problem solved.

Other evidence suggesting that lower levels of consciousness can occur in pretense is that children exhibit the illusion of independent agency in their descriptions of interactions with imaginary friends, in ways that are nearly identical to creative writers' descriptions of being guided by their characters (rather than the other way around). Taylor, Carlson, and Shawber (2007) reported that among preschoolers with imaginary companions (which occurs in approximately 33%–50% of children), one-third of the imagined characters were described as being outside of the child's control. Some were regarded more like enemies than friends, and were uncooperative and unpredictable. For example, one child described her pretend friend as bothering her when she tries to read, to the extent that she sometimes has to shut and lock her door to keep the friend out. It is important to keep in mind that this was a nonclinical, typically developing sample, and that descriptions of uncontrollability were fairly common. As well, children age 3–4 years are not generally confused about the distinction between fantasy and reality; they "know," when pressed, that their imaginary companions are only pretend and will even begin to worry about the *interviewer's* grasp on reality after a lengthy list of questions about the friend (Taylor, 1999). Preschoolers who engage in more frequent role play (including having imaginary companions and impersonating others) are also more dissociative (at a subclinical level), which might be indicative of a more componential sense of self (Carlson, Tahiroglu, & Taylor, 2008). Consistent with this interpretation, Taylor and Carlson (1997) found that high-fantasy children performed significantly better than low-fantasy children on theory-of-mind tasks, in which they need to understand the subjectivity of mental states, and this was independent of intelligence.

In children's imaginative play, as in creativity in science and art, we see that descending back down the ladder of consciousness need not be the mark of a brain disorder (e.g., blindsight), or a fundamental breach with reality (e.g., schizophrenia), or a regression to an infantile or automaton state of mind; instead, it might paradoxically indicate a relatively advanced stage in thinking, on the way to having a new take on an old situation, that is, grounded innovation (see Schooler, Chapter 12, this volume).

CONCLUSION

Consciousness develops, most likely in a hierarchical fashion with recursive reprocessing of information at higher levels of reflective awareness.

But what goes up must come down, that is, with increasing automaticity of skill in a given domain, thinking about the known becomes less effortful, more implicit or tacit, hence drawing a distinction between objective and personal knowledge. Nonattended but enlightened information can influence action and discovery, as in science, the arts, and children's play. To understand how, we need to put things back together again. It is possible that back-grounding of the known frees up resources for new associations and creative syntheses to be formed and, eventually, articulated consciously in verbal thought. Bumping up against a new problem or aspect of a situation (e.g., a fact that doesn't fit a theory or belief; disliking something about one's painting in progress; uncertainty in play) can propel one to make existing knowledge again explicit so that it can be consciously examined, alongside a feeling *in* (not necessarily about) the situation, thereby integrating objective and tacit knowledge structures and viewing things from a more enlightened yet deeply personal (attached) perspective.

DISCUSSION WITH STEPHANIE CARLSON

Is "theory of mind" an appropriate term to describe the ability to distinguish one's own mental states from those of others?

Learning to walk requires that children learn about balance and gravity, among other things. However, when a child learns to walk, no one argues that the child has learned a theory of physics. Walking is just a physical skill that children develop, based largely on learned responses. Why not refer to *theory of mind* as an interpersonal skill that one develops, like walking? The reason *theory of mind* is preferable is that interpersonal development in children is not simply the learning of a set of responses one gives to other children. Interpersonal interactions require that one form mental representations of other people's mental representations. The ability to form representations of others' representations is more than just a skill (in the sense that walking is a skill), so the term theory of mind is apt.

There is evidence that children form representations of others' representations, even at a very young age. This is evident in pretend play. When a child engages in pretend play, he or she has to make assumptions about the state of mind of the other player, beginning with the understanding that the other player is pretending.

How immersive is pretend play?

Pretend play can be extremely immersive. For instance, children who pretend to play a game like "Peter and the Wolf" can become genuinely scared of the wolf. There are many cases of children becoming afraid of monsters that the children invented themselves. Likewise, children who have imaginary friends often imbue their imaginary friends with a sense of independent agency. For example, a child's imaginary friend might refuse to play a game the child wants to play, and the child may become frustrated with the imaginary friend. Clearly, pretend play can be very immersive. However, this does not mean that children are incapable of distinguishing imagination from reality; when children are pressed, they will acknowledge the difference between reality and unreality.

Parents often play with their children by pretending to be serious about something silly. For example, a parent may pretend to be serious about using a banana as a telephone. Why is this common?
Parents may unintentionally (or perhaps intentionally in some cases) be teaching children about theory of mind. This exercise requires that children make sense of a parent's behaviors by understanding that what appears to be serious behavior is actually playful behavior. In other words, children need to understand their parents' mental states for the game to work. There is research illustrating that when parents pretend to do something seriously, they exaggerate the motions so as to give children cues that they are really playing.

Does humor help develop consciousness?
Humor is helpful in developing children's understanding of what is real and what is unreal. Often the things that children find humorous are discrepancies between what is expected and what is experienced. For example, children may laugh when a father puts a bucket on his head. Presumably the discrepancy between what is expected and what actually occurred is the element that children find funny. Children as young as one year experience actions discrepant with expectations as humorous.

REFERENCES

Baldwin, J. M. (1892). Origin of volition in childhood. *Science, 20*, 286–287.

Baumeister, R. F., Schmeichel, B. J., DeWall, C. N., & Vohs, K. D. (2007). Is the conscious self a help, a hindrance, or an irrelevance to the creative process? In A. M. Columbus (Ed.), *Advances in psychology research*, 53 (pp. 137–152). Hauppauge, NY: Nova Science Publishers.

Beck, D. M., & Carlson, S. M. (2008, June). Psychological distancing and the Less is More task. In Giesbrecht, G (Organizer), *Creating space for self-regulation: Psychological distancing in the development of executive function, emotion regulation, and theory-of-mind.* Paper symposium presented at the annual meeting of the Jean Piaget Society, Quebec City, Canada.

Boysen, S. T., Berntson, G. G., Hannan, M. B., & Cacioppo, J. T. 1996. Quantity-based inference and symbolic representations in chimpanzees (Pan troglodytes), *Journal of Experimental Psychology: Animal Behavior Processes, 22*, 76–86.

Bunge, S., & Zelazo, P. D. (2006). A brain-based account of the development of rule use in childhood, *Current Directions in Psychological Science, 15*, 118–121.

Carlson, S. M. (2005). Developmentally sensitive measures of executive function in preschool children. *Developmental Neuropsychology, 28*, 595–616.

Carlson, S. M., & Beck, D. M. (2009). Symbols as tools in the development of executive function. In A. Winsler, C. Fernyhough, & I. Montero (Eds.), *Private speech, executive functioning, and the development of verbal self-regulation* (pp. 163–175). New York: Cambridge University Press.

Carlson, S. M., Davis, A., & Leach, J. G. (2005). Less is more: Executive function and symbolic representation in preschool children. *Psychological Science, 16*, 609–616.

Carlson, S. M., Davis-Unger, A. C., & White, R. E. (2009). *Representation and role-play: The relation between individual differences in executive function and pretense.* Manuscript in preparation, University of Minnesota, Minneapolis, MN.

Carlson, S. M., Mandell, D. J., & Williams, L. (2004). Executive function and theory of mind: Stability and prediction from age 2 to 3. *Developmental Psychology, 40*, 1105–1122.

Carlson, S. M., & Moses, L. J. (2001). Individual differences in inhibitory control and children's theory of mind, *Child Development, 72*, 1032–1053.

Carlson, S. M., Tahiroglu, D., & Taylor, M. (2008). Links between dissociation and role play in a non-clinical sample of preschool children. *Journal of Trauma and Dissociation, 9*, 149–171.

Carlson, S. M., & Zelazo, P. D. (2008). Symbolic thought. In M. M. Haith & J. B. Benson (Eds.), *Encyclopedia of infant and early childhood development* (Vol. 3, pp. 288–297). London: Elsevier.

Carson, S. H., Peterson, J. B., & Higgins, D. M. (2003). Decreased latent inhibition is associated with increased creative achievement in high functioning individuals, *Journal of Personality and Social Psychology, 85*, 499–506.

Diamond, A., Barnett, W. S., Thomas, J., & Munro, S. (2007). Preschool program improves cognitive control. *Science, 318*(5855), 1387–1388.

Hughes, C., & Ensor, R. (2007). Executive function and theory of mind: Predictive relations from ages 2 to 4. *Developmental Psychology, 43*, 1447–1459.

James, W. (1890/1950). *The principles of psychology* (Vol. 1). New York: Dover.

Jung, C. G. (1933). Psychology and literature. In *Modern Man in Search of a Soul.* New York: Harcourt, Brace.

Kant, I. (1952). *The critique of judgment* (J. C. Meredith, Trans.). Oxford: Oxford University Press (Original work published in 1790).

Karmiloff-Smith, A. (1995). *Beyond modularity: A developmental perspective on cognitive science.* Cambridge, MA: MIT Press.

Libet, B. (1985). Unconscious cerebral initiative and the role of conscious will in voluntary action, *Behavioral and Brain Sciences, 8*, 529–566.

Metzinger, T. (2006). Conscious volition and mental representation: Toward a more fine-grained analysis. In N. Sebanz & W. Prinz (Eds.), *Disorders of volition* (pp. 19–48). Cambridge, MA: MIT Press.

Mischel, W., Shoda, Y., & Rodriguez, M. 1989. Delay of gratification in children, *Science, 244*, 933–938.

Moses, L. J. (2001). Executive accounts of theory-of-mind development. Commentary on "Meta-analysis of theory-of-mind development: The truth about false belief." *Child Development, 72*, 688–690.

Pellicano, E. 2007. Links between theory of mind and executive function in young children with autism: Clues to developmental primacy, *Developmental Psychology, 43*, 974–990.

Perner, J., & Lang, B. (2000). Theory of mind and executive function: Is there a developmental relationship? In Baron-Cohen, S., Tager-Flusberg, H., & Cohen, D. (Eds.), *Understanding other minds: Perspectives from developmental cognitive neuroscience* (2nd ed., pp. 150–181). New York: Oxford University Press.

Piaget, J. (1977). *The development of thought: Equilibration of cognitive structures* (A. Rosin, Trans.). Oxford: Viking.

Poe, E. A. (1846, April). The philosophy of composition. *Graham's Magazine of Literature and Art, 28, 4*, 163–164.

Polanyi, M. (1958). *Personal knowledge: Towards a post-critical philosophy*. Chicago: University of Chicago Press.

Rubin, K. H., Fein, G. G., & Vandenburg, B. (1983). Play. In P. H. Mussen (Ed.), *Handbook of child psychology: Vol. 4. Socialization, personality, and social development* (pp. 693–774). New York: Wiley.

Russell, J. (1996). *Agency: Its role in mental development*. Hove, UK: Taylor & Francis/ Erlbaum.

Sabbagh, M. A., Xu, F., Carlson, S. M., Moses, L. J., & Lee, K. (2006). The development of executive functioning and theory of mind: A comparison of Chinese and U.S. preschoolers. *Psychological Science, 17*, 74–81.

Sawyer, R. K. (1997). *Pretend play as improvisation: Conversation in the preschool classroom*. Mahwah, NJ: Erlbaum.

Taylor, M. (1999). *Imaginary companions and the children who create them*. New York: Oxford University Press.

Taylor, M., & Carlson, S. M. (1997). The relation between individual differences in fantasy and theory of mind. *Child Development, 68*, 436–455.

Taylor, M., Carlson, S. M., & Shawber, A. B. (2007). Autonomy and control in children's interactions with imaginary companions. *Proceedings of the British Academy (Issue on Imaginative Minds), 147*, 81–100.

Taylor, M., Hodges, S. D., & Kohanyi, A. (2003). The illusion of independent agency: Do adult fiction writers experience their characters as having minds of their own? *Imagination, Cognition and Personality, 22*, 331–338.

Tulving, E. (1985). Memory and consciousness. *Canadian Psychology/Psychologie canadienne, 26*(1), 1–12.

Vygotsky, L. S. (1933). Play and its role in the mental development of the child, *Soviet Psychology, 5*, 6–18.

Wegner, D. M. (2002). *The illusion of conscious will*. Cambridge, MA: MIT Press.

Zelazo, P. D. (2004). The development of conscious control in childhood, *Trends in Cognitive Sciences, 8*, 12–17.

Zelazo, P. D. (2006). The dimensional change card sort (DCCS): A method of assessing executive function in children, *Nature Protocols, 1*, 297–301.

Zelazo, P. D., Carlson, S. M., & Kesek, A. (2008). The development of executive function in childhood. In C. Nelson & M. Luciana (Eds.), *Handbook of developmental cognitive neuroscience* (2nd ed.) (pp. 553–574). Cambridge, MA: MIT Press.

Zelazo, P. D., Carter, A., Reznick, J. S., & Frye, D. (1997). Early development of executive function: A problem-solving framework. *Review of General Psychology, 1*(2), 198–226.

Zelazo, P. D., Gao, H., & Todd, R. (2007). The development of consciousness. In P. D. Zelazo, M. Moscovitch, & E. Thompson (Eds.), *The Cambridge handbook of consciousness* (pp. 405–432). New York: Cambridge University Press.

Zelazo, P., Müller, U., Frye, D., & Marcovitch, S. 2003. The development of executive function: Cognitive complexity and control—revised, *Monographs of the Society for Research in Child Development, 68*, 93–119.

10 Freedom, Neural Mechanism, and Consciousness

Adina L. Roskies

Some worry that our growing understanding of brain mechanisms of behavior poses a threat to our common attributions of freedom and responsibility. There are two ways in which the threat has been characterized. On the one hand, it has been suggested that neuroscience will answer the factual question at the center of the compatibilism/incompatibilism debate. This debate hinges the question of whether we have free will in part upon a further question: Is the world (or are we) deterministic or indeterministic? Let us call this the question of determinism. Much of the philosophical literature has framed discussions about free will in the context of the question of determinism. Many take it for granted that people are natural incompatibilists, believing that freedom is incompatible with determinism. By answering the determinism question, some think neuroscience will thus settle the question of free will, and probably in the negative (Smilansky, 2000). On the other hand, despite the focus on determinism, philosophical discussions of free action typically involve a number of concepts such as deliberation or the weighing of reasons, decision, intention, control, and the absence of constraint (see, in this volume, Mele; Holton; and Searle). These are high-level, for the most part, psychological, phenomena. It is possible that neuroscience will challenge those psychological concepts, showing them to be false constructs, and that freedom, which relies upon them, is equally illusory. (Interestingly, no one seems worried that neuroscience will demonstrate that we do have free will).

In the first part of the paper, I argue that neuroscience will not be a challenge to freedom in the first way. In the second part, I explore a strategy for understanding decision making that illuminates the question of free action in a manner neutral with respect to the question of determinism, and consider whether it poses a challenge to freedom conceived in the second way. Finally, I consider the relevance that consciousness may have for the preceding debate.

PHILOSOPHICAL AND FOLK CONCEPTIONS OF FREE WILL

Determinism is the thesis that the state of the world at a given time plus the laws of nature uniquely determine the state of the world at every other time. In other words, given an exhaustive specification of the physical state of the universe at any given time, as well as perfect knowledge of the physical laws, one could, in principle, predict with certainty the physical state of the universe at any other time. The negation of determinism is indeterminism: Given the complete specification of the physical state of the universe and all the laws, multiple possible futures could ensue. If indeterminism is true, there are random events, not causally necessitated.

Determinism entails that there is only one course the evolution of the universe could take, given facts about its makeup. Many people think that it is self-evident that determinism precludes free will: If there is only one course the universe could take, and we are part of that universe, we could not do other than we do, and thus, we do not have real choices or options, and so no free will.

While at first blush indeterminism seems the only hope for the preservation of free will, a closer look makes indeterminism seem as unfriendly to freedom as does determinism. Indeterministic events are random events; what it means to be indeterministic is that there is an element of randomness. But what we think we have when we have free will are actions that are *caused by us*, for which *we can be held responsible*. But for us to cause or determine the course of events, they cannot be random. It therefore remains puzzling how appeals to indeterminism could save free will, or at least the free will worth wanting.

Philosophical approaches to the problem of free will can be categorized as compatibilist or incompatibilist. Compatibilists hold that free will is compatible with the truth of determinism,[1] while incompatibilists hold that freedom is impossible if we are deterministic systems. There are numerous articulated philosophical positions within these divisions, but they needn't concern us here. The burden of the compatibilist is to show how freedom and responsibility can exist in a deterministic universe, or in a universe in which the actors are deterministic systems. The burden on the incompatibilist is to show how freedom and responsibility can exist if our actions are random events.

Outside the realm of academic philosophy, a question that has come increasingly to the fore is whether the advances in the sciences of the mind will demonstrate or otherwise convince us that we lack free will. Of some concern seems to be what the effect of scientific advances will be on the beliefs and attitudes of soccer moms and Joe The Plumbers, not so much on the beliefs and attitudes of academics breathing the rarified air atop the ivory tower. Whether the sciences will or will not undermine the ordinary man's confidence in free will and responsibility depends in part upon the nature of the common sense notions of freedom, as well as on the ability of the sciences to address questions fundamental to these views. If the folk are incompatibilists, then evidence that our actions or choices are determined will spell trouble for the folk's faith in freedom. If the folk are compatibilists, the sciences may affect the folk's views in other ways. We may thus be worried about the practical consequences advances in neuroscience might have for freedom. Another concern is, of course, with the theoretical consequences neuroscience may have for freedom: What can science contribute to our understanding of free will and responsibility, if anything? The first part of this paper will largely concern the attitudes of the folk; the second part will concern the impact of neuroscience on theories about free will.

Many people have thought it self-evident that the folk's conception of free will is incompatibilist; others have argued that it is clearly compatibilist. Recent work in experimental philosophy by some of my colleagues and myself has revealed that common sense views of freedom and responsibility are not as straightforward as many have supposed. Nahmias and colleagues (Nahmias, Morris, Nadelhoffer, & Turner, 2005, 2006) provided people with scenarios of a deterministic universe and asked whether people in that universe were free and responsible. Their results suggested that people are natural compatibilists. In contrast, Nichols and Knobe's results pointed to incompatibilism when they probed people's intuitions about freedom and responsibility (Nichols & Knobe, 2007).

Nichols and I recently ran an experiment to try to adjudicate between these disparate findings. To our surprise, we found that people's judgments of freedom and responsibility were affected not just by the nature of the agents and their world, that is, local features of the experimentally defined situation, but also by the hypothetical nature of our own world (Roskies & Nichols, 2008). More specifically, when probed to make judgments about freedom and responsibility, people's responses were linked to whether the scenario they were posed was set in our own or an alternate universe. When the universe was explicitly not ours and deterministic, people tended to judge agents to be less free and responsible than in identical scenarios when the universe was our own and deterministic.

Although this experiment makes sense of the apparent conflict between the data of Nahmias and Nichols and Knobe, and shows both results to accurately reflect people's concepts, it is less clear how the nature of those concepts should be interpreted. One might argue that the folk conception of free will is compatibilist because people in our own universe are held responsible and thought to be free even if that universe is deterministic. However, one might instead argue that the folk conception is incompatibilist, since whether or not the universe is deterministic affects the degree and scope of responsibility judgments. Several psychological explanations of what is going on are available. Many of them paint the seeming compatibilist judgments in our own universe to be an effect of bias operating over a generally incompatibilist concept. For instance, Nichols and Knobe's results suggest that judgments of responsibility and freedom are modulated by the degree of engagement of emotional systems in the comprehension of the given scenario. However, it is also possible that our results are not properly interpreted in terms of bias, but rather provide an accurate representation of a coherent but complex concept: according to this view, the folk concepts of freedom and responsibility are complex hypothetical concepts dependent upon the actual nature of our own universe, whose structure is well-represented by the philosopher's technical apparatus of two-dimensional possible-world semantics (Roskies & Nichols, 2008). On this view, neither camp accurately characterizes the view of the folk because the folk's position is more nuanced than either. A final possibility is that the folk concept is fundamentally confused.

Regardless of the correct way of interpreting the views of the folk, the foregoing discussion suggests that we may be on the wrong track in thinking that a scientific answer to the question of determinism will alter the folk's conception of freedom. Though the folk's abstract and unsituated view about the nature of freedom may be described as incompatibilist, our results suggest that their situated views about responsibility, and to a slightly lesser extent freedom, are not dependent upon the answer to the question of determinism. Moreover, I have argued elsewhere that neuroscience cannot answer the scientific question of whether or not we are deterministic systems (Roskies, 2006). While I will not go into any detail about this question here, I will summarize my arguments thus: Neuroscientific techniques provide neither the fineness of grain nor the breadth of information that would be needed to answer the question of determinism in a way relevant to the free will debate. What looks like stochastic activity or randomness at one level of neuroscientific investigation may look deterministic at a finer-grained level, or when more of the preceding state of the system can be described. In other cases, what looks like deterministic behavior may be the result of aggregate stochastic events. Neuroscience can never provide total information and thus cannot provide a definitive answer to the question of determinism. If anything will provide such an answer, our best physical theory will, and not a neuroscientific finding. Consideration of what science can deliver and of what effect such deliverances might have on the judgments of the folk both lead independently to the conclusion that neuroscience will not affect our views on freedom and responsibility by way of answering the question of determinism. The suspicion that by trying to answer the question of determinism we are looking in the wrong place is further strengthened, I think, by the fact that no answer to the question of determinism makes it apparent how our will can be free: The philosophical problem of free will would not dissolve with either a positive or negative answer to the question of determinism.

RETHINKING THE FUNDAMENTAL ISSUES

The abovementioned discussion supports two theses: *(1)* Whether or not we are free or responsible does not rest on the question of determinism (see, e.g. Roskies, 2006), and *(2)* factors other than determinism are integral to assessments of freedom and responsibility.

Taking the first thesis seriously enables us to reframe the free will debate in ways that I think are productive. It allows us to investigate simple mechanisms of decision making without requiring that we attempt to ascertain whether or not those mechanisms are deterministic or stochastic, and it prompts us instead to pay attention to the nature of the processes that underlie choice or decision making in simple situations, and to the features of these processes that do or do not correspond to the psychological processes that we often invoke when reasoning about responsibility. In my view, pursuing this course will allow us to see how choice can be instantiated in a brain and what further features of brain activity we must strive to understand in order to really get a handle on the processes that we deem essential for attributions of freedom and responsibility to agents.

With our attention thus diverted from determinism, we are free to focus upon the interesting questions raised by the second thesis: What are the other factors that matter for attributions of freedom and responsibility? For the remainder of the paper, I will consider what neuroscience can tell us about freedom and responsibility once these concepts are considered independently of the determinism issue.

DECISION MAKING

The work of Bill Newsome, Michael Shadlen, and colleagues provides one of the best examples of how decision making occurs at the neural level. These neuroscientists explore decision making in nonhuman primates and are able to record in real time from one or a few neurons while the awake monkey performs decision tasks. Here I will focus on Shadlen's work in particular, for it nicely illustrates the type of insight into decision making that neuroscience can provide.

Shadlen records from monkey cortex while monkeys make perceptual decisions under uncertainty. These decisions involve deciding to make a certain response based upon a judgment about a visual stimulus. Shadlen's work involves characterizing the firing properties of neurons in a variety of brain areas involved in decision making using single-cell recordings, and relating these processes to aspects of the stimulus and/or decision outcome. In addition, he has developed mathematical models and abstract descriptions of the processes at work. I believe that systems described in the monkey can be taken to be a model for neurally based decision-making systems more generally, including in the human. At any rate, it provides an excellent starting point for investigating the neural bases of decision processes.

Briefly, monkeys are trained to view stimuli of dots moving randomly to the right and left, and to make judgments about the net motion direction of the stimulus. By varying the percentage of dots moving right and those moving left, judgments of net motion can be made more or less difficult. Monkeys are trained to report their judgment by moving their eyes (making a saccade) to one of two visual targets, to the right or left of the random dot stimulus. Rightward saccades indicate that the monkey's decision is that the net motion is to the right; leftward saccades indicate it is to the left. Psychometric curves of the monkeys' performance (measures of reaction time and accuracy for different net motion strengths) are nearly indistinguishable from those of humans performing the same task, showing that choice probability and response time are related to stimulus difficulty in the same way for monkeys and for humans. These behavioral measures suggest that the decision processes in the human and monkey are, indeed, relevantly similar.

Distinct populations of neurons in particular cortical areas are sensitive to specific stimulus parameters. In investigating the neural bases of decision making, Shadlen harnesses the well-established fact that cells in areas MT, MST, and LIP are sensitive to motion in particular directions. Recordings from cells in area MT show that neurons there are sensitive to the momentary net motion of the randomly moving dots in the cell's receptive field (the region of visual space to which the cell can respond). These cells are tuned to motion in a specific direction. Cells that prefer rightward motion fire more strongly the greater the strength of the stimulus motion to the right, and they are inhibited by leftward motion; those that prefer leftward motion show the same sensitivity to momentary motion in the leftward direction (Newsome, Britten, & Movshon, 1989). Cells in area MST, another region of cortex specialized for processing visual stimuli, have larger receptive fields and some have more complex motion sensitivities, but they also tend to also represent the momentary motion strength (Celebrini & Newsome, 1994; Shadlen & Newsome, 2001).

However, things look different when recording from the lateral interparietal area (LIP). Cells in this region tend to fire during the planning and execution of an eye movement. Rather than being characterized according to their "receptive fields," as sensory neurons are, LIP neurons have a motor component and are characterized by their "response fields," the regions of visual space to which the eyes move when they fire (Shadlen & Newsome, 2001). Interestingly, a large number of LIP neurons carry information about both sensory and motor processes. When recording from LIP neurons whose response fields coincide with one of the visual saccade targets of the perceptual decision task, many are found that show sustained activity in response to the visual motion stimulus in that direction. Unlike the sensory neurons that represent momentary levels of activity in their preferred direction, these neurons show activity that correlates with the temporal integral of motion in the direction of their response field. These neurons look as if they are computing an estimate of total information for motion in that direction throughout the course of the trial. Not surprisingly, these cells get input from the sensory regions described earlier. Activity in LIP neurons rises as the cells accumulate information. Perhaps most interestingly, firing rates ramp up until firing reaches a particular level, at which point the monkey executes the saccade and the neurons cease firing. This level acts as a decision threshold: The monkey executes a saccade in the direction of the response field of the LIP cells to first reach threshold firing rates. The time it takes for activity to rise to the threshold level is dependent upon the perceptual features of the stimulus (motion strength over time). Firing ceases after a response has been made. Moreover, the firing is dependent upon whether or not the monkey is asked to respond at will or is asked to withhold his response until cued to respond. LIP neurons maintain their firing in the absence of the visual stimulus if the monkey is asked to wait until cued in order to respond. Thus, unlike the sensory cells in MT and MST that are stimulus-driven, these LIP neurons can continue to fire in the absence of sensory stimulation (Gold & Shadlen, 2007): they are not stimulus bound. This is essentially the pattern of firing one would expect to see for a neuron involved in a decision-making process: It can represent evidence accumulated over time; firing levels can be sustained in the absence of the stimulus, signifying the independence of the decision from the inputs it operates over; and the activity continues until either a criterion level is reached, at which point a response is generated, or until neurons representing accumulated evidence for a different choice lead to an eye movement to the other target, at which point firing also ceases. Furthermore, electrical stimulation of LIP neurons can influence the monkey's decision, indicating that LIP plays a causal role in the decision process (Hanks, Ditterich, & Shadlen, 2006). Whether that role corresponds more to deliberation leading up to a decision, or the decision itself, remains unknown.

Shadlen and colleagues (Gold & Shadlen, 2007; Wong et al., 2007) have characterized the dynamics of this system mathematically, modeling it as a race to threshold. According to this model, populations of neurons with specific response properties represent different "hypotheses," in this case, hypotheses about the direction of stimulus motion. The firing rates of these groups of neurons represent the strength of evidence for those hypotheses based upon accumulated evidence from the environment, in this case, the perceptual stimulus. As evidence for or against each hypothesis is integrated, the firing rates approach or recede from a criterion level of firing, which represents the decision point of the animal. This is the point at which he has "made up his mind" about the net direction of motion. The first group to reach this threshold "wins," driving the animal's motor response.

The picture painted so far is one of sensory neurons tuned for particular stimulus features feeding into higher areas in which information is pooled over time and space. Neurons coding for alternative choices and actions accumulate information until some threshold of activation for some outcome is reached, at which point a decision is made and a response generated. There is a gradual transformation of information from the purely sensory realm to sensory-motor representations, and ultimately an activation of the saccadic motor system. This framework for transforming sensory information to action can be thought of as the skeleton of a decision-making system.

I think this is a model of decision making in general. However, it will be objected that decisions such as this are not representative of decisions that we make, and when we worry about free choice, we are not worried about choosing among such value-neutral options as leftward or rightward motion, or about things as bottom-up as perceptual decision making. One might also object that usually when we talk about "freely deciding," we are deciding *to do* something, not deciding *that* something is the case (see Mele, this volume). This is true. But rather than dismissing the information we glean from monkey cortex as irrelevant to understanding choice and decision making in the realms that do interest us, we should ask what more would be necessary for this sort of model to be applicable to the sorts of decisions that humans make and care about.

There seem to be two main aspects of human decision making that are absent from this model. One is in the inclusion of value in decision making. We are often called upon to decide among options on the basis of values that we assign to them, such as which has the better outcome, which is the more morally worthy, or which avoids the most harm. The values for different options can vary, they can depend upon shifting preferences, and they can be updated or revised. Nothing in the perceptual decision task thus described addresses this important feature of decision making. The second aspect that seems relevant is that our decisions are often between options that are complex, propositional, and discursive. Aggregate leftward and rightward motion seem to be poor stand-ins for decisions about ratifying bills for bailout packages, accepting or offering marriage proposals, and the like.

I think both these deficiencies can be accounted for using this same model, with additional neuroscientific investigation and a little imagination. For example, the work of Glimcher, Platt, Newsome, and others enriches our understanding of the decision-making system by showing how consideration of value can be integrated into this basic picture. These groups have shown that by manipulating the expected rewards for correct action or for particular types of decisions, or by manipulating probabilities of outcomes, both the decision and the levels of LIP activity are altered (Dorris & Glimcher 2004; Glimcher, 2002; Platt & Glimcher, 1999; Sugrue, Corrado, & Newsome, 2004). So, for example, offering a reward that the monkey likes better for one sort of decision can bias the monkey's choice of saccade target. At the same time, the firing rates of LIP neurons with response fields in the direction of the preferred reward choice show increased activity in proportion to the desirability of the reward (based on quality, magnitude, or both). These experiments show that LIP neurons can integrate information about reward or value into the decision-making process, and that the incorporation of value has causal consequences for the decision. In addition, by varying the probability of the reward or of the stimulus direction, researchers can also alter the firing rates of LIP neurons and the probability of decisions in directions consistent with decision theory. Researchers in this area suggest that these neurons represent measures of the subjective utility of the option.

A growing body of work in neuroscience has gone far in elucidating a network of subcortical and frontal brain regions that are involved in representing reward and expectation. This network is likely contributing information regarding reward and probability that is integrated by the LIP neurons. Altered levels of LIP activity change the time course and error rates of decision making, just as altering value and probability can alter our decisions under uncertainty. Thus, both perceptual and reward contingencies play a role in the dynamics of decision-related activity in LIP.

The second factor, richness of representation, can also be approached neuroscientifically. Admittedly, in philosophical discussions, talk about decision making rarely gets couched in terms of representation; even less often is there talk of neural activity and mechanistic models. Questions have been raised about whether common folk psychological constructs, such as beliefs and desires, correctly describe the brain at any level (Churchland, 1981). Decisions are usually conceived of as abstract, complex cognitive tasks that issue in intentions, not as perceptual tasks that issue in motor action. Usually what matters in decision making gets framed in terms of having and deliberating about reasons (see Yang and Shadlen, 2007), not firing rates or receptive fields. Are the folk psychological notions of decision making compatible with the simple neurobiological picture I have painted?

It might take a little stretching to get there, but I think so. At least a number of these constructs have close analogues in the neural realm. As mentioned before, populations of MT and MST neurons can be taken to represent particular hypotheses about the stimulus (motion is to the right; motion is to the left). The firing rates of these neurons may represent the strength of the perceptual evidence in favor of those hypotheses. The strength of this evidence plays a causal role in determining LIP activity, and the ultimate decision is represented by the plan to saccade in a particular direction. One might think of the LIP neuron populations that represent particular decision outcomes as propositions coding desired states of affairs. Whether they can be properly thought to represent intentions (e.g., intention to respond to the right; intention to respond to the left) is an open question, as is the question of whether intentions should be conceived of as propositions or in some other way. One might worry that such analogies seem convincing in simple perceptual tasks such as the one I discuss, but that this task is not really representative of human decision making. However, in conceiving of the neuronal populations as representing particular propositions, one can imagine analogous neural systems governing much more abstract, less stimulus-bound decisions. There could be a population of neurons that represents the proposition to stay in my current position on the couch watching TV, another population of neurons that represents getting up to switch the channel, and yet another that represents getting up to put on my shoes and drive to store for a pint of Ben and Jerry's. Indeed, since I can think these things, *something* in my brain must be representing them. It is almost assured that some configuration of neural firing does represent propositions like these, and there appears to be no limit on how articulated those propositions can be. The line between *deciding to* and *deciding that* is not as clear as we may have thought, and the brain representations that combine perceptual information and response information illustrate this. There is, in principle, no reason that the most abstract propositions cannot be represented by neural activity, although how to understand or decipher the relevant neural codes may be difficult or nigh impossible. Investigating perceptual decision making is a way of taking a nearly intractable problem and framing it in a way that makes it scientifically approachable, allowing us to infer what the more complex instantiations of the problem might be.

Thus, we might think of the neural activity that feeds into the ultimate levels of processing prior to plans or actions as representing the integrated force of value-weighted propositions. So, for example, in deciding whether to help the lady who has tripped on the curb, we can imagine a number of neural populations representing competing and congruent considerations, including the empathetic input from emotional systems that impinge on the "Stop and help"–representing neurons. These are also affected by neurons explicitly representing "Do unto others..." and related immediate inferences. Other populations representing the negative consequences of missing the 10 a.m. meeting modulate the population that impinge on the "keep walking"–representing neurons, and so on. These neuronal populations both represent the reasons for and against particular decisions and/or actions and are causally potent in producing the final outcome. So in this framework, we do act for reasons, and because of reasons, and despite all the work being done by neurons, there seems to be no impediment to these reasons being as complex and propositional as you please. In showing how neuronal populations can represent and update information, and in showing how reward and probability can modulate the responses of such neuronal populations, we can see the most important and abstract aspects of philosophical views of decision making embodied.

Worth noting is that the question of whether the neurons in this system are deterministic or not seems to be moot. At the grain at which these studies investigate the phenomenon, neuronal activity appears stochastic, though closely correlated with macroscopic variables such as stimulus strength and reward expectation. The decision-making process, conceived of as a race-to-threshold model, is purely mechanistic; it matters not whether the mechanisms are deterministic or truly stochastic.

Nonetheless, my sense when thinking of the system in this way is that it is making a decision in just the way we expect decisions to be made. The system weighs the evidence for competing alternatives, by weighting and accumulating information about empirical evidence and potential reward (Dorris & Glimcher, 2004). This suggests that our views about decision making at the folk psychological level are not undermined, but rather ratified, by the current neuroscience. The neuroscientific picture, as it stands now, does not pose a challenge to our commonsense views.

Of course, a number of open questions remain with respect to our understanding of this system, and it is likely that answers to these questions will color whether we think of actions as freely chosen or of ourselves as responsible agents. For example, we know that LIP can encode reward probability and value information, as well as visual motion information. What other types of information can it encode? What other sorts of inputs can affect LIP activity? More broadly, we do not know whether LIP alone drives the decision, or whether other brain regions independently contribute to or mediate a decision that occurs downstream or upstream of LIP.

Another fundamental question is what happens in decision cases that are less closely tied to stimulus properties or motor activity. Shadlen and colleagues proved that LIP decisions are not stimulus bound, by showing that LIP activity is maintained in the absence of a stimulus while the animal is asked to wait before executing his motor plan. Nonetheless, the inputs to these processes are sensory inputs. Many of the decisions we make have far fewer apparent sensory components; the failures of radical empiricism suggest that reducing all representations to sensory building block is not feasible. How are more abstract decision domains represented? I have suggested that populations of neurons can represent propositional content, but we have little understanding of how this is actually implemented. Furthermore, LIP neurons seem to represent eye movement action plans, but if the decision about the random dot direction is indicated by moving a lever rather than by an eye movement, a different set of neurons is involved in the task. We can therefore ask whether LIP really represents the motion direction decision, or a much more constrained decision (such as motion direction in the context of this particular task configuration), or whether the decision about motion direction is represented elsewhere entirely, ultimately affecting and being affected by the LIP cells in the goal of task execution. The answer is still unclear.

Not all our decisions result in immediate action, or many don't necessitate any action in particular. A decision to choose to attend a particular college is made well in advance of actually going and does not imply any particular bodily movements. Are there other brain areas that are specialized for decisions that are more abstract than ones heavily based on sensory input or resulting in immediate or proximate motor output? Which college to go to, whom to vote for in an election, and so forth, are decisions that seem to be significantly different from the sort of decision easily studied in the laboratory, and although we can imagine these sorts of decisions on a model based on perceptual decision making, it would be nice to validate our suspicions. However, because we lack an understanding of the how the brain represents these more abstract domains, we also are left with little guidance in terms of what to look for and where in the brain to look.

Finally, it remains entirely mysterious what establishes the threshold or criterion for the decision in the model just discussed. What factors go into setting the level, can it be adjusted, and how can it be adjusted? One might think that we lack a certain sort of necessary control if the threshold is blindly anchored to an arbitrary level. However, if certain reasons (i.e., populations of neuronal firing that represent states of the world, values, etc.) can set or alter the threshold for particular decisions depending on circumstances, then many may share the intuition that the attainment of the requisite threshold seems to be more our decision than it would be otherwise.

CONSCIOUSNESS AND FREEDOM

Thus far, nothing has been said about consciousness. Some readers might object that decision making, or decision making relevant to discussions of freedom, necessarily involves consciousness. While I disagree that all decision making requires consciousness, I am far less clear about whether consciousness plays a necessary role in free will, and if so, what role it must play.

It does seem intuitively correct that consciousness of some sort is necessary for freedom: It doesn't seem to make sense to ask whether a river, a falling rock, or even an oak tree is free. So the presence of consciousness may be a necessary condition for freedom, in that any agent, to be considered a free agent, must be conscious. But what kind of consciousness is necessary, and what role must it play? We can delineate a number of potential roles for consciousness in free action.

My general proposal is that awareness or conscious access to reasons for action is necessary for an action to be free (also see Baumeister, this volume). Consider what we are aware of when we make decisions. We obviously don't have any introspective access into the decision process itself, at least not as I have characterized it here. In making a decision, we are completely unaware of the busily firing, opposing populations of neurons, the summing of activity and comparison to a criterion value, or to the process (still mysterious) of setting the criterion itself. We do not have access to the implementation details of the decision process. What we do have access to, at least sometimes, are some of the propositions to which our actions or choices are or should be sensitive (not all; see Dijksterhuis, Bos, Nordgren, & van Baaren, 2006). That is, we are often aware of reasons for our choices. These reasons could take the form of sensory evidence, or propositions describing that evidence ("the dots are moving rightward"), or they could take the form of more abstract propositions ("I will get a better education there" or "I've always wanted to live in a big city"). If we have no access to any propositions relevant to our choices, then we truly do seem like automatons, not acting *for* reasons, but merely acting in a way describable from the outside in terms of reasons. In such cases it is doubtful that people would consider the actor an agent or hold it responsible for its actions—at the very least, such scenarios suggest that there is a certain kind of control that is lacking. In these cases I would suggest we do not act freely. So my proposal is that the importance of consciousness in decision making or in acting freely is in providing access to the semantic content of our reasons—in allowing the reasons for which we act to be understood by us, integrated into our discursive conception of the world, trafficked with other people in the context of asking for and giving justification. Consciousness of content seems essential. How this occurs, what neural substrates make it possible, remains one of the deepest mysteries of science.

That said, there are more questions one can ask about the role of consciousness. For example, one might think that mere consciousness of reasons may not be enough to make freedom possible. For if consciousness made the agent aware of the reasons for action, but otherwise disconnected from the process of deliberation, and unable to affect it in any way, one might think that consciousness would be too impotent to ground freedom, or that the conscious agent wouldn't have anything more of import than the zombie agent we don't think of as free. We can call this the "spectator view" of consciousness. On this view, the machinery of deliberation churns mechanistically, following some inevitable course, while the conscious agent merely looks on but is not part of the decision-making apparatus.

If that seems too weak for the required role for consciousness, let us add something. Perhaps in addition to providing awareness of reasons, the agent must be able to consciously endorse or take a "pro-attitude" toward the reasons involved in the deliberation. Thus, the agent not only would be conscious of the content of the deliberation, but would also have emotional or other appraisals of those reasons, or some way of distinguishing reasons more in line with its own agency from those less so. While this seems coherent on the face of it, it is not clear what this extra ingredient would amount to in the mechanistic picture I have described above. For according to my account of decision making, reasons are already weighted, or given values, in the way in which they are neurally represented. One might think there is nothing more to endorsement than a certain type of valuing, or that reasons that are in line with the agent's character or self-perception are just those that are given high weight, and thus, there is nothing more to be said about endorsement than is already built into the picture I have drawn.

A still stronger role might be required for consciousness than the spectator role or the endorsement role. We might call this role "engagement." The engagement role answers well to many people's intuitions about freedom. For example, there has been longstanding interest in the role of conscious intention in *driving* action. Challenges to that view, such as some think are posed by the work of Benjamin Libet, have been taken by many to pose a problem for freedom. For example, many people think Libet's work demonstrates that our brains make our decisions before we are aware of consciously intending them, and that because of the relative timing of consciousness of intention and signals preceding action, conscious intention cannot be causally potent in driving action. They conclude that this shows the will not to be free. I disagree both with this interpretation of his experiments, and with the inference about their relevance for freedom. My arguments for this are spelled out elsewhere (Roskies, forthcoming). Consciousness of intention may be one way that consciousness can play a role in free action, but not the only way in which engagement can occur. My proposal can be considered an alternative proposal for consciousness to be engaged in free action. Consciousness can be engaged in deliberation in that consciousness of reasons for action may play an active role in modulating the assessment of relative values, and in weighting and reweighting values in the light of new evidence. Thus, rather than being an impotent spectator, the agent is consciously involved in assessing and reassessing the values of available reasons for action and in so doing becomes an active and engaged part of the machinery of deliberation. This form of engagement occurs during the decision process, but it does not mean that intentions to act need be conscious at any prescribed time during the decision/action process.

This possibility brings up another potential role for consciousness in free action. This is the possibility that consciousness of self is necessary for something to be an agent to which responsibility can be attributed, and self-ascription of reasons is an important aspect of what is involved in making decisions in a free and responsible way. This differs from my original proposal in the following ways. Consciousness may be involved in assessing the concordance of values with what one might call one's self-conception. Consciousness of self requires more than just awareness of content; it requires a conceptualization of oneself as an enduring agent. This may involve recognizing oneself as an agent with interests, future plans, and past history. Self-ascription of reasons would then involve not only being aware of reasons weighing for or against potential options, but also explicitly embracing or endorsing those reasons, taking them as reasons *for me*, as an agent, with my particular interests, desires, past, and so forth. This may be a more full-blown version of endorsement than merely adopting a pro-attitude, which one could imagine occurring in the absence of an explicit concept of self. While neuroscience is making some headway in articulating the ways in which aspects of self are represented in the brain, progress has been largely in representations of bodily components of self-representation. Very little is yet understood about agential self-representation, or self-awareness beyond bodily self-awareness, so at least at this time, neuroscience has little to contribute here.

What if neuroscience were able to explain or characterize consciousness or self-consciousness—would that undermine our views of freedom? Again, I doubt it. It seems that neuroscience may be able to articulate or describe precise implementations of the vague concepts mentioned above, but nothing in these concepts seems likely to be undermined by what neuroscience will discover. I do not think it will be able to show that there is no such thing as consciousness, and thus no free will, for either it will explain consciousness or we will conclude that we haven't yet explained it. While it may make the notion of a unitary enduring self seem illusory, our conception of freedom does not depend upon the truth of that notion.

DISCUSSION WITH ADINA L. ROSKIES

Will brain science ever be philosophically useful? Will it answer the question of free will?

Neuroscience has a variety of wonderful and useful tools—including fMRI and the ability to record activity from single neurons. These tools are useful for providing insights into brain functioning. However, if the question of free will is hinged on the metaphysical determinism/indeterminism question, then it seems unlikely that brain science will be useful in directly addressing this question. Ultimately the determinism/indeterminism question is one for physics and not for neuroscience. There is some belief that physics has already answered the question of determinism, and that the answer provided by quantum mechanics is that the universe is indeterministic. However, there is not a consensus on this.

Formulating the question of free will in terms of determinism and indeterminism seems to be the wrong way of formulating it, especially if the goal is to have the question answered by brain science. Brain science can provide a lot of insight into decision making, emotions, cognition, and other similar topics, but it does not seem able to answer the question of free will. What may appear at first to be deterministic behavior may actually be aggregate behavior that is caused by many (seemingly) indeterministic mechanisms converging together. A closer look at those seemingly indeterministic mechanisms may reveal that they are really deterministic when reduced further. It seems that this cycle of determinism/indeterminism only ends at the level of quantum physics. Neuroscience, as it is currently conceived, does not concern itself with particular molecules or subatomic particles and where they happen to be. In short, it seems unlikely that neuroscience will be able to answer the question of free will.

Imagine a scenario in which a scientist implanted electrodes into a human subject, having identified each electrode as associated with a particular decision. However, rather than just recording activity, these electrodes are stimulated to cause specific decisions to be made. Further, suppose you are able to implant a sense of having consciously made those decisions in the subject, so that they have the experience of free will. Would that speak to the question of free will or the lack thereof?
It is already clear from the research program of Dan Wegner and others that people make mistakes about whether they acted volitionally. The position that people are never wrong about whether they acted volitionally is untenable. However, just because people sometimes make mistakes about it does not mean that they are always wrong about it. By stimulating the right areas, the subject in this hypothetical experiment might make all kinds of mistaken judgments about whether his actions were freely chosen. A more important question is what happens when the experiment is over, the electrodes are removed, and the subject returns home? The subject may or may not act in a way that denies the possibility of free will. In either case, the fact that a person's volition could seemingly be circumvented does not speak to the larger issue of whether free will exists.

Are studies on monkeys helpful in answering the question of free will in humans? Wouldn't humans act decidedly differently under the same experimental conditions?
Monkeys are usually trained with food rewards (punishments also work for training monkeys, but ethical concerns prompt the use of rewards). Humans also desire food and can experience it as a reward. However, when humans are subjected to conditions they do not like, they act in decidedly different ways from monkeys. For instance, there are some

cases of humans going on hunger strikes, even to death. Thus, some humans might refuse to participate in such a study.

However, monkeys are not completely passive either. They sometimes refuse to cooperate. This may be an indication that they object in some sense, but the desire for food rewards is strong enough that they usually learn tasks well anyway. Humans who objected would probably do the same thing if the rewards were sufficient.

Are saccades decisions?

These saccades are not something that monkeys naturally do. An experimenter cannot simply place a monkey in front of the display and gather useful data. The required behavior requires a lot of training, and the monkeys have to learn to fixate on a certain place and to saccade to a particular place. It is clear that there is a lot going on mentally, but it is unclear whether the saccade is the decision or the saccade is the effect of a decision. It is theoretically possible the monkeys are saying the equivalent of "Now!" to themselves and then moving their eyes, but there is no information on that.

NOTES

1. Some compatibilists maintain that determinism is a necessary condition for freedom and/or responsiblity; others hold weaker positions, claiming merely that determinism doesn't preclude freedom or responsibility.

REFERENCES

Celebrini, S., & Newsome, W. T. (1994). Neuronal and psychophysical sensitivity to motion signals in extrastriate area MST of the macaque monkey. *Journal of Neuroscience, 14*(7), 4109–4124.

Churchland, P. (1981). Eliminative materialism and propositional attitudes,. *Journal of Philosophy, 77*(4), 67–90.

Dijksterhuis, A., M. W. Bos, L. F. Nordgren, & R. B. van Baaren (2006), On making the right choice: The deliberation-without-attention effect, *Science, 311*(5763), 1005–1007.

Dorris, M. C., & Glimcher, P. W. (2004). Activity in posterior parietal cortex is correlated with the relative subjective desirability of action,. *Neuron, 44*(2), 365–378.

Glimcher, P. W. (2002). Decisions, decisions, decisions: Choosing a biological science of choice,. *Neuron, 36*(2), 323–332.

Gold, J. I., & Shadlen, M. L. (2007). The neural basis of decision making,. *Annual Review of Neuroscience, 30*(1), 535–574.

Hanks, T. D., J. Ditterich, & M. N. Shadlen (2006). Microstimulation of macaque area LIP affects decision-making in a motion discrimination task,. *Nature Neuroscience*, *9*(5), 682–689.

Nahmias, E., Morris, S., Nadelhoffer, T., & Turner, J. (2005). Surveying freedom: Folk intuitions about free will and responsibility,. *Philosophical Psychology*, *18*(5), 561–584.

Nahmias, E., Morris, S., Nadelhoffer, T., & Turner, J. (2006), Is incompatibilism intuitive?, *Philosophy and Phenomenological Research*, *73*, 28–53.

Newsome, W. T., Britten, K.H., & Movshon, J.A. (1989), Neuronal correlates of a perceptual decision, *Nature*, *341*, 52–54.

Nichols, S., & Knobe, J. (2007). Moral responsibility and determinism: The cognitive science of folk intuitions,. *Nous*, *41*(4), 663–685.

Platt, M. L., & Glimcher, P. W. (1999). Neural correlates of decision variables in parietal cortex,. *Nature*, *400*(6741), 233–238.

Roskies, A. L. (2006). Neuroscientific challenges to free will and responsibility,. *Trends in Cognitive Sciences*, *10*(9), 419–423.

Roskies, A. L., & Nichols, S. (2008), Bringing moral responsibility down to earth, *Journal of Philosophy*, *105*, 371–388.

Shadlen, M. N., & Newsome, W. T. (2001). Neural basis of a perceptual decision in the parietal cortex (area LIP) of the rhesus monkey,. *The Journal of Neurophysiology*, *86*(4), 1916–1936.

Smilansky, S. (2000), *Free will and illusion*. Oxford: Oxford University Press.

Sugrue, L. P., Corrado, G. S., & Newsome, W. T. (2004). Matching behavior and the representation of value in the parietal cortex,. *Science*, *304*(18, June), 1782–1787.

Wong, K.-F., Huk, A. C., Shadlen, M. N., & Wang, X.-J. (2007). Neural circuit dynamics underlying accumulation of time-varying evidence during perceptual decision making,. *Frontiers in Computational Neuroscience*, *1*(November), 1–11.

Yang, T., & Michael N. Shadlen, M. N. (2007). Probabilistic reasoning by neurons,. *Nature*, *447*(7148), 1075–1080.

11 (Virtual) Reality, Consciousness, and Free Will

Jim Blascovich

In this chapter, I examine the relationships among various aspects of reality, consciousness, and free will. The ideas expressed here emerged during the last decade as I began using digital immersive virtual reality technology (IVET) to study social influence and social interaction processes experimentally (cf. Blascovich et al., 2002; Loomis, Blascovich, & Beal, 1999; McCall & Blascovich, in press). To be sure, I believe that the studies we conducted using digital IVET, papers we presented, and articles we published answer many questions about social influence processes generally and thereby are relevant to any social situation (e.g., Bailenson, Blascovich, Beall, & Loomis, 2003; Hoyt & Blascovich, 2007; Hoyt, Blascovich, & Swinth, 2003; McCall, Blascovich, Young, & Persky, 2009).

In addition, many other studies, papers, and articles answer questions about social influence process specifically within immersive digital situations that allow visual representations and behaviors of participants that are not possible in the natural environment (e.g., Bailenson, Beall, Loomis, Blascovich, & Turk, 2004; Beall, Bailenson, Loomis, Blascovich, & Rex, 2003). The latter are important because they address social influence processes within the increasingly ubiquitous digital virtual worlds "inhabited" by an ever-increasing proportion of the Earth's population.

However, a more general story pertinent to the issues that are the foci of this volume has emerged. This is my initial attempt to tell this story, and I appreciate the forum to do so.

My ideas about reality, consciousness, and free will that have emerged from observing individual and social behavior in digital immersive virtual environments began introspectively during and after my initial experience in an immersive digital virtual environment. Walking by the open door of a colleague's lab, I saw a person wearing what I later learned was a head-mounted display (HMD). It completely encased the upper portion of her face including her eyes. Watching her walk around, I realized that her motor behaviors were driven not by the physical environment, the high tech perception laboratory, in which I saw her, but rather by the virtual one she was transported to via the HMD. Intrigued, I asked my colleague Jack Loomis, whose lab it was, if I could experience what this immersive virtual reality stuff was all about. He welcomed me to do so.

Wearing the HMD and other devices that informed the computer controlling the system of my exact position and my visual point of view at any given time (i.e., every 40 ms) in the three-dimensional space (i.e., the lab I was in physically), I found myself in a digital three-dimensional immersive virtual environment. It was a simple one with a textured floor and a dull sky above. Subsequently, a square hole or pit opened up in the floor. The pit looked to be about 3 m square and deep enough so that I could not see its bottom from the oblique viewing angle I had from my eye height of about 1.5 m vertically from the floor and standing 3 m away horizontally. I was instructed to walk to the edge of the precipice and look down. I did so cautiously. Looking down the hole, I estimated it to be about 10 m deep. Admittedly, I was frightened. As I looked down, a narrow wooden board appeared spanning the chasm. Jack asked me to try walking across it. I demurred for a bit bantering nervously but then complied. I "walked the plank" not only with trepidation but also struggling to keep my balance.

To this point, I was consciously immersed in the virtual world with no thoughts of the outside physical environment. However, while standing at the edge of the abyss my mind wandered back to the physical environment. I began trying consciously to convince myself that there was no pit in the physical laboratory floor underneath my feet. Metaconsciously, I was amazed that I could not consciously control my fear response and could not will it away no matter how hard I tried, even when closing my eyes. It was this experience, which I have come to label "a clash of consciousness" that motivated me to think about issues associated with perceived reality, consciousness, and free will.

PERCEIVED REALITY

Roger Shepard (1990) typifies perceptual psychologists who have joined other perceptionists and philosophers such as Plato, Descartes, Aldous

Huxley (1954), and many others when he made reference to perception as hallucination. Among other dichotomies, such perceptions or hallucinations can be parsed into those people consider "real" and those they consider "virtual," via a metaphysical belief that can be labeled "psychological relativity." More specifically, people contrast their experience of grounded reality—for most of us what is labeled the "natural" or "physical" world—with all other realities they experience—those labeled "virtual" worlds. By definition, grounded reality holds some sort of primacy (i.e., people believe their grounded reality is "real") over virtual realities even though what actually constitutes reality, grounded or virtual, is never totally sensed. Furthermore, what is sensed does not pass through to our perceptions but rather is mediated by cognitive or mental processes that sometimes filter out much of what is sensed and sometimes inserts things for which there are no corresponding sensory data, as in cases of imagery and dreams as well as visual hallucinations and illusions.

Upon reflection, one quickly realizes the arbitrary relativity of "grounded" versus "virtual" worlds. If one's grounded reality were a digital one, or even an elaborate physical environment much like a movie set, then the natural world would be virtual relative to it. This latter statement represents a familiar theme in cultural artifacts such as Stephen King novels (e.g., *The Shining*) and Wachowski brothers' movies (e.g., *The Matrix*).

Furthermore, permanence is not a necessary condition of grounded reality. What constitutes grounded reality can change back and forth over time. To illustrate such flux, recall the "prism glasses" experiments (e.g., Stratton, 1896) in which individuals continuously wore prismatic spectacles that effectively turned the grounded environment upside down during their waking hours. These individuals adapted after a relatively short phase transition period with right side up becoming the original upside down and vice versa. And it was transitive, so that when the glasses were removed, participants went through a reverse "phase transition" and the world righted itself.

As another example, a recent study we completed crossed visible social stigma (present or absent) and reality (grounded vs. virtual) using digital immersive virtual environment technology. Naïve participants met another participant (actually a confederate) when both arrived at our laboratory. This other "participant" either bore a "port-wine" facial birthmark or not. We know from our decade-long history of stigma research (e.g., Blascovich, Mendes, Hunter, & Lickel, 2000; Blascovich, Mendes, Hunter, Lickel, & Kowai-Bell, 2001) that a person with such a birthmark evokes a pattern of cardiovascular responses associated with threat in other persons with whom she or he is interacting, even in a cooperative situation. Furthermore, we know from pilot studies that a similar response is evoked when one interacts with a digital agent (i.e., a human-appearing, nonhuman entity such as a computer algorithm) bearing such a birthmark in a digital immersive virtual environment (i.e., one perceptually surrounding the individual).

However, this new study differed from the earlier ones in the following way. Immediately after the participant met the confederate, both were immersed in a digital immersive virtual environment in which they played a cooperative word-finding game (i.e., a version of the popular game, Boggle), the same one used in the original physiological studies (Blascovich et al., 2001). However, the digital representation of the confederate, her avatar, either bore or did not bear a facial birthmark orthogonally to whether the confederate bore it physically or not, essentially a classic 2 × 2 experiment.

Interestingly, during the first task minute, participants were threatened only if the confederate they had met bore a birthmark before the immersion. By the fourth task minute, participants were threatened only if the avatar bore the birthmark regardless of whether the confederate bore it physically or not. These results demonstrate that social perceptions and their concomitant neurophysiological consequences can change during grounded-reality- to virtual-reality phase transitions even when participants likely have knowledge of the reality change.

MECHANISMS OF VIRTUAL TRAVEL

It can be safely assumed that humans are not completely neurophysiologically equipped to sense all extant external stimuli. It also can be safely assumed that humans are neurophysiologically equipped to create and perceive stimuli that are not there. People's minds wander constantly from grounded to virtual realities and even among virtual realities. Sometimes people's mind wanderings are consciously provoked as when they are said to "tune out" of a reality; sometimes they are not consciously provoked as when they are said to "zone out" of a reality (Smallwood & Schooler, 2006). Furthermore, over the millennia, humans have discovered and developed "technologies" to augment mind wandering, that is, to "travel virtually." Digital technology is only the latest in a long history of such technologies.

Some of these technologies work endogenously and involve the absorption of substances by the body. The most obvious of these are so-called mind-altering agents that we know of as hallucinogens such as psilosyban, mescaline, LSD, angel dust, and so forth. Some are reasonably benign medically; some are lethal. However, they point to a basic human need to escape grounded reality now and then even if it means, or perhaps because it means, losing consciousness of grounded reality.

Media tools work exogenously via the senses. Although communication media are functional for purposes other than for virtual travel, the ubiquity of communication media technologies and the development of newer and more powerful ones that have increased over the millennia at a seemingly exponential rate suggest strongly that our species somehow needs to leave grounded reality for greener virtual pastures perhaps more often than we realize (Klinger, 2008). In addition, given that humans are gregarious creatures, it is not surprising that we like company on our virtual *soirées* even if the company consists of fictional or fantastical others.

Humans have communicated among themselves for as long as anyone knows. Nonverbal signals such as gestures and paralanguage probably preceded spoken language, and spoken language preceded written language. By communicating symbolically via nonverbal signals and spoken language, humans developed ways to elicit their intended meanings in others (cf. Mead, 1934). With written language, humans enjoyed a communication technology that they could use to travel virtually to many places past, present, and future. In an important sense, nonverbal and verbal (spoken and written) languages were the first meaningful communication technologies, and the first hard evidence of our species' consciousness.

But language is not and, as far as we can tell, was not ever, constrained by grounded (i.e., physical) reality. In this vein, storytelling relied on language to transport individuals to places other than their grounded realities. Soon, words, gestures, and paralanguage became augmented by graphics: first, with two-dimensional representations as in cave art; and later with three-dimensional representations as in sculpture. Arguably, theater was the first major "multimedia communication technology." In theater, written scripts integrate storytelling, graphics (e.g., scenery), and actors (i.e., sentient agents), making dynamic immersive virtual reality experiences possible for actors and audiences alike.

In the arena of written language, the integration of inventions including ink, paper, and quill pens over more than a thousand years facilitated knowledge transmission via manuscripts. For a long while afterward, monasteries, where monks lived in groups, thrived. An important and time-consuming part of the monks' calling was hand-copying religious writings in order to preserve them and to keep religious stories alive.

No doubt, the most important communication media technology to follow was the invention of the modern printing press. In the tradition of the religious nature of most hand-copied manuscripts, the first book that Gutenberg printed was the Bible. With the invention of the printing press, stories, in addition to religious ones, could be disseminated broadly. This revolutionary technology made transmission of fiction and nonfiction to wide audiences possible. Readers then as today could transport themselves mentally to places other than their grounded realities easily by reading and, perhaps, also knowing that they were sharing the experience with other readers.

More than 300 years later, in the early 1820s, prior centuries of human effort and inventions led to the photograph. People were stunned by the possibilities of this new media. Some were in awe and some were afraid (Marien, 2006). Three-quarters of a century later, motion pictures appeared. The first naïve audience to view a film was a French one. They watched Lumiere's short film entitled *Arrival of a Train at La Ciotat Station*. The audience's point of view was quite close to the railroad tracks and looking toward an approaching train. The film proved quite frightening for many members of the audience (Gunning, 1989). Apparently, some even fled the building. Like my personal experience with Jack Loomis' digital virtual pit, Lumiere's moviegoers were not able to consciously control their fear responses.

Electricity made even more powerful media tools possible. Personal two-way communication devices such as the telegraph and telephone appeared. These instruments made real-time communication possible. Later, electronics came into being, leading to the invention of radio and television that improved prior mass media technologies such as newspapers by allowing simultaneous transmission of information to multitudes of individuals instantaneously.

Digital computing arrived in the 1940s with the invention of the first general-purpose digital computer in 1946. The development of solid-state electronics led to mainframe computers in the 1950s and 1960s and eventually to the powerful personal computers we know of today. In the early 1990s, the "Internet" and "World Wide Web" were coupled. Clearly, this communication network has revolutionized human communication as we know it, making instant two-way and even N-person-way worldwide communication possible. Together with advances in personal computing technology and graphics software shared social, digital virtual environments, such as Second Life, came on the scene (Boellstorf, 2008).

We can safely assume that humans are neurophysiologically equipped to experience virtual worlds consciously (e.g., daydreaming) and unconsciously (e.g., sleep dreaming). Beyond innate endogenous mechanisms, humans have created both endogenous and exogenous technologies to augment their virtual experiences. These endogenous and exogenous technologies help humans mentally travel to virtual places.

The Role of Consciousness in Virtual Travel

In my view, humans are able to travel virtually because of their faculties for unconscious, conscious, and metaconscious information processing (i.e., automatic mental processes, deliberate thought processes, and thinking about thinking, respectively). These processes cut across human mental abilities in the areas of perception, cognition, motivation, and emotion.

Humans' facility for virtual travel is functional. Virtual travel facilitates planning for the future and goal setting, via imagination of what the future might be or can be like, for example. For future planning, virtual travel is likely to be driven primarily by high-level or conscious processes.

Virtual travel is also functional in another way. Humans' ability to reflect metaconsciously on their own existence induces scientifically unanswerable questions (e.g., Why do we exist? What will happen to us after we die? Where were we before we were born?). These questions induce anxiety and even terror. Being able to escape mentally by traveling to virtual realities helps keep such angst out of our minds. Such virtual travel is likely to be driven primarily by automatic or unconscious processes.

HOW DIGITAL IMMERSIVE VIRTUAL ENVIRONMENT TECHNOLOGY WORKS

Digital immersive virtual environment technology (IVET) can be used to provide sensory input, including synthetic visual, auditory, haptic, olfactory and even taste information to users, though most system implementations focus on visual and auditory information (Blascovich et al., 2002). The immersive aspect is facilitated by the elimination of outside visual and auditory information by encasing individuals in an "envelope" created by limiting the visual and auditory fields via head-mounted visual displays and headphones or by display screens completely surrounding the user, and by providing stereoscopic visual and auditory stimuli (see Figure 11.1 for an illustration).

Truly immersive IVET systems rely on the integration of hardware and software systems. An IVET system must track users' body and head movements to determine their position in virtual space as well as their literal point of view. Because users are relatively unconstrained in terms of movements in an immersive virtual environment, tracking systems must and can keep up with even very quick movements. Video, inertial, magnetic, and other tracking systems have been developed that meet these requirements.

The tracking information is streamed to the control computer that, in turn, identifies users' positions and points of view in virtual space and creates a set of three-dimensional coordinates by which to identify and select appropriate information from a three-dimensional sensory

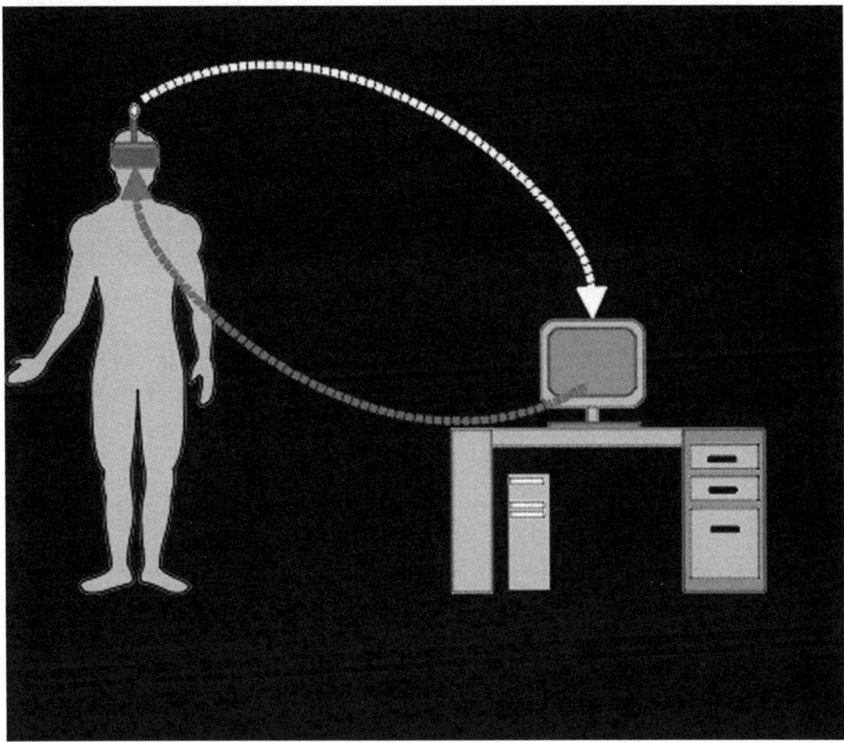

Figure 11.1. Immersive virtual environment technology illustration.

information database. The appropriate sensory information is then rendered (i.e., displayed) to the users. This cycle occurs very quickly, usually occurring at about 50 Hz or every 40 ms, preventing user disorientation. The end result is that users can move around freely in much the same way that they do in the physical world and receive appropriate sensory information "on the fly."

In order to construct a digital virtual world, developers construct a three-dimensional database necessary to their purposes. This is done in software and involves modeling software to create digital virtual spaces including "indoor" and "outdoor" venues, and scripting software to implement dynamic aspects of the world including the movements of digital human representations and objects.

SOCIAL INFLUENCE IN VIRTUAL ENVIRONMENTS

As noted above, humans are gregarious creatures and are relatively rarely content to virtually travel solo. Rather, much more often than not, our virtual wanderings involve graphic representations of virtual others whether they are known to us in grounded reality or not. Paramount to understanding social interaction in virtual environments is familiarity with social psychology, more particularly social influence processes. The term "social influence" refers to people's effects on each other, which, of course, take many forms: for example, conformity, attitude change and persuasion, performance facilitation or inhibition, individual and group identity, and contagious antisocial and prosocial behaviors.

How does social influence occur in IVET-mediated virtual environments? During the 15 years in which we've empirically examined social influence and interaction using digital immersive virtual environment technology, we've developed and refined a theoretical model addressing that question. Our *threshold model of social influence within immersive virtual environments* is based on interactions among four major factors. These dimensions are: *Agency, Communicative Realism, Response System, Self-Relevance,* and *Context.*

Agency or *Theory of Mind* concerns humans' attributions about others' sentience. At the superordinate level, these attributions range from totally nonsentient to sentient. Applying this dimension to digital virtual environments in our model, attributions about the sentience or agency of any "others" present varies between *agent* and *avatar* (see the abscissa in Figure 11.2a). The convention we follow (Bailenson & Blascovich, 2005) defines an agent as a digital representation that can appear in human or other form but that is driven and controlled completely by computer algorithms. The same convention defines an avatar as a digital representation of an actual person in real time that can appear in human or other form that is driven and controlled by that individual's tracked and rendered behaviors. Anything in between can be thought of as a *cyborg* combining features of agents (i.e., computer algorithms) and avatars (i.e., actual human-controlled actions). Neither agents nor avatars need to have all algorithms or actions, respectively, represented in digital virtual worlds.

There are two ways in which conscious attributions of agency can be made: assumption and deduction. Assumed attributions are what an individual assumes to be the case based on externally provided information before entering or during a digital virtual environmental experience. For example, one can be told by any number of sources (e.g., an experimenter) that a digital human representation is that of a computer algorithm and, hence, an agent, or that the digital human representation is that of an actual person in real time and, hence, an avatar (cf. Hoyt, Blascovich, & Swinth, 2003).

If one has no basis for assumption, then the attribution of agency may be deduced from, or induced by, the behaviors of the representation itself within the context defined by the virtual environment. In a digital

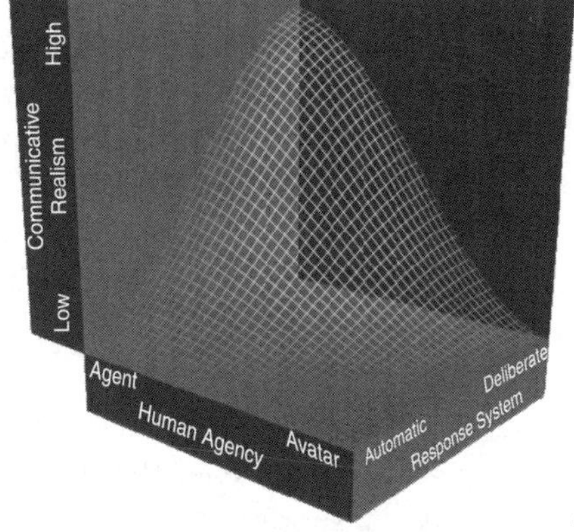

A. High Self-relevance

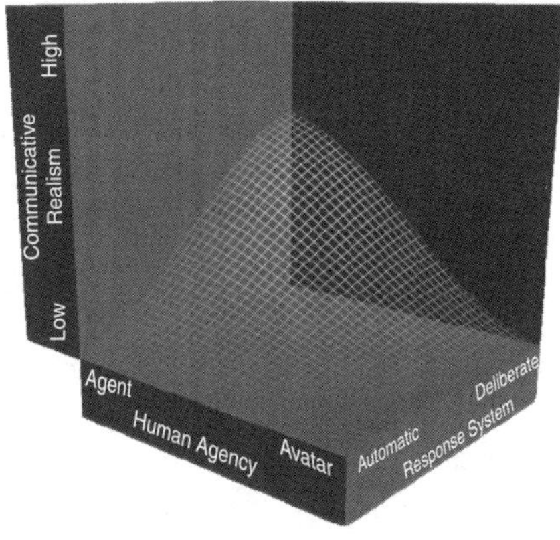

B. Moderate Self-relevance

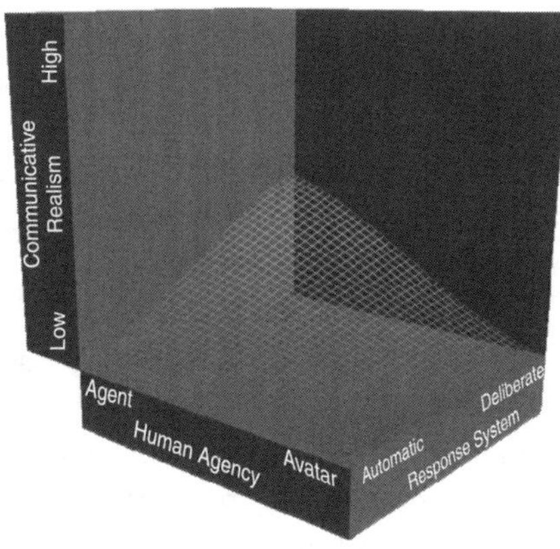

C. Low Self-relevance

Figure 11.2. The threshold model of social influence within immersive virtual environments.

immersive virtual environment, when a digital human representation speaks to or moves toward a person or when a person speaks to or moves toward the digital human representation), the person can consciously look for auditory and visual signs that point toward sentience or nonsentience. This is kind of a personal *Turing Test* users sometimes employ. If a user cannot tell whether the representation is an agent or a human from the vocalizations and movements, she or he is likely to conclude that it is an avatar and interact with it accordingly.

Whether arrived at by assumption or logic, what is most important for agency attributions in virtual reality is the belief that a person holds about a human representation. If a digital representation is believed to be an avatar, it is an avatar. Agency attributions are also important in grounded reality where people sometimes treat sentient individuals such as custodians as nonsentient persons (cf. Goffman, 1961) and where people sometimes treat nonsentient individuals such as those in persistent vegetative states as sentient (e.g., Terry Schiavo's body before the life support was removed).

Communicative Realism refers to the recognizable signal quality of communicative acts. Within digital immersive virtual worlds, communicative realism can be said to vary from low to high (see ordinate in Figure 11.2a). While not as necessary in digital virtual environments for representations that users assume are avatars (i.e., actual people), communicative realism is a very important aspect for representations that users assume are agents (i.e., computer algorithms). In this situation, communication processes can operate automatically or unconsciously in powerful ways. That is, even though people may be conscious of the fact that a representation is an agent, bottom-up processes often operate to attenuate the implications of that knowledge on social influence within digital virtual environments.

According to our model, communicative realism is a latent variable that involves three decreasingly important manifest communication variables: movement realism (e.g., postures, gestures, facial expressions, and proxemic behaviors), anthropometric realism (human-like morphology and articulation of body parts), and photographic realism (the fidelity of recognizable individuals). Anthropometric realism serves human movement realism in the sense that many human movements cannot be made without recognizable human body parts such as arms, legs, faces, and so forth. Photographic realism serves only to connote identity, including group identity, as might be revealed by organismic characteristics such gender and race, and specific personal identity. Even these markers of identity do not require what we commonly think of as high-fidelity photorealism (e.g., caricatures).

Importantly, others' movements are known to give rise to low-level central nervous system processes involving mirror neurons that project to areas of the brain controlling various mental processes that cause us to treat others, even those we believe to be agents, as sentient at some level, perhaps even unknowingly. Movement realism by digital agents (and avatars) can easily compensate for lack of anthropometric and photorealism, something we all experience from viewing animations produced by cartoonists.

The third dimension in our model is *Response System Level,* which varies from automatic to deliberate (see z-dimension in Figure 11.2a). Social influence can affect automatic or uncontrolled processes as well as deliberate or controlled processes. Over the past two decades, social psychologists have become more and more aware of the ubiquity and strength of "implicit" or automatic social influence effects. This is true for social interactions in both grounded and virtual reality (as the birthmark study described above demonstrates). Indeed, unconscious social influence processes appear similar in both types of reality. When a digital agent smiles, users smile back, just as in grounded reality (Bailenson & Yee, 2005). When a digital agent makes a loud noise, users exhibit a startle response, just as in grounded reality.

Figure 11.2a depicts relationships among agency, communicative realism, and response system level in a highly user-relevant context. The surface within the three-dimensional framework is what we label the "threshold of social influence." This threshold predicts the occurrence of social influence effects as a function of the three factors. At or above the threshold surface, social influence affects should occur. Below the surface they should not.

For example, if agency is high (i.e., the user believes the representation is an avatar), then both communicative realism and response system level need not be high in order for social influence effects to occur. For example, an avatar consisting merely of a "smiley face" can be enough to elicit positive affect in terms of automatic user behaviors such as a returned smile or in terms of a deliberate user response such as a verbal "Thank you!" On the other hand, if agency is low (i.e., the user believes the representation is an agent), then social influence will occur as a positive function of the degree of communicative realism (e.g., high movement realism) for deliberate user responses such as conversation. A high level of communicative realism is not necessary for automatic user responses even to an agent.

Self-relevance is the final factor in our model. It can vary from high to low. Self-relevance can simply be thought of as the personal meaningfulness of a social interaction. This is as true in digital immersive virtual environments as it is in grounded reality. Some social interactions are casual or are relatively unimportant transactions. Some are more important, especially when they invite evaluation by others such as performances in games. Some are very important such as the development of a romantic relationship. Figures 11.2b and 11.2c depict the lower-surfaced thresholds of social influence for moderate- and low-self-relevant contexts.

IMPLICATIONS FOR CONSCIOUSNESS AND FREE WILL

As stated at the outset, my thoughts regarding consciousness and free will largely stem from our work using digital immersive virtual technology to examine and explore social influence processes. A major caveat is that I have nothing to add to the discussion and debate regarding the so-called "hard consciousness problem" (Chalmers, 1999), that is, "What is consciousness?" Furthermore, I have nothing to add to the debate on the existence of free will.

What I do have something to say about is what Steven Pinker (2007) termed the "simple consciousness problem." That is, "What are the forms of consciousness and what functions do they play?" I defer to the processes of consciousness delineated by Schooler (2002). These include unconscious, conscious, and metaconscious processes (i.e., automatic mental processes, deliberate thought processes, and thinking about thinking, respectively). Furthermore, the interaction of these processes seems to limit any notion of "free will" to "will."

Forms of Consciousness

Digital immersive virtual environment technology provides a valuable empirical model for investigations of the "simple" consciousness problem. As exemplified by the "birthmark" study delineated above, digital IVET sets the stage—and allows researchers to control it—for scientific investigations of the operation of and interactions among unconscious, conscious, and metaconscious processes.

In the birthmark study, recall that the association of the stigmatic birthmark with a specific face in grounded reality carried over into the virtual world whether or not the avatar was facially birthmarked. Participants exhibited implicit (cardiovascular) evidence of threat based on that association; that is, when the physical person had had the birthmark, threat occurred. Within a few minutes, however, the original association was overcome by the avatars' appearance in the digital immersive virtual environment; that is, when the avatar bore the birthmark and participants exhibited implicit (cardiovascular) evidence of threat based on the new association.

In between, a sort of phase transition must have occurred in which mental processes of some sort mediated the change in associations. It is this period that is quite interesting. In the conditions in which the avatar did not bear the birthmark, whether the person behind it bore it physically, or in which the avatar did bear a birthmark that the person behind it didn't have, one can reasonably assume that the transition period included more metaconscious processing involving participants than the veridical conditions. The "magic" appearance/disappearance would likely have been noticed and participants may have wondered why. That wonderment itself likely induced metaconscious processing during which participants were able to recognize that they were in two places, one physical and one virtual, simultaneously. Resigned to completing the experience, these conscious and metaconscious processes faded, and participants were immersed in the virtual word-finding game.

These speculations are as yet unconfirmed by data, but it would be a relatively simple thing to investigate via a replication in which participants in the appropriate conditions were interrupted for thought-listing purposes or even by using the paradigm to investigate central neurophysiological processes associated with unconscious and conscious mental processes. If our speculations about metaconscious processing are correct, the phase transition period would be fertile ground for examining brain activity in some form to determine if higher-order thinking (i.e., metaconscious processing) can be distinguished from first-order thinking (i.e., conscious processing).

Free Will

As suggested above, much work over recent decades has demonstrated the importance and resilience of automatic or unconscious processes underlying social influence. Social influence effects seem driven strongly by nonverbal communicative behaviors, a type of communication of which interacting people are often unaware. Some of this work (cf. Ferguson & Bargh, 2004) involves mimicry of others' movements such as facial expressions, gestures, and so forth. Such effects occur in digital immersive virtual environments even when people interact with digital human representations known to be agents (Bailenson & Yee, 2005). In addition, gaze behavior, including eye movements and mutual gaze, is an important underpinning of social influence processes (Argyle & Cook, 1976; Bailenson et al., 2003).

As described above, digital IVET tracks and renders the movements and actions of users in near real time. Ordinarily, if a participant turns to the right to look at a particular digital human representation, his avatar also does so immediately and veridically. However, because the tracking-to-rendering process runs through a computer, veridical rendition does not have to be the case. For example, a person's gaze can be redirected to another avatar in the virtual world without his or her knowledge. Indeed, if there are multiple other avatars in the virtual world, that person's gaze can be directed to each of the multiple avatars (from their viewpoints), simultaneously producing what we have termed a "nonzero sum gaze," a type of the more general "transformed social interaction" (Bailenson et al., 2004) that can be manipulated.

The point here is that in digital virtual environments, bottom-up processing by a targeted person can be engineered easily by manipulation of protagonists' nonverbal movements and cues without their knowledge. Such cues affect target individuals unconsciously, leading among other effects to automatically primed goals. Subsequently, targeted individuals may consciously "choose" to do something, but with far less free will than they might perceive. This rationale is consistent with empirical literature demonstrating what is termed "automated will" by some (e.g., Bargh, Gollwitzer, Lee-Chai, Barndollar, & Trotshel, 2001). However, digital immersive virtual environment technology provides far more powerful priming tools.

DISCUSSION WITH JIM BLASCOVICH

What are the potential dangers of people's increasing reliance on technology? Some forms of virtual reality are so compelling and exciting that they can seem preferable to grounded reality. Some video games, for example, offer a virtual reality in which ordinary people are transformed into indestructible, sexy, powerful, even godlike figures. Such virtual realities can be very seductive and can make grounded reality boring by comparison.

This poses two problems. The first is addiction. When the Internet or video games become the central aspect of a person's life, the term addiction may apply. Pharmacological agents can produce addictions, which are known to be harmful in a variety of ways. Virtual worlds may produce similar addictions. The second, related problem is that one can become neglectful of important responsibilities in grounded reality because virtual reality can be so thrilling that the mundane requirements of daily life suffer. This can be called *reality hangover.*

One case illustrates the potential for addiction and reality hangover (though one should be cautious in generalizing from individual cases). A South Korean man died after 50 consecutive hours of playing an online video game, apparently of exhaustion. The virtual reality in which he was immersed was so compelling that he neglected food, drink, and sleep. This example is extreme, but there are many examples of people neglecting close relationships (and hygiene) in favor of gaming, Facebook, or online chats. Thus, the main potential danger of an excessive reliance on technology seems to be neglect of grounded reality, perhaps especially neglect of close relationships.

What are the potential benefits of technology and virtual worlds?
In some ways, effective use of technology may enhance relationships (though most likely the benefit is stronger for casual friendships than for close relationships). Through social networking, Second Life, online games, Twitter, chat rooms, and other media, one need not be physically present in order to interact with others. One's virtual representations are widely available for social interaction, as are the virtual representations of one's friends and family.

Interactions in virtual space may be especially welcome for people who have difficulty making social connections in grounded reality, such as those with extreme social anxiety or other phobias. In particular, they may find it easier to satisfy belongingness needs virtually. Additionally, virtual worlds may offer relief to individuals who are under acute stress. That is, virtual worlds can be an excellent escapism tool, permitting people relief from an unpleasant reality.

Have virtual realities always existed, or are technology-based virtual realities a qualitatively new experience?
Reading or hearing stories can be very immersive experiences, and these have been widespread throughout human history. Thus, some form of immersion in a virtual reality is probably a common aspect of human life. One of the biggest effects that technology has had is that immersion in a virtual world can be happen extremely quickly now. As technology advances, permitting constant kinesthetic feedback to be provided, deep immersion in a virtual world will happen even faster than it does now.

Younger people have more experience with virtual realities than do adults. Does this affect how they behave in virtual environments?
Some anecdotal evidence is informative. Using a head-mounted display, researchers have rendered a three-dimensional world in which there is a virtual pit. Across the virtual pit there is a virtual board, which seemingly enables one to cross the pit. Adults and children handle the task of traversing the pit very differently. Adults are very cautious, and about 50% of them will not cross the pit (for fear of falling into the pit), and about 25% of adults who do cross require some help. Nearly all children cross quickly and easily. It seems children may be better able to distinguish between virtual and grounded reality, perhaps as a product of experience.

The virtual world is not constrained by the laws of physics. What are the implications for social interactions in virtual worlds?

A person can only look one person in the eyes at once in grounded reality. One feature of some virtual environments is *nonzero-sum gaze,* which means that a person can seemingly maintain eye contact with several people at once. Studies in virtual worlds have demonstrated that speakers are more persuasive and their words are easier to remember when they maintain eye contact with each individual member of the audience relative to control conditions. Looking someone in the eye one-on-one has this effect in grounded reality, and one feature of the virtual environment is that the effect of direct eye contact can be exploited.

Similarly, a person can emerge as a leader of a group by virtue of how his or her virtual representation is rendered. For example, if a group of people is gathered around a virtual table, the person who is rendered as standing at the end of the table will presumably be the leader of the group (or will at least be in a good position to become the group leader).

Currently, people react to interpersonal cues (e.g., eye gaze, standing) in the virtual world in much the same way that they do in the natural world. That may change if interpersonal interactions in virtual space routinely exploit the fact that the laws of physics do not apply.

REFERENCES

Argyle, M., and Cook, M. (1976). *Gaze and mutual gaze.* Cambridge University Press, London.

Bailenson, J., Beall, A. C., Loomis, J., Blascovich, J., & Turk, M. C. (2004). Transformed social interaction: Decoupling representation from behavior and form in collaborative virtual environments, *Presence: Teleoperators and Virtual Environments, 13,* 428–441.

Bailenson, J., & Blascovich, J. (2005). Avatars. In W. S. Bainbridge (Ed.). *Berkshire Encyclopedia of Human-Computer Interaction.* Great Barrington, MA: Berkshire Publishing Group.

Bailenson, J. N., Blascovich, J., Beall, A. C., & Loomis, J. M. (2003). Interpersonal distance in immersive virtual environments, *Personality and Social Psychology Bulletin, 29,* 819–834.

Bailenson, J. N., & Yee, N. (2005). Digtal chameleons: Automatic assimilation of nonverbal gestures in immersive virtual environments, *Psychological Science, 16,* 814–819.

Bargh, J. A., Gollwitzer, P. M., Lee-Chai, A., Barndollar, K., & Trotshel, R. (2001). The automated will: Nonconscious activation and pursuit of behavioral goals, *Journal of Personality and Social Psychology, 81,* 1014–1027.

Beall, A. C., Bailenson, J. N., Loomis, J. M., Blascovich, J., & Rex, C. S. (2003). Non-zero sum gaze in immersive virtual environments. In *Proceedings of HCI international, 2003, (Crete)*. Lawrence Erlbaum Associates.

Blascovich, J., Loomis, J., Beall, A., Swinth, K., Hoyt, C., & Bailenson, J. (2002). Immersive virtual environment technology as a research tool for social psychology, *Psychological Inquiry, 13*, 103–125.

Blascovich, J., Mendes, W. B., Hunter, S., & Lickel, B. (2000). Challenge, threat, and stigma. In T. Heatherton, R. Kleck, M. R. Hebl, & J. G. Hull (Eds.), *The social psychology of stigma* (pp. 307–333). New York: Guilford.

Blascovich, J., Mendes, W. B., Hunter, S. B., & Lickel, B., & Kowai-Bell, N. (2001). Perceiver threat in social interactions with stigmatized others, *Journal of Personality and Social Psychology, 80*, 253–267.

Boellstorf, T. (2008). *Coming of age in second life: An anthropologist explores the virtually human*. Princeton, NJ: Princeton University Press.

Chalmers, D. (1999). Facing up to the problem of consciousness. In J. Shear (Ed.) *Consciousness: The hard problem*. Cambridge, MA: MIT Press.

Ferguson, M. J., & Bargh, J. A. (2004). How social perception can automatically influence behavior. *Trends in Cognitive Sciences, 8*, 33.

Goffman, E. (1961). *Asylums*. New York: Penguin.

Gunning, T. (1989). An aesthetic of astonishment: Early film and the (in)credulous spectator, *Art and Text, 34*, 114–133.

Hoyt, C., & Blascovich, J. (2007). Leadership efficacy and women leaders' responses to stereotype activation, *Group Processes and Intergroup Relations, 10*, 595–616.

Hoyt, C., Blascovich, J., & Swinth, K. (2003). Social inhibition in immersive virtual environments, *Presence: Teleoperators and Virtual Environments, 12*, 183–195.

Huxley, A. (1954). *The doors of perception and heaven and hell*. New York: Harper Brothers.

Klinger, E. (2008). Daydreaming and fantasizing: Thought flow and motivation. In K. Markman, B. Klein, and J. Suhr (Eds.), *Handbook of imagination and mental simulation* (pp. 227–241). New York: Psychology Press.

Loomis, J. M., Blascovich, J., & Beall, A. C. (1999). Virtual environment technology as a basic research tool in psychology, *Behavior Research Methods, Instruments, and Computers, 31*, 577–564.

Marien, M. W. (2006). *Photography: A cultural history: 2nd edition*. New York: Laurence King.

McCall, C., & Blascovich, J. (in press). How, when and why to use digital experimental virtual environments to study social behavior. *Personality and Social Psychology Compass*.

McCall, C., Blascovich, J., Young, A., & Persky, S. (2009). Proxemic behaviors as predictors of aggression towards black (but not white) males in an immersive virtual environment, *Social Influence, 5*, 1–17.

Mead, G. H. (1934). *Mind, self and society*. Chicago: University of Chicago Press.

Pinker, S. (2007, January 19). The mystery of consciousness. *Time*.

Schooler, J. W. (2002). Re-representing consciousness: Dissociations between consciousness and meta-consciousness, *Trends in Cognitive Sciences, 6*, 339–344.

Shepard, R. N. (1990). *Mind sights: Original visual illusions, ambiguities, and other anomalies, with a commentary on the play of mind in perception and art.* New York: W. H. Freeman.

Smallwood, J., & Schooler, J. C. (2006). The restless mind, *Psychological Bulletin, 132,* 946–958.

Stratton, G. (1896). Some preliminary experiments on vision without inversion of the retinal image. *Psychological Review, 3,* 611–617.

12 What Science Tells Us about Free Will

Jonathan W. Schooler

The very first act of a will endowed with freedom should be to sustain the belief in the freedom itself. I accordingly believe freely in my freedom. I do so with the best of scientific consciences. . .

—William James (James, 1899/1946, p. 192)

Advances in the science of thought and action put undeniable constraints on traditional notions of free will. As we come to understand the unconscious processes that drive behavior (e.g., Bargh & Ferguson, 2000), the neurocognitive mechanisms that underpin it (e.g., Crick, 1994), and the discrepancies between intentions and actions (e.g., Wegner, 2002), it seems ever more difficult to conceptualize what role the experience of personal agency might play. Indeed, on the basis of such challenges many scientists (e.g., Bargh, 2008; Blackmore, 1999; Wegner, 2002) and philosophers (e.g., Churchland, 1995) have argued that the time has come for us to abandon the notion of the self as a free agent. As Francis Crick (1994) put it:

> You, your joys and your sorrows, your memories and your ambitions, your sense of personal identity and free will, are in fact no more than the behavior of a vast assembly of nerve cells and their associated molecules. Who you are is nothing but a pack of neurons.

The suggestion that advances in the mind sciences necessarily force us to abandon long-held notions of free will raises important questions regarding the impact of communicating this message. The philosopher Smilansky (2000) suggests that: "Humanity is fortunately deceived on the free will issue, and this seems to be a condition of civilized morality and personal value. . .there would be considerable room for worry if people became aware of the absence of libertarian free will" (p. 505). On a brighter side, others have suggested that an appreciation of the lack of genuine free will may lead people to be more forgiving of criminal behavior, viewing punishment more from the pragmatic perspective of correction and deterrence, and less from a vengeful perspective of retribution (Greene & Cohen, 2004).

Although challenging, the question of what impact changing views on free will might have on people's moral behavior and judgments need not be confined to the philosopher's armchair. Rather, we can investigate the impact of exposing people to arguments regarding the absence of free will and assess whether those arguments have any impact on their ethical behavior or judgments. As will be discussed, recent studies taking this approach have found evidence that telling people they lack free will not only impacts on their belief about free will, but also influences their ethical behavior and judgment.

The finding that people's moral appraisals and actions may be influenced by hearing that science has ruled out the existence of free will adds increased urgency to the question of whether or not this conclusion is warranted. Addressing the age-old issue of whether or not free will exists is far less straightforward (particularly for behavioral scientists) than assessing the consequences of a belief in free will. Nevertheless, given that scientists' views on free will can impact on people's ethical behavior, it seems appropriate that scientists with diverging opinions chime in on this important issue. Having now spent a fair bit of time reviewing this topic, I find myself struck by how compelling seemingly contradictory arguments appear to be. Hard determinists' assertions that free will is a mere illusion are difficult to dismiss. Compatabilists' claims that we can maintain personal responsibility even in a universe ruled by cause and effect seem compelling. Yet it also seems premature to rule out libertarians' arguments that there might still be some way in which conscious choice could have a genuine causal impact. In the second section of this chapter, I review a selection of arguments from various alternative camps with the goal of illustrating my sympathy with many of the disparate views that have been presented. Given the cogence of the many alternative views of free will, I conclude that while the argument that science rules out free will is certainly a tenable hypothesis, at present it should be treated as such, and not as an irrefutable truth upon which all sensible people must necessarily agree. In short, I suggest that a belief in free will is still an option for those so inclined to choose it.

THE VALUE OF A BELIEF IN FREE WILL

Given how entrenched the notion of free will is to our sense of ourselves, each other, and our legal institutions, it does not require a huge leap of imagination to worry that exposure to the argument that free will is an illusion could have significant consequences. If personal responsibility depends on a sense that one could have behaved differently, then it stands to reason that people's sense of personal responsibility might be undermined by the conclusion that a combination of genetic and environmental factors compels them to behave as they do. And if people lose the sense of personal responsibility, then it follows that they might feel less compunction to act in an ethical manner themselves, and less indignation when others behave badly. After all, it is not really their fault.

Although philosophers have long speculated about the impact of a belief in free will on moral behavior and judgments, it is only recently that experimentalists have begun to empirically examine the issue. Experimental philosophers were the first to empirically address this question by asking people to assess personal responsibility within the context of imagining a purely deterministic universe. Nahmias, Morris, Nadelhoffer, & Turner (2005) had subjects assume that determinism is true and then judge whether an agent was blameworthy under those circumstances. They found that subjects tended to say that the agent was blameworthy despite living in a deterministic world. However, using a somewhat different design, Nichols and Knobe (2007) presented subjects with a description of an alternate universe that is deterministic, and they found that subjects tended to say that agents were not responsible in that universe. The apparent disparity between these studies was at least partially resolved by Roskies and Nichols (2008), who compared people's assignment of responsibility when the universe that was characterized as deterministic was either our own or some imaginary alternative universe (see also Roskies, Chapter 10, this volume). Participants were more likely to find agents culpable when the deterministic universe was our own (replicating Nahmias et al.), and less culpable when it was some imaginary other universe (replicating Nichols & Knobe).

The finding that participants in these studies tended to continue to hold people responsible when considered in the context of a deterministic universe (at least when it is our own) ameliorated these researchers' concerns about the impact of scientific dismissals of free will. As Roskies and Nichols (2008) observed:

> The upshot of this is that these worries about how neuroscientific understanding will undermine the social order are misplaced . . . if

> people came to believe in determinism, it seems likely that they would not significantly change their practices of attributing responsibility. (378)

While these conclusions are seemingly reassuring, there are important limitations to these investigations. First, these studies involve hypotheticals—asking people to imagine the universe being one way or another, and to imagine how they would feel under those situations. Given that people are notoriously bad at predicting their future feelings (Gilbert, 2006), it is quite possible that their conjectures about possible assignments of responsibility could be markedly different from how they would really feel were they to actually believe the world was deterministic. Furthermore, these studies merely asked people to speculate about responsibility, they did not assess what impact a belief in free will versus determinism had on actual moral behavior. Thus, while an important first step, these initial studies leave open the possibility that encouraging people to genuinely believe that free will is an illusion could have important effects on their actual moral behavior.

The Impact of Anti–Free Will Sentiments on Cheating

A recent series of studies by Vohs and Schooler (2008) addressed the above concerns by examining the impact of exposing participants to *genuine scientific claims* that science has shown that people lack free will on their *actual moral behavior*—willingness to cheat. In the first experiment, participants read one of two excerpts from Francis Crick's *The Astonishing Hypothesis*. In one excerpt, people were exposed to an expansion of the quote mentioned earlier in which Crick espouses the view that science has definitively shown that free will is an illusion. In a second excerpt, Crick talks about consciousness but makes no mention of the merits of the concept of free will. After reading one of these passages, participants completed a questionnaire regarding their beliefs about free will and then engaged in what they believed was an unrelated activity of completing mental arithmetic problems. Drawing on a cheating paradigm developed by von Hippel, Lakin, and Shakarchi (2005), participants were told that there was a glitch in the program and that after the problem was presented, they needed to press the space bar in order to prevent the computer from inadvertently giving them the answer before they had solved it themselves. Furthermore, participants were told that although the experimenter would not know whether they had pressed the space bar, they should try to solve the problems honestly on their own. In short, a failure to press the space bar enabled them to get the answer without solving it themselves, in effect, to cheat.

The results revealed several ways in which participants were impacted by reading the Crick essay dismissing the existence of free will. First, participants who read the anti–free will passage revealed a reduced degree of belief in free will relative to participants who read the control passage. Most importantly, those individuals who were exposed to the anti–free will passage were significantly more likely to cheat on the mental arithmetic test, and this increase in amoral behavior was mediated by a reduced belief in free will.

A second experiment conceptually replicated the first while addressing several possible concerns. In Experiment 1, amoral behavior was assessed by failure to press the space bar. While participants were explicitly told that they needed to press the space bar in order to perform honestly, it is possible that their failure to press it in the anti–free will condition was not due to an increased tendency for amoral behavior so much as a greater degree of passivity. Experiment 2 addressed this issue by introducing an active measure of amoral behavior—enabling participants to overpay themselves for their performance. A further innovation of Experiment 2 was the introduction of a pro–free will condition.

In this second experiment, participants received one of three treatments. In one condition, participants read a series of statements designed to induce a feeling of determinism. Sample statements included, "Ultimately, we are biological computers—designed by evolution, built through genetics, and programmed by the environment." The participants' task was to read each statement and think about it, and then when instructed, they were to turn the page and read another statement. This task is modeled after the oft-used Velten mood induction task (Velten, 1968). In another condition, participants read statements that were designed to bolster beliefs in free will, such as "I am able to override the genetic and environmental factors that sometimes influence my behavior." A third group of participants read neutral statements. The cheating opportunity was set up such that participants self-scored a cognitive test on which they were to be paid $1. Ostensibly because of an unexpected errand, the experimenter left the room and allowed participants to score their exam and then pay themselves for their performance on the test. The money that participants paid themselves thus served as proxy for their claimed scores on the exam, and could be compared to veridical scores from participants who took the exam and were not allowed to self-score. The research question was whether participants would give themselves differential amounts of money as a function of whether they had been encouraged to believe in free will, or determinism, or whether their beliefs were left unchanged.

The results showed that after participants read statements that told them their actions were predetermined and therefore not under their control, they cheated more—as evidenced by more money taken in this condition compared to the control condition and the free will condition. Reading statements that bolstered participants' belief in free will did not affect cheating behavior, as these participants paid themselves as much money as did participants whose scores were known. Once again, we found that participants' beliefs changed, with people who were exposed to the anti–free will passage expressing a reduced belief in free will relative to the other conditions. Interestingly, there was no effect of exposure to the pro–free will passages on participants' belief in free will, suggesting that people's default belief is in free will.

There are a number of important lessons to extract from Vohs and Schooler's experiments. First, the results suggest that individuals' beliefs about free will can be significantly influenced by exposure to claims that science has cast doubts on the existence of free will. Such a finding is in and of itself of importance as it was far from clear a priori that participants' opinion about an issue as fundamental as the existence of free will could be influenced by exposure to relatively brief arguments against the concept. Although we did not assess the long-term impact of anti–free will passages, the ease with which we were able to at least temporarily influence people's attitudes on the subject suggests that regular exposure to scientific claims that free will is an illusion could lead to enduring changes to their attitudes about free will.

Clearly, the most striking finding of the Vohs and Schooler study was that exposure to anti–free will sentiments increased their amoral behavior—inducing passive cheating in Experiment 1 and active cheating in Experiment 2. These findings suggest that prior arguments that exposure to scientific refutations of free will could negatively impact on moral behavior may have some merit after all. Of course, allowing a computer to provide answers for problems or slightly overpaying themselves for problems solved are relatively mild moral infractions that in no way constitute the type of "unprincipled nihilism" (Smilansky, 2000, p. 189) that some have feared dismissal of the concept of free will might induce. None of the participants exposed to the anti–free will message assaulted the experimenter or ran off with the payment kitty. Nevertheless, these findings do suggest that discouraging a belief in free will can lead to demonstrable increases in certain amoral behaviors.

The Impact of Anti–Free Will Sentiments on Helpfulness and Aggression

Given the potential implications of the Vohs and Schooler study, it is important to assess the degree to which other types of antisocial behaviors might be encouraged by discouraging a belief in free will. Recently a series of studies by Baumeister, Masicampo, and Dewall (2009) provided evidence that reading anti–free will statements undermines prosocial behavior in several additional ways, including reducing participants' willingness to help others and increasing their tendency to behave aggressively.

In Experiment 1 of Baumeister et al., participants engaged in one of the three statement-reading conditions used in Experiment 2 of Vohs and Schooler. They then read hypothetical scenarios in which they had to indicate how likely they would be to help out in each situation at the present moment. The scenarios included situations such as giving money to a homeless person and allowing a fellow classmate to use one's cellular phone. The results revealed that participants who had read the anti–free will sentiments reported being significantly less likely to help out in these situations than individuals who read the pro–free will or control statements. No differences were found on either helpfulness or belief in free will between the control and pro–free will participants, suggesting again that people's pre-existing views are generally pro–free will.

Experiment 2 of Baumeister et al. examined the relationship between anti–free will sentiments and participants' willingness to engage in actual helping behavior. In this study, participants' beliefs in free will were assessed using the same free will scale used in the other experiments, and then participants read about a fellow student whose parents had been killed in a car accident and who was going to have to drop out of school unless she could find someone to help her out financially. Following a false debriefing, participants were given the opportunity to engage in volunteer behavior to help out this student. The results revealed that disbelief in free will was associated with a lower tendency to volunteer to help. This study thus demonstrated that the negative relationship between anti–free will sentiments and helping behavior generalize to pre-existing beliefs and to situations in which participants believe that they will actually be called on to help.

Experiment 3 of Baumeister et al. examined the relationship between anti–free will sentiments and aggression. In this study, participants read either the pro– or anti–free will passages and then were given an opportunity to add varying amounts of hot sauce to crackers that they believed were going to be eaten by another participant who did not care for spicy food. The results once again revealed a relationship between belief in free will and prosocial behavior, such that those participants who read the anti–free will statements endorsed more anti–free will sentiments on the free will scale and served up more hot sauce to participants who they knew would not like it.

Accounting for the Negative Impact of Anti–Free Will Sentiments on Prosocial Behavior

The above studies suggest a variety of situations in which encountering and/or endorsing anti–free will sentiments reduces prosocial behaviors, raising the important question of what the mechanism of this effect might be. Although there are several mechanisms that remain viable alternative accounts of this important effect, several of the less interesting interpretations have been ruled out. One possibility is that reflecting on the notion that free will does not exist is a depressing activity, and that the results are simply the consequence of increased negative affect. However, both Vohs and Schooler and Baumeister et al. assessed mood and found no impact of the anti–free will statements on mood, and no relationship between mood and prosocial behavior. Another possibility is that participants were responding to demand characteristics. Perhaps they inferred that if the experimenter was having them read statements dismissing free will that the experimenter expected them to behave badly. However, Baumeister et al. specifically addressed this issue by including an additional validation study in which participants read the pro– or anti–free will statements and then indicated their judgments regarding the possible expectations of the author of those statements, including "The person who wrote those statements probably would want me to be kind and helpful," and "The person who wrote those statements would probably want me to be mean and cruel." Reading these statements had no effect on participants' beliefs about experimenter expectancies, arguing against the suggestion that the impact of these manipulations were due to demand characteristics.

Regarding the conceptually more interesting (i.e., nonartifactual) accounts of the impact of anti–free will statements, some progress has been made in isolating the mechanism, but again more research is required. Two related possibilities are that discouraging a belief in free will reduces participants' sense of personal accountability or agency. To address this issue, Baumeister et al. included an additional validation study in which they examined the impact of reading the pro– or anti–free will sentiments on both participants' belief in free will (using the same scale mentioned in the earlier studies) and their perceived accountability and feelings of agency. Perceived accountability was assessed by statements such as "I am held accountable for my actions" and agency by statements such as "Right now, I feel active." The result revealed that whereas the pro– versus anti–free will statements significantly impacted people's reported belief in free will, they neither affected their perceived accountability nor agency.

Baumeister et al. argue that the absence of an impact of anti–free will sentiments on participants' reported accountability and personal agency argues against a role of either of these constructs in mediating the relationship between endorsing anti–free will statements and prosocial behavior. Nevertheless, it might still be the case that some implicit sense of these constructs might be involved. Just as priming achievement-oriented goals can influence participants' tacit sense of achievement without them explicitly realizing it (Bargh, 2005), so too might discouraging a belief in free will tacitly minimize individuals' sense of accountability or agency, without people explicitly realizing this change. Future research might profitably explore this issue by examining whether implicit measures of these constructs are affected by anti–free will sentiments.

Another possible way in which encountering anti–free will sentiments might reduce prosocial behavior is by reducing the energy that individuals are willing to expend. As Baumeister et al. (2009) observe:

> Volition and self-control require the person to expend energy, and these expenditures enable them to act prosocially. Apparently disbelief in free will subtly reduces people's willingness to expend that energy. Hence, disbelief in free will serves as a cue to act on impulse, a style of response that promotes selfish and impulsive actions such as aggressing and refusing to help. (p. 267)

Although it may be premature to conclude that this is necessarily the mechanism underlying these effects, the notion that encountering anti–free will sentiments subtly reduces the energy that people have available to expend in the service of prosocial behavior seems quite plausible. In the future, this hypothesis might be more directly tested by examining the relationship between encountering anti–free will sentiments, and other measures known to be sensitive to "ego depletion" (Baumeister, Bratslavsky, Muraven, & Tice, 1998; Baumeister, Chapter 3, this volume; Vohs, Chapter 5, this volume) that do not have any explicit moral element. For example, it has been found that when individuals resist eating chocolate chip cookies, they experience a reduced capacity to persevere on anagrams that (unbeknownst to them) are unsolvable. If encountering anti–free will sentiments produces a similar reduction in available mental energy, then it might have comparable reduction in the effort individuals are willing to expend on solving anagrams.

While more research will be needed to isolate the precise psychological mechanisms underlying the impact of encountering anti–free will statements, two conclusions so far seem clear: *(1)* a belief in free will leads to a variety of prosocial behaviors, and *(2)* encountering anti–free will sentiments can undermine the advantages of this belief. These conclusions naturally lead to the question that is likely to be burning in at least some reader's minds. If discouraging a belief in free will is such a potent psychological manipulation, are its effects necessarily all bad, or might there be at least some contexts in which a benefit to anti–free will views might be observed? I consider this question in the next section.

The Impact of Anti–Free Will Sentiments on Retribution

In an influential review, Greene & Cohen (2004) speculated that as society increasingly comes to understand the true basis of human behavior, legal judgments will decreasingly rely on antiquated concepts of free will. Rather than endorsing retributivist views of punishment as a worthy end in itself, the abandonment of a belief in free will lead, they suggest, to an increasingly consequentialist approach to punishment, focusing on social benefits such as the prevention of future transgressions through deterrence. As Greene and Cohen put it:

> As more and more scientific facts come in, providing increasingly vivid illustrations of what the human mind is really like, more and more people will develop moral intuitions that are at odds with our current moral practices... The law will continue to punish misdeeds, as it must for practical reasons, but the idea of distinguishing the truly, deeply guilty from those who are merely victims of neuronal circumstances will ... seem pointless. (p. 1778)

The speculation that reduced beliefs in free will may discourage retributive thinking suggests a context in which anti–free will statements might have positive consequences—namely, encouraging people to be more forgiving and behave less vindictively.

A recent study by Shariff, Greene, and Schooler (2009) addressed this issue. In this study, participants first read either control passage with no relevance to the issue of free will or descriptions of scientific findings that were characterized as suggesting that the brain is the ultimate arbiter of people's choices. Subsequently, they read a murder scenario in which, a high school senior loses his temper in a bar and beats another man to death. Participants then read sentencing arguments by the defense and prosecutor that were designed to reduce the consequentialist impact of prison sentencing. Specifically, they read an argument by the defense team in which it is argued that instead of being sent to prison, he should be sent a treatment facility that has demonstrated a 100% success rate at curing youths of their aggression and preventing recidivism. The defense team reminds the court that no deterrence benefits will be gained from additional detention beyond the time spent at the treatment facility. The prosecution agrees but nonetheless argues for prison time as an appropriate (retributive) punishment. Finally, participants were asked to indicate the amount of prison time, if any, that they would recommend for the defendant, following his time in the treatment facility.

The results revealed a significant impact of reading the anti–free will sentiments. Participants who read the anti–free will passage recommended on average between 2 and 5 years additional imprisonment following the 5 years in the treatment facility, whereas those reading the control passage recommend between 5 and 10 years. The finding that anti–free will sentiments can significantly temper people's retributive tendencies can reasonably be characterized as a positive impact of endorsing anti–free will sentiments. Although some may feel that revenge for revenge's sake is an appropriate human reaction, many, I expect, would view the advancement of a worldview that enables forgiveness as a genuinely positive development.

Summary of the Impact of a Belief in Free Will

Collectively, the above findings demonstrate that the issue of whether or not free will exists is not simply an obscure philosophical debate confined to the ivory tower. Rather, beliefs on this issue have important effects on both people's own moral behavior and their assessment of the behavior of others. On the negative side, exposure to anti–free will sentiments can lead to detrimental effects on a variety of moral behaviors, including increasing cheating (both passive and active), reducing helpfulness (both hypothetical and actual), and increasing aggression. On the positive side, anti–free will sentiments reduce retribution, suggesting that it may enable people to be more forgiving.

Were the relationship between beliefs in free will and morality exclusively limited to people's enduring pre-existing beliefs, and were such beliefs found to be resistant to influence, then these findings might easily be dismissed as being of little relevance to the old debate regarding the possible impact of scientific claims of discrediting free will. But, to the contrary, the present findings suggest that people's views about free will are volatile and highly sensitive to the messages of scientists. Given that these views also appear to influence their moral behavior (see also Pizarro and Helzer, Chapter 7, this volume), it seems appropriate that we carefully assess what science can currently tell us about the existence of free will.

THE STATUS OF FREE WILL

In the following section, I review what I find to be some of the most compelling cases both for and against the existence of free will. Let me be up-front about my conclusion. In my view, there are many extremely compelling arguments on all sides of this issue. Those who have concluded that science simply leaves no room for free will (hard determinists) have some very good arguments. But then again, those who claim that at least some version of free will can exist within a purely deterministic world (compatibilists) also make a good case. While the libertarian view that conscious deliberation can have a causal role in adjudicating between actual alternative futures is perhaps the hardest case to defend, in my view it, too, cannot be ruled out. Thus, the conclusion that I find myself reaching is that scientists are entirely justified in expressing their opinions regarding the implications of science for conceptualizing free will. However, I believe that scientists should express those conclusions as representing their personal interpretation of the evidence and not as an articulation of indisputable scientific fact. To do otherwise is to make the very same mistake that religions have made over the millennia–articulating faith as fact, and potentially vilifying those who do not see the world as they do.

Hard Determinism–Free Will Is an Illusion

From a logical standpoint, the case that free will is merely an illusion is probably the easiest to make. The arguments for a hard determinist perspective are both numerous and compelling. These include:

Argument by Analogy

Everything else in the universe appears to follow the law of cause and effect. Why then should conscious choice be the one exception to this rule? If we can explain all other phenomena without recourse to deliberate intention, then surely we can do the same for human behavior. As Dennett (1991, p. 251) put it, "in biology, we have learned to resist the temptation to explain *design in organisms* by positing a single great Intelligence that does all the work ... We must build up the same resistance to the temptation to explain *action* as arising from the imperatives of an internal action-orderer who does too much of the work."

Argument from Neuroscience

Neuroscience is increasingly demonstrating the direct correspondences between thoughts and brain activity. Given that all thoughts are the product of brain activity, it follows that human choices can be understood simply as the product of the neural activity that underpins it (Crick, 1994).

Argument from Genetics

Human behavior is powerfully determined by genetic influences. Twins separated at birth share startling correspondences not only in their temperaments but also in their likes and dislikes (Segal, 1999). Even moral behaviors have a fundamental genetic component as evidenced by the heritability of qualities such psychopathology (Jang, 2005) and addiction (Loughead et al., 2008). If people's choices and moral behavior can be traced to their genetics, then people are no more in control of their actions then they are of their inherited genetic code.

Argument from Environmental Influences

Those aspects of human behavior that are not accounted for by genetic influences can readily be posited to be a result of environmental factors. Environmental stressors such as poverty, lack of education, poor nutrition, and history of abuse are all known to have a powerful impact on the unfolding of people's lives, influencing not only the opportunities that people are able to realize, but also even the likelihood that they engage in criminal activity (Cassel & Bernstein, 2007).

Argument from Nonconscious Processes

Increasingly, we are coming to understand the powerful unconscious mental processes that drive many of our actions. Though the actual nature of these processes is only now being appreciated, their existence and implication for free will has long been acknowledged. As Spinoza

(1677/1951) put it, "men believe themselves to be free, simply because they are conscious of their actions, and unconscious of the causes whereby those actions are determined" (p. 134). Just a few of the many examples of unconscious mental processes known to influence behavior outside of awareness include the observations that: *(1)* priming goals (e.g., completing an anagram involving cooperation) can unconsciously influence people's behavior (how cooperatively they behave) (Bargh, Gollwitzer, Lee-Chai, Barndollar, & Trötschel, 2001), *(2)* major life choices (e.g., where people end up locating) can be influenced by similarities between the letters in peoples names and in their choices (e.g., there are more Veronicas in Virginia) (Pelham, Mirenberg, & Jones, 2002), and *(3)* people are often unaware of the actual reasons for their behavior yet nevertheless are readily willing to confabulate justifications (Nisbett & Wilson, 1977). If people are so routinely unaware of the real reasons for their behaviors, then why should we think their behaviors are a consequence of deliberate choices?

Argument from Illusions of Will

Recent research has demonstrated that people can be easily duped into taking responsibility for actions over which they could have had no control. When, for example, people hear the name of an object in close temporal proximity to a cursor landing on that object, they perceive themselves as having deliberately moved the cursor to that location even when they had no actual control (Wegner & Wheatley, 1999). Such findings suggest that the experience of intention causing action is the product of an illusory inference stemming from the frequent co-occurrence of thoughts followed by actions (Wegner, 2002). Thoughts no more cause actions than lightning causes thunder.

Argument from the Timing of Intention and Brain Activity

Accumulating evidence suggests that the brain activity associated with conscious decisions often occurs well before an individual is aware of having made the decision (Libet, 1985). If the brain has already made up its mind by the time the individual is aware of the decision, then what possible role could the consciousness of the choice have?

This is an impressive set of arguments and far from exhaustive. Admittedly, there are significant counterarguments that can be mustered against at least some of these arguments. For example, Libet (the discoverer of the finding that brain activity often precedes awareness of conscious choices) has argued that conscious will might circumvent its otherwise after-the-fact status by having a capacity for inhibition (sometimes referred to as "free wont") (Libet, 1999, 2003). However, these counterarguments have in turn been countered (for example, to date there is no evidence that the capacity to restrain behavior is any more under conscious control than the capacity to initiate it) (Velmans, 2003). This is not to say that the case for hard determinism is an open and shut case (as will be seen, my argument is quite the contrary), but simply that it is very understandable why so many people would find it so persuasive.

Compatibilism—Free Will and Determinism Are Not Mutually Exclusive

Intuitively, compatibilism makes great sense as it acknowledges two observations that seem very difficult to deny. First, this view recognizes that science is premised on the fundamental notion that all phenomena, both physical and mental, can be understood as the product of a chain of causes and effects. At the same time, compatibilism acknowledges that human existence is riddled with the need to make real decisions about genuine options. Given the seemingly self-evidentiary nature of both the supremacy of the law of cause and effect, and the existence of genuine choosing, it follows that both must be true. The challenge is conceptualizing precisely how these two constructs can coexist. Though a variety of different versions of compatibilism have been proposed, two general elements are often invoked.

Two Sides of the Same Coin

According to this view, causal brain processes and free will represent different facets of the same phenomena. Yes, our brain controls our actions, but yes, we also control our actions because we are our brains. Conscious desire doesn't spawn or lead to neural processes any more than neuronal activity spawns or leads to conscious experience. The experience of conscious free will is the first-person perspective of the neural correlates of choosing (Velmans, 2002).

Emergent Properties

Another complimentary approach to the compatabilists' perspective is to argue that free will is an emergent property that arises from a particular set of conditions surrounding the physical systems of our genetic brains steeped in our environmental culture. For example, Dennett (2003) suggests that free will is a unique capacity that emerged as a consequence of evolution and culture. As Dennett puts it: "Free will is real, but it is not a preexisting feature of our existence . . . it is an evolved creation of human activity and beliefs." (p. 13). A related form of emergence suggests that higher-order mental processes emerge from but are not reducible to lower-level neural processes. These processes occurring at the macrobehavioral level can modulate lower levels and thereby introduce a capacity for genuine agentic control (Bandura, 2008).

The attraction of compatibilism stems at least in part from the inherent appeal of the middle ground. So often when there is a long-standing debate (e.g., nature/nurture), the answer lies somewhere in the middle. Surely, therefore, there must be some way to simultaneously acknowledge that people are susceptible to the same causal forces as all other things in nature, while recognizing that they have the capacity to make real choices. The fact that we cannot precisely explain how these two concepts mesh reflects a significant challenge, but arguably no greater a challenge than that raised by the hard determinists' view that the experience of genuine choice is entirely illusory, or the libertarians' view (to be discussed next) that free will relies on an "extra something."

Libertarianism—The Existence of Genuine Choice

As Samuel Johnson observed long ago, "All theory is against the freedom of the will; all experience for it." (Boswell, 1924). Experientially, the sense of having a causal role in one's actions is overwhelming. If I want to lift my hand up, I do. And if I don't, I don't. Even more striking are the acts of will in which I must apply enduring effort. While there are many actions where one experiences ambiguity regarding the source (did I really mean to scratch that itch?), there are others in which it feels overwhelmingly evident that my experience of exerting will was causally involved. In such cases, people have the distinct sense of being "the ultimate creators (or originators) and sustainers of their own ends and purposes" (Kane, 1996, p. 4). While some are prepared to accept such experiences as mere illusions, others feel there has to be something real about them. Although the libertarian view appears to be the default view among laypeople (Baumeister et al., 2009; Vohs & Schooler, 2008), it is often characterized as a minority view among both scientists and philosophers (Bloom, 2004).[1] Nevertheless, there are a number of compelling arguments for keeping it in the running. These include:

The Experience of Free Will

The experience of free will is overwhelmingly compelling. As Searle (1984) observes, "The experience of freedom, that is to say, the experience of the sense of alternative possibilities, is built into the very structure of conscious voluntary, intentional human behavior" (p. 98). Although subjective experience is often considered a rather dubious source of evidence, it does inform our views of reality. For example, from a scientific perspective there is really no direct evidence that subjective experience exists at all, leading some to conclude that qualia itself is an illusion (Dennett, 1991). Nevertheless, many feel that despite the lack of objective evidence, experience is self-evident, as even the illusion of experience would itself have to be experienced (Schooler & Schrieiber, 2004; Searle, 1997). Although clearly not as self-evident as experience, volition has a similar self-evident subjective quality. The evidentiary significance of the experience of volition has weighed differently in various authors' speculations about free will. Some (e.g. Searle, Chapter 8, this volume; Shariff, Schooler, & Vohs, 2008) have considered it an important observation that gives teeth to the potential genuineness of free will but not necessarily proof of its existence. Others, however (e.g., Griffin, 1996; Whitehead, 1929), view it as a pivotal fact in the case for a libertarian view of free will. For example, Griffin distinguishes between hard-core and soft-core common sense with the former corresponding to notions that are so intrinsic to our nature that "they cannot be consistently denied" and the latter to "merely parochial notions that can be denied without pain of implicit inconsistency" (p.16). Examples of hard-core common sense include such things as the reality of the external world, the past, the future, and conscious experience, whereas soft-core commons sense include now defunct claims (such as the notion that the world is flat), as well most current scientific theories, which, while compelling, could in principle be similarly overturned by new evidence. In keeping with Whitehead, Griffin concludes that the experience of personal agency is so intrinsic to our day-to-day experience that it must be considered a hard-core common sense, giving it greater ontological status than the soft-core intuition of determinism. As Griffin puts it:

> "if we cannot really give up our intuition about freedom because it is inevitably presupposed in practice, we should instead turn our critical eye to those (soft-core) intuitions that seem to 'force us' to deny freedom in our scientific and philosophical theories" (p. 166)

The Functionality of Libertarianism

Closely related to the experiential argument for libertarianism is that of pragmatism. A belief in free will is a very useful thing. It underpins both the sense of moral culpability (see Pizarro and Helzer, Chapter 7, this volume) that prevents us from doing what we think we shouldn't and personal agency that gives us the get-up-and-go to do what we think we should. Although the utility of free will alone is clearly insufficient to justify its acceptance, if one is faced with deciding between alternative metaphysical views, each of which are irresolvable based on the extant evidence alone, then considering the pragmatics of the alternative views is a reasonable, if not fail-safe, approach. If a particular view is one that feels right to me, if it affords significant functionality, and if it remains a logically viable alternative, then this is a reasonable justification for me to maintain that view as long as I can. This call to pragmatism was one of the key reasons that William James (James, 1907) remained sympathetic to the libertarian view despite acknowledging the viability of the deterministic perspective.

Indeterminism

A precondition for the self to have a causal role in its actions is that it be possible that the individual could have done otherwise. If all of one's future actions are already 100% determined, then it seems the experience of making a genuine decision between real alternatives has to be illusory. Thus, a necessary precondition for free will is that the future not be written in stone. In recent years, libertarians have suggested that the degree of freedom necessary for genuine free choice might be provided by quantum indeterminacy. As Searle (Chapter 8, this volume) observes:

> ... It looks as if, if there is any factual reality to the conscious experience of non-determinism, that is to say freedom, there must be some connection between consciousness and quantum indeterminacy.

It is often pointed out that quantum indeterminacy offers little solace for libertarians because having one's choices influenced by a combination of deterministic forces and some random quantum element still leaves no room for the conscious chooser. However, Searle (Chapter 8, this volume) argues that this is a "fallacy of composition" by which it is assumed that "what is true of the elements of a system will be true of the entire system." Accordingly, it is at least possible that human choice could be subject to the nondeterminism observed at the quantum level without necessarily also acquiring the randomness associated with that level of analysis. As Searle observes,

> What I am suggesting is the logical possibility, though empirical unlikelihood, that the higher-level consciousness of voluntary, free decision-making would manifest the lack of causally sufficient conditions characteristic of the quantum level without inheriting the randomness of that level.

In short, by demonstrating the reality of indeterminacy in at least one level of nature, quantum mechanics reveals the possibility that free will could in principle be able to select between genuine alternative futures. If free will introduces a principled, rather than random way of adjudicating between these alternatives, then the possibility of individuals being at least occasionally "the ultimate creators (or originators) and sustainers of their own ends and purposes" remains viable.

The Importance of Effort

If genuine free will does exist, given all the evident influences that are outside of our control, it clearly must be highly constrained in the situations to which it could even conceivably apply. For William James (1899/1946), the existence of genuine free will was limited to situations that depend on voluntary attention, which "*consists in the effort of attention by which we hold fast an idea*" (p. 187). According to James, these incidences of sustained voluntary attention necessary for careful deliberation provide the window for the introduction of genuine free choice: "Our acts of voluntary attention, brief and fitful as they are, are nevertheless critical, determining us, as they do, to higher or lower destinies" (p. 189). Kane (1996) similarly suggests that the impact of genuine free will might be limited to relatively rare difficult decisions, what he refers to as "self-forming actions," in which individuals are torn between competing visions of what they should do or become. Ultimately, for Kane, James, Searle, and others sympathetic to the libertarian perspective, it is at these critical junctures in which individuals willfully sustain attention in the service of making conscious deliberate decisions that individuals are most likely to have a truly causal impact on the direction of their lives.

The Value of Establishing Habits of Mind

If individuals devote great resources to thinking through their decisions at critical junctures and establishing a policy of how they wish to behave under certain circumstances, then this policy may enact itself automatically in cases in which it applies. In this manner, even if people act automatically at the moment that the choice is made, they may still be implementing an intention that is consistent with a well-thought-out goal. Like a sailor in high seas who can set a general course despite being unable to control the moment-to-moment motion of her craft, the deliberate establishment of personal policies of action may enable the will to exert an impact on one's course of action, despite the unconscious turbulence that moves us at any particular moment.

Agency as a Fundamental Aspect of the Universe

Some have argued that consciousness and agency, like mass and gravity, are fundamental aspects of the universe. The notion, termed "panpsychism" or "panexerperientialism," that all elements of the universe possess varying degrees of consciousness, has been held by a number of distinguished scholars including Leibnitz (1714/1989), Spinoza (1660/1955), James (1907), Whitehead (1929), and more recently, Chalmers (1995) and Griffin (1996). Although not all who favor panexperientialism see volition as a necessary element (e.g. Chalmers, 1995; Spinoza, 1660/1955), this perspective provides a way of conceptualizing how free will might exist, namely, as an inherent property not only of humans but also of all constituents of the universe.

Whitehead and his intellectual heir Griffin propose the existence of a hierarchy of compound individuals with ever-increasing degrees of sentience and volition. Inorganic materials, though constituted by elements each possessing an iota of consciousness, involve aggregations that do not compound into larger experiences. As a consequence, the agency inherent in inorganic material cancels itself out, leaving little trace of its presence (with the possible exception of the atomic level, where randomness can be viewed as the will of individual particles). In contrast, organic structures are assumed to enable the mental combination of constituent elements, creating ever-larger coherent mental experiences. Accordingly, cell organelles possess a small element of sentience and volition, compounding into the increasingly greater experiences of individuals cells, brain networks, and ultimately human beings. Experience and agency grows as individual sentient elements amass into larger sentient individuals, somewhat akin to the way mass and gravity increase with larger physical compounds. It is well beyond the scope of this chapter to do justice to Whitehead's theory of panexperientialism, but suffice to say that one of the most brilliant philosophers of the twentieth century articulated a comprehensive and highly innovative vision for how free will manifests in the physical world. Readers are encouraged to see Griffin (1996) and Hunt (2009) for recent perspectives on Whitehead's views.

The Limits of Current Understanding

Many readers presented with the suggestion that consciousness and free will might be inherent aspects of matter are likely to believe science long ago dismissed such fanciful notions. However, a final, albeit related, core element of libertarian arguments is an acknowledgment that science is a long way off from a full understanding of the relationship between consciousness and physical reality (Chalmers, 1995), leaving room for the possibility of a host of potential ways in which consciousness might have a causal impact. James believed that this critical window of uncertainty surrounded the exertion of conscious effort in the service of a deliberate decision, noting that "the predetermination of the amount of my effort of attention can never receive objective proof" (p. 192). This led him to conclude that "such psychological and psychophysical theories as I hold do not necessarily force a man to become a fatalist or a materialist" (p. 192). Eccles (1986), Hameroff (2006), Kane (1996), Penrose (1987), Stapp (2007), and others also pin their hopes for a resolution of the causal impact of consciousness on various yet-to-be-determined relationships between consciousness and physical reality.

Increasingly it seems scientists have to be careful about what they claim is impossible. Additional dimensions of reality, parallel universes, time travel, and other concepts that used to be considered exclusively the domain of science fiction now are seriously entertained as physical possibilities (for a review, see Kaku, 2005). If time, as is often suggested, can be thought of as akin to another dimension of space, then perhaps, like space-time, it too is multidimensional. If so, it might be possible to move forward in time to alternative outcomes, each representing a different value in this additional temporal dimension. Accordingly, we might move forward not only in time but also the temporal equivalent of left and right. From this perspective, free will might be the capacity of consciousness to control, perhaps through effort or interpretation, which direction in time the next moment realizes. Such ideas are admittedly far-fetched, but so too is the notion that universes might be constantly splitting off as is currently suggested by the many-worlds account of quantum physics (Everett & DeWitt, 1973). The point is simply that there is so much still unknown about the nature of reality and its relationship to consciousness, that we must be very careful in imposing constraints on what that relationship will eventually prove to be.

Final Reflections on Alternative Conceptualizations of Free Will

Ultimately, each of the three approaches to conceptualizing the issue of free will has two things in common: each makes a compelling case, and each relies on a promissory note that future evidence will support its particular view. Hard determinism is able to bring an impressive array of empirical evidence to bear on the issue, but it requires one to accept that, in principle, it should be possible to perfectly predict all human behavior. Compatibilism has the strength of offering the middle-ground compromise position but requires one to accept that it will be possible to understand how genuine choice can be exist in a world in which the future is written in stone. Libertarianism fits most naturally with our personal intuitions, but it requires us to accept that some account will emerge for how consciousness can serve as a cause unto itself.

Many, perhaps most, will disagree with the above characterizations, seeing one of these views as clearly more compelling than the others. Importantly, however, those very same people may differ with respect to which view they see as the only reasonable one. The fundamental fact is that smart, well-reasoned people subscribe to all three perspectives. Some might argue that to suggest that we keep an open mind on this issue is akin to keeping an open mind on all scientific facts. Surely, I am not suggesting that we keep an open mind on whether or not the world is flat. If libertarians with their flighty dualist notions are given the same credence as hard-nosed scientifically minded determinists, what is to stop us from giving creationists equal room on the platform with evolutionists?

Ultimately, the progress of science requires a balancing act. On the one hand, scientific progress depends on the accumulation of knowledge. If the gaining of new facts does not enable us to draw new conclusions, then the enterprise of science is fundamentally bankrupt. On the other hand, science needs to be wary of overgeneralizing what it knows and prepared to fundamentally revise preconceived notions in the face of new evidence. The evidence is simply overwhelming that the Earth is round, and that evolutionary processes take place. However, the evidence in the case of the free will debate is not of this nature, at least not yet.

Were this to be simply an academic issue, then scientists' perennial tendency to overstate the evidence for their respective positions would be of little consequence. But, as the first half of this chapter demonstrates, this debate is not simply limited to the ivory tower. Like it or not, scientists' opinions can influence both what people think and how they behave. Throughout history scientists have made premature claims with dangerous societal ramifications. For sure, we should continue to explore the illusions of free will, and the many ways in which our behaviors are influenced without our knowledge or intention. But we also should explore the potential ways in which conscious choice might have a genuine impact on our futures. The time may come when society will have to adjust itself to the scientifically validated conclusion that the experience of free will is a complete illusion, but that time is not yet upon us, and it may never be.

If science is not yet in a position to give people a definitive answer on the question of free will, what then should we tell them? My view is that scientists should inform the public of the facts but encourage them to make up their own minds. Let's face it: ultimately, the question of free will boils down to metaphysical questions about the nature of the human spirit and its potential to transcend the limits of physical reality. Beliefs about the nature of one's own being involve deeply personal questions on which all of us must make important leaps of faith. It is an inescapable fact that there are certain metaphysical presumptions that precede empirical observations. For example, there is no way to know that one is not simply dreaming his or her entire life. The determination of whether beings other than oneself are actually sentient is similarly empirically intractable. Ultimately most of us conclude that reality is real and that others have consciousness, not because we can prove these views but because the experience of reality and other minds is so compelling. For many people, the experience of a personal spirit is as phenomenologically evident as reality itself. Not all of us share that intuition, but recognition of the personal assumptions and phenomenological appraisals underlying our own views of reality may give us greater sympathy for how the same facts can be reasonably interpreted from different metaphysical perspectives. Time and time again, history has shown the dangers of metaphysical dogmatism. Rather than using science as a pulpit for indoctrination to our own personal metaphysics, let's simply be frank with the public about what we know as scientists and what we believe as individuals, and then encourage people decide what they think for themselves.

DISCUSSION WITH JONATHAN W. SCHOOLER

For the talk, J. Schooler focused on a metaphor briefly alluded to in the chapter in which free will is likened to sailing. Like a helmsman, free will sets a course but remains at the mercy of forces out of its control. Moment-to-moment actions may appear to be lacking volition, but nevertheless, with effort and good luck people often end up in the vicinity of where they wanted to go. Moreover, it was suggested that all people are collectively sailing on the equivalent of a giant shock wave moving through a space-time multiverse. Through intention and perhaps interpretation, people may influence which branch of the multiverse they traverse, thereby providing the possibility of genuine alternative futures.

Isn't the helmsman in the sailing metaphor completely controlled by circumstance? If so, does the metaphor really capture the problem of free will?
The sailing metaphor assumes free will. The metaphor was designed to address the question, "If there were such a thing as free will, what would it be like?" The main point of the sailing metaphor is that free will must be constrained in fundamental ways. It must be constrained by environmental and genetic factors, and it must be susceptible to unconscious forces. The metaphor is designed to illustrate how control might operate among strong and persistent forces.

The question of free will is indeed separate and is better addressed by the proposition that there are multiple potential futures in which people are able, through the choices they make, to cause one of several possible alternatives to unfold.

One thing that is true about sailing is that different helmsmen have different levels of experience sailing. Is it true that there might be experience effects, such that the older one gets, the better one is able to understand one's limitations and motivations?
It is possible that when people become mindful of this metaphor, it may give them the sort of heuristic that will enable them to gain from experience in ways that they might not have otherwise. Regardless of whether the explicit use of the metaphor actually is helpful, the basic idea is to give people a way to think about consciousness and free will in a way that is helpful.

Nature has given people boats that vary to a great extent. Some people have sleek boats, and others clearly do not. However, experience can teach a person how to get the most out of the boat one has.

Can the claim that we are all on the same wave of consciousness be reconciled with the claim that we can all branch off into multiple universes?
The argument is not that there are multiple universes, but that there are multiple potential universes. Making choices and directing attention in one direction or another causes the realization of the possible next *present-time*. There are a variety of possible next present-times, or

possible bifurcations. For instance, if a person chooses coffee over tea, he or she pushes everyone over to a universe in which that person consumed coffee.

However, it is still possible to reconcile the idea of a single wave of consciousness with the idea that people can individually choose between genuine alternative futures. Accordingly, if each of us faces alternative on coming futures then the individual decision that each of us make enables each of us to slightly impact on how reality unfolds for everyone. Indeed, from this vantage we are all slightly contributing to the way in which the collective wave of consciousness progresses.

Can the helmsman fall out of the boat?

In one way, if consciousness could continue without the body. That would be one way of falling out.

Can a zombie or robot direct the boat?

The sailing metaphor assumes consciousness, which is to say that the sailing metaphor is a model for how consciousness plays itself out in this reality. What consciousness is, in reality, is a separate question. One possible answer to that is that consciousness is actually a wave moving through the multiverse. This wave of consciousness is not to be confused with the sailing metaphor, in which waves are metaphorical.

ACKNOWLEDGMENTS

I thank Ben Baird and Tam Hunt for helpful comments on earlier drafts of this manuscript. The writing of this chapter was supported by a grant from the William Grant Foundation.

NOTE

1. It would be quite interesting to conduct a formal poll of philosophers and scientists to determine precisely what the distribution of opinions on this topic really is. Because libertarianism is such a taboo position, I suspect that there may be more closet sympathizers with it than is currently recognized.

REFERENCES

Bandura, A. (2008). Reconstrual of "free will" from the agentic perspective of social cognitive theory. In J. Baer, J. C. Kaufman, & R. F. Baumeister (Eds.), *Are we free? Psychology and free will.* Oxford, UK: Oxford University Press.

Bargh, J. A. (2005). Bypassing the will: Towards demystifying the nonconscious control of social behavior. In R. Hassin, J. S. Uleman, & J. A. Bargh (Eds.), *The new unconscious* (pp. 37–58). New York: Oxford University Press.

Bargh, J. A., (2008). Free will is un-natural. In J. Baer, J. C. Kaufman, & R. F. Baumeister (Eds.), *Are we free? Psychology and free will.* Oxford, UK: Oxford University Press.

Bargh, J. A., & Ferguson, M. L. (2000). Beyond behaviorism: On the automaticity of higher mental processes, *Psychological Bulletin, 126,* 925–945.

Bargh, J. A., Gollwitzer, P. M., Lee-Chai, A., Barndollar, K., & Trötschel, R. (2001). The automated will: Nonconscious activation and pursuit of behavioral goals. *Journal of Personality and Social Psychology, 81* (6), 1014–1027.

Baumeister, R. F., Bratslavsky, E., Muraven, M., & Tice, D. M. (1998). Ego depletion: Is the active self a limited resource? *Journal of Personality and Social Psychology, 74,* 1252–1265.

Baumeister, R. F., Masicampo, E. J., & Dewall, C. N. (2009). Prosocial benefits of feeling free: Disbelief in free will increases aggression and reduces helpfulness. *Personality and Social Psychology Bulletin, 35*(2), 260–268.

Blackmore, S. (1999). *The meme machine.* Oxford, UK: Oxford University Press.

Bloom, P. (2004). *Descartes' baby: How the science of child development explains what makes us human.* New York: Basic Books.

Boswell, J. (1924). *The life of Samuel Johnson.* (The first edition, 1791, reprinted with the appendix, "the principal corrections and additions," 1793.) London: Navarre Society.

Cassel, E., & Bernstein, D. A. (2007). *Criminal behavior.* Mahwah, NJ: L. Erlbaum Associates.

Chalmers, D. (1995). Facing up to the problem of consciousness. *Journal of Consciousness Studies, 2*(3), 200–219.

Churchland, P. M. (1995). *The engine of reason, the seat of the soul: A philosophical journey into the brain.* Cambridge, MA: MIT Press.

Crick, F. (1994). *The astonishing hypothesis: The scientific search for the soul.* New York: Simon & Schuster.

Dennett, D. C. (1991). *Consciousness explained.* Boston: Little, Brown, & Co.

Dennett, D. C. (2003). *Freedom evolves.* London: Allen Lane.

Eccles J. C. (1986). Do mental events cause neural events analogously to the probability fields of quantum mechanics? *Proceedings of the Royal Society of London. Series B, Containing Papers of a Biological Character. Royal Society (Great Britain)*, 227 (1249), 411–428.

Everett, H., & DeWitt, B. S. (1973). *The many-worlds interpretation of quantum mechanics: A fundamental exposition.* Princeton, NJ: Princeton University Press.

Gilbert, D. T. (2006). *Stumbling on happiness.* New York: A. A. Knopf.

Greene, J., & Cohen, J. (2004). For the law, neuroscience changes nothing and everything. *Philosophical Transactions of the Royal Society of London. Series B, Biological Sciences, 359* (1451), 1775–1785.

Griffin, D. R. (1996) *Unsnarling the word-knot: Consciousness, freedom and the mind-body problem.* Eugene, OR: Wipf & Stock.

Hameroff, S. (2006). Consciousness, neurobiology and quantum mechanics: The case for a connection. In J. Tuszynski (Ed.), *The emerging physics of consciousness.* Berlin, Germany: Springer.

Hunt, T. (2009). *The better story: A narrative for the future.* Manuscript in preparation.

James, W. (1907). *Pragmatism.* Cambridge, MA: Harvard University Press.

James, W. (1946). *Talks to teachers on psychology.* London: Longmans, Green, and Co. (Original work published 1899)

Jang, K. L. (2005). *The behavioral genetics of psychopathology: A clinical guide.* Mahwah, NJ: Lawrence Erlbaum Associates.

Kaku, M. (2005). *Parallel worlds: A journey through creation, higher dimensions, and the future of the cosmos.* New York: Doubleday.

Kane, R. (1996). *The significance of free will.* New York: Oxford University Press.

Libet, B. (1985). Unconscious cerebral initiative and the role of conscious will in voluntary action, *Behavioral and Brain Sciences, 8,* 529–66.

Libet, B. (1999). Do we have free will? *Journal of Consciousness Studies, 6*(8), 47–57.

Libet, B. (2003). Can conscious experience affect brain activity? *Journal of Consciousness Studies, 10*(12), 24–28.

Leibniz, G. (1714/1989). Monadology. In G. W. Leibniz, Philosophical Essays, R. Ariew and D. Garber (Eds. & Trans.), Indianapolis, IN: Hackett Publishing Company.

Loughead, J., Wileyto, E. P., Valdez, J. N., Sanborn, P., Tang, K., Strasser, A. A., et al. (2008). Effect of abstinence challenge on brain function and cognition in smokers differs by comt genotype. *Molecular Psychiatry,* 14(8), 820–826. doi: 10.1038/mp.2008.132.

Nahmias, E., Morris, S., Nadelhoffer, T., & Turner, J. (2005). Surveying freedom: Folk intuitions about free will and moral responsibility. *Philosophical Psychology, 18*(5), 561–584.

Nichols, S., & Knobe, J. (2007). Moral responsibility and determinism: The cognitive science of folk intuitions. *Nous, 41*(4), 663–685.

Nisbett, R.E., & Wilson, T. D. (1977). Telling more than we can know: Verbal reports on mental processes, *Psychological Review, 84,* 231–259.

Pelham, B. W., Mirenberg, M. C., & Jones, J. T. (2002). Why Susie sells seashells by the seashore: Implicit egotism and major life decisions. *Journal of Personality and Social Psychology, 82,* 469–487.

Penrose, R. (1987). Quantum physics and conscious thought. In B. J. Hiley & F. D. Peat (Eds.), *Quantum implications: Essays in honour of David Bohm.* London: Routledge & Kegan Paul.

Roskies, A. L., & Nichols, S. (2008). Bringing moral responsibility down to earth. *The Journal of Philosophy, 105*(7), 371.

Schooler, J., & Schreiber, C. A. (2004). Experience, meta-consciousness, and the paradox of introspection, *Journal of Consciousness Studies, 11,* 17–39.

Searle, J. R. (1984). *Minds, brains, & science: The 1984 Reith lectures.* London: British Broadcasting Corporation.

Searle, J. (1997). *The mystery of consciousness.* New York: Review Press.

Segal, N. L. (1999). *Entwined lives: Twins and what they tell us about human behavior.* New York: Dutton.

Shariff, A. F., Greene, J. D., & Schooler, J. W. (2009). His brain made him do it: Encouraging a mechanistic worldview reduces punishment. *Under revision.*

Shariff, A. F., Schooler, J., & Vohs, K. D. (2008). The hazards of claiming to have solved the hard problem of free will. To appear In J. Baer, J. C. Kaufman, & R. F. Baumeister (Eds.), *Are we free? Psychology and free will* (pp. 181–204). New York: Oxford University Press.

Smilansky, S. (2000). *Free will and illusion.* New York: Oxford University Press.

Spinoza, B. (1955). *The chief works of Benedict de Spinoza.* New York: Dover Publications.

Spinoza, B. de (1951). *Ethics* (proposition III, part II). In R. H. M. Elwes (Ed. & Trans.), *Spinoza: The chief works* (Vol. 2). New York: Dover (Original work published 1677).

Stapp, H. P. (2007). Quantum mechanical theories of consciousness. In S. Schneider & M. Velmans. (Eds.), *The Blackwell companion to consciousness.* Malden, MA: Blackwell.

Velmans, M. (2002). How could conscious experiences affect brains? *The Journal of Consciousness Studies, 9*(11), 3–29.

Velmans, M. (2003). Preconscious free will. *Journal of Consciousness Studies, 10*(12), 42–61.

Velten, E. (1968). A laboratory task for the induction of mood states. *Behavioral Research and Therapy, 6,* 607–617.

Vohs, K. D., & Schooler, J. 2008. The value of believing in free will: Encouraging a belief in determinism increases cheating, *Psychological Science, 19,* 49–54.

Von Hippel, W., Lakin, J. L., & Shakarchi, R. J. (2005). Individual differences in motivated social cognition: The case of self-serving information processing. *Personality and Social Psychology Bulletin, 31,* 1347–1357.

Wegner, D. M. (2002). *The illusion of conscious will.* Cambridge, MA: MIT Press.

Wegner, D. M., & Wheatley, T. (1999). Apparent mental causation: Sources of the experience of will: What cognitive mechanism makes us feel as if we are acting consciously and willfully? *American Psychologist, 54*(7), 480–492.

Whitehead, A. N. (1929) *Process and reality: An essay in cosmology.* New York: Free Press.

INDEX